C000182657

Staying Spiritually Fresh

Yan Hadley

New Life Publications

New Life Publications
80 Lime Avenue

Groby

Leicester LE6 0EN

Tel: 0116 2356992

ISBN: 978-0-9531107-4-2

Typeset and cover by: Barratt Ministries, Manchester
Printed by The MPG Books Group in the UK
Published by: New Life Publications, Leicester

Dedication

This book is dedicated to my wife, Gail, who is a consistent encouragement and immense support to me and the ministry.

I thank God for your love and friendship, and for believing in me. The example of your commitment, prayerfulness and unwavering faith is always such a great inspiration, for which I am very grateful.

Contents

Acknowledgements

My grateful thanks to everyone who has encouraged me and played a part in seeing this, my sixth book, published.

Particular appreciation also goes to those who have sacrificed their personal time in meticulously proof-reading the manuscript: Helen Cockram in Cheshire, Gail Hadley in Leicester, Beryl Maskell, in Surrey and Pat Sampson in Lincolnshire.

Foreword

There is no-one reading this book who will not go through a desert experience at some phase in their lives. For many people, these times are only short periods of feeling distant from God, or being discouraged and unsure of His purpose for them. With some, it is weariness due to activity that hasn't been fully reliant on the Holy Spirit. There will also be those who, through the culmination of various pressures, are physically and emotionally drained, as well as being spiritually burnt-out. Sadly, there are a greater proportion of people who, through apathy, have drifted from God and are suffering the consequences of their neglect. Whatever the reason, there is the need for every believer to stay spiritually fresh, and be vigilant against the danger of becoming dry and barren.

The title for this book arose out of a preaching topic God gave me three years ago. It created more interest than any other I've spoken on in thirty-four years of Christian ministry. While itinerating full-time and sharing this message, people's immediate response was extremely positive. Leaders and Church members came for prayer, speaking of how they had grown discouraged, weary and spiritually dry. A significant number shared with me how they had considered leaving the Church, giving up their ministry or, in several cases, even contemplated suicide.

In almost every place I visited, someone would make an approach at the end of the service and ask if this message, I'd just preached, was available on DVD or CD. There were those who even asked if they could copy the written notes, while others suggested that I wrote a book on the subject. Through these people, the Lord impressed upon me the importance of addressing this issue. It was to be in a way that would reach a greater number who were struggling, and in a format giving much more detail than would be possible with just a sermon.

My burden to make this subject matter available was increased greatly, when looking around at the plethora of other Christian books. I found a wide variety of topics giving practical help, but nothing that focussed specifically on maintaining spiritual freshness.

Argentinean evangelist Luis Palau said, "When you face the perils of weariness, carelessness, and confusion, don't pray for an easier life. Pray instead to be a stronger man or woman of God." Similarly, my prayer is, that in reading the following pages you will be helped, encouraged, and strengthened in your desire to be your very best for the Lord.

Chapter 1

The Need to Stay Spiritually Fresh

With the pace of life as it is today, together with its many associated pressures, we can so easily feel run down, stressed out and find ourselves in a position of being weary and tired. God has an exciting destiny for our lives, and to be able to effectively fulfil His call we must remain spiritually fresh. We must seize every opportunity that He brings across our path, facing the challenges that confront us with the enthusiasm of being *'more than conquerors'* in every circumstance of life. Therefore, right from the outset of this book, let me state three of the most important reasons why it is crucial that we maintain this spiritual vigour:

1. Our Worship Of God
2. Our Warfare Against Satan
3. Our Witness To A Dying World

Firstly, Our Worship Of God

When we think about our worship of God, the commandment given in Deuteronomy 6:5 is, *'You shall love the Lord your God with all your heart, and with all your soul, and with all your might."* This involves the totality of our

11

being - every breath that is within us worshipping Him for who He is. It is impossible to do that unless we are spiritually fresh. Jesus emphasises the importance of acceptable worship in saying, *"... true worshippers will worship the Father in spirit and truth, for such the Father seeks to worship him"* (John 4:23b). Now, for Jesus to say the Father is seeking such people clearly indicates that these are not easy to find; God has got to seek them out! You can be in a church full of people that look very pious. They might express the right words and be demonstrating the correct actions, yet they are not necessarily *'true worshippers'* – those who love God with their whole being.

The Bible shows us God's hatred towards worship that isn't flowing from sincerity and is not expressed in the dynamic reality of faith in the book of Revelation. Here, He addresses the church at Laodicea in chapter 3:16, and His rebuke to these Christians is, *"So, because you are lukewarm, and neither cold nor hot, I will spew you out of my mouth."* These are extremely strong words, but they merely express the strength of God's desire for our worship to be vibrant and heartfelt, and this can only be the case when we are spiritually fresh.

Secondly, Our Warfare Against Satan

The Bible teaches us in Ephesians 6:12-13 that we are in a spiritual war. We are warned that our fight is not against flesh and blood, but against *"the principalities and powers, against the world rulers of this present darkness, against the spiritual hosts of wickedness in heavenly places."* There is a battle we are all called to be a part of, yet it is one that we are ill-equipped for unless we are vibrantly alive spiritually. Paul, when writing to his young disciple Timothy, refers to the Christian as a soldier at war and says that we are to *"Fight the good fight of faith...*" (1 Timothy 6:12). Furthermore, his warning is, "*No soldier on service gets entangled in civilian pursuits, since his aim is to satisfy the one who enlisted him*" (2 Timothy 2:4).

Unless we maintain a spiritual vitality, we will be vulnerable rather than vigilant against the trickery of Satan's wiles. The Christian has got to be alert at all times, otherwise he faces almost certain defeat and will be robbed of his full and rightful inheritance that Jesus came to bring.

The scriptures could not be clearer when they speak of Satan coming against not just the Church, but also your life and mine. We are warned that he will attack with strong defiance as a "*roaring lion*" (1 Peter 5:8), and also with subtle deception as an "*angel of light*" (2 Corinthians 11:14). Unless we are spiritually fresh we are going to find ourselves suddenly taken by surprise; entangled in all manner of bondage, and easily deceived, so that we are drawn away from God and no longer walking in His will. When Paul was teaching the Ephesian Christians, his concern for them was that they would not be taken advantage of in this way, so he exhorts them to be spiritually aware and strong, saying, "*Stand strong in the Lord and in the strength of his might*" (Ephesians 6:10).

Thirdly, Our Witness To A Dying World

How can the brightness of our testimony shine out effectively to others unless we have an enthusiastic and passionate faith? If we are apathetic or half-hearted in any aspect of our Christian living then rather than reflecting the glory of God, a dullness in what we present to others will be seen. We are, as Ambassadors for Christ, called to be witnesses of the one who has defeated the devil, taken the sting out of death and who has overcome the world!

13

Therefore, there ought to be something about us that is distinctive and stands out in stark contrast to mere religion; something that catches the attention of others. As our colleagues, neighbours and unconverted family observe our lives they should see something in us that causes them to at least be curious. They may not understand quite what it is, but they'll want what they see! If we are not spiritually fresh then we just offer dead religion and irrelevant tradition; a life of meaningless rules and regulations.

Jesus said, *"If salt has lost its taste it is no longer good for anything but to be thrown out and trodden underfoot"* (Matthew 5:13). This is what happens when we are not spiritually fresh; we lose that 'saltiness' – the ability to create in others a thirst and interest for God.

The Bible states that in the last days there will be those who have a *"form of godliness but who deny its power"* (2 Timothy 3:5). Real Christianity is very different; when we are spiritually fresh we become a radiant and irresistible force that people notice! The reality of this is seen in the Old Testament in Exodus 34. When Moses came down from the mountain, having had a remarkable encounter with the Lord, he was never the same again! The Bible says in verse 35, *"the skin of his face shone."* The glory of God was upon him; people noticed he was radically different and this should be so with us also. The same was true in the New Testament with the early church. Ordinary, uneducated fishermen stood out; their bold uncompromising faith was obvious to all and resulted in the religious leaders being astonished: *"they took note that these men had been with Jesus"* (Acts 4:13, NIV).

There is a very revealing verse in John 1:4 where it speaks of the source of the impact Jesus had upon those He met. Here it says of Christ, *"In him was life, and the life was the light of men."* There was a supernatural quality of life in Jesus that was so dynamic that it shed light into the darkness of other people's lives. It is a challenge for us all to reflect upon the quality of life that ought to be within us. This is truly awesome in the context of 2 Corinthians 4:6: *"It is the God who said, "Let light shine out of darkness," who has shone in our hearts to give the light of the knowledge of the glory of God in the face of Christ."* We are called to be carriers of the glory of God; to possess a distinctiveness that will draw other people to the reality they see in us.

The Responsibility Is Ours

Maintaining the vitality and the freshness of our spiritual lives is a major responsibility for us all and if we neglect this we can start to feel oppressed, weak, weary and dry. If we aren't careful we can slowly come to the place of being WORN OUT, BURNT OUT and unable to GIVE OUT! God's will for us all is a consistently, vibrant, victorious life, which is why Jesus said in John 10:10, *"I came that they may have life, and have it abundantly."* Jesus did not come to make us religious, nor did He come to make us narrow-minded - He came to bring something so liberating; a life wonderfully exciting and extraordinary – life in all its fullness!

The scriptures clearly express the heart of God, warning us not to allow ourselves to grow tired and dry. His Word gives every encouragement to stay spiritually fresh: In Galatians 6:9 we read, *"Let us not grow weary in well doing."* For each of us this is a problem we will face from time to time. We can be working hard, walking faithfully, serving God, doing everything we know how best to do, yet find ourselves getting weary in the good that we are doing. This

15

is particularly so if we have some responsibility in the church. Even though we may be involved in good work, fulfilling this with all sincerity and faithfulness, we can still start to grow weary carrying it out.

Isaiah the prophet speaks of the believer, in chapter 40:31, as being able to, *"mount up on wings as eagles, to run and not grow weary, to walk and not grow faint."* In looking at the picture of the eagle rising up and soaring to great heights we are reminded that the characteristic of this bird is to fly with ease, in a way that seems almost effortless, and not to be frantically flapping its wings. The eagle is able to ascend to tremendous heights as it soars on the currents of the wind. In the same way God enables every child of His to rise above their problems and to look at life from the vantage point of a divine perspective as they live in the dimension of the Holy Spirit.

There is a fascinating verse in Psalm 18:29, that speaks of the vigour and vitality that should characterise our lives. David says,*"By you I can crush a troop; and by my God I can leap over a wall."* It doesn't matter what age we are, what level of fitness we have, or what physical infirmities may be upon our body. By the Spirit of God we will know a supernatural energy to serve Him in a way which previously would have been impossible in our natural ability. This is the enthusiastic service that Paul spoke to the Corinthian Christians about when he said, *"Be steadfast, immovable, always abounding in the work of the Lord..."* (1 Corinthians 15:58).

God's grace towards us is remarkable and enables us to remain consistent even in times of great trial and pain. When we experience seasons of difficulty and frustration Psalm 84:6-7 shows us that still we can maintain this good level of spiritual freshness: *"As they go through the valley of Baca they make it a place of springs; the early rains also cover it with pools. They go from strength to strength."* The valley of Baca was always known as a dry and desolate place. It was representative in the scriptures of a place of sorrow and was spoken of as the 'valley of weeping'. In looking closely at this verse we notice that negative circumstances do not adversely change these people, rather they change the environment around them! – *"they make it a place of springs."*

With the busyness and stresses of modern day life, people today can so easily begin to feel tired and worn out and some, having lost their zeal, find themselves living in mediocrity; just going through the motions of their faith. Let us consider five reasons for this spiritual fatigue that affect us all:

1. Disconnection With God

Whenever we are not rightly connected to God, the one who is the source of our total supply, we lose the power we need to maintain our spiritual strength. If something clouds our communion and relationship with the Lord there then follows a drifting away and a backsliding begins. We lose the enthusiasm we once had. The one sure thing to bring that disconnection is always sin. Just as Samson was robbed of his strength, you and I also, through compromise, are brought to a place of weakness spiritually. This is because unresolved guilt will always defeat and deflate us.

We therefore need to keep short accounts with God. There is nothing more draining than living in denial and nothing more invigorating than honesty and having a clean heart. Confession is most certainly good for the soul; it restores our emotional and physical energy, as well as our relationship with God. Any denial in our lives brings us into a place of deception. 1 John 1:8 says, *"If we say we have no sin, we deceive ourselves, and the truth is not in us."*

What occurs when the truth is not in us is that spiritual darkness comes in, overshadowing our revelation of God. We find ourselves rendered powerless because we have lost the intimacy and joy we once had with the Lord. Jesus spoke of this to the church at Ephesus in Revelation 2:4, when He said, *"I hold this against you: you have forsaken your first love"* (NIV). If our daily work and living is not issuing from a passion of love, then no matter how much we do, it is unacceptable to God and unfulfilling to ourselves.

2. Discouragement

I can guarantee that for any person who feels discouraged in any way, about anything, it will have the effect of making them feel dry and empty inside. Discouragement saps all the joy and enthusiasm from our lives and causes our motivation to grind to a halt! We come to the place of feeling weary and thinking, 'why bother', in some cases to the point of wanting to give up! Whether it is a series of problems that have worn us down, or perhaps we've been hurt, disappointed, or let down by someone, weariness is the result. This is especially so where our hopes have been dashed, or our dreams shattered - any discouragement will eat away at us and bring spiritual dryness into our lives. This is what the Bible means when it says, *"... a downcast spirit dries up the bones"* (Proverbs 17:22b).

Discouragement comes upon us when we least expect it and can be totally irrational. At such times we need to recognise the problem as a spiritual attack that has the potential to render us powerless. Unless we deal with the problem immediately we'll find ourselves being sucked into a dark hole of despair that will be very difficult to get out of. When David found himself under this kind of attack he took decisive action by speaking to his own life. He said, *"Why are you downcast, O my soul? Why so disturbed within me? Put your hope in God..."* (Psalm 42:5a, NIV).

3. Distraction

It is so easy to become distracted with the busyness of life today. There are numerous demands made upon our time and a multitude of voices all clamouring for our attention. Unless we are determined to keep Jesus at the centre of our lives, gradually we will become preoccupied with things that steal our time and cause us to feel dissatisfied in our relationship with God. This also leaves us frustrated with a list of goals that remain unfulfilled, simply because secondary things have taken our attention.

These distractions may be seemingly innocent pursuits such as hobbies, music, sport, or relationships – even our children or grandchildren can begin to take that primary place Christ should occupy in our lives. In so doing, they become the means of weakening the relationship God wants us to have with Him. Whenever Jesus is not the motivating factor of our lives and other things come in, we start to feel dry and weary inside.

4. Deception

To stay spiritually fresh we must consciously be walking in the centre of God's will. The devil will do all he can to lead us from a position of clarity and security. He knows full well that if he can bring uncertainty, confusion or blindness into our lives, then he can take advantage over us and wear us down. So many Christians today haven't got a clue as to what the will of God is for them, and are completely unaware of how vital this assurance is to their spiritual well-being.

Whenever we are not confidently walking in the will of God and are being misled, either knowingly or unknowingly, then we start to do things in our own strength. There is no surer way of experiencing spiritual fatigue than struggling to make things succeed in our own ability. This is why God says, *"Not by might, or by power, but by my Spirit, says the Lord of hosts"* (Zachariah 4:6).

5. Doubt

Every time there is an element of uncertainty about a decision we've made, or need to make; some aspect of our life where guidance is important, but we are not fully assured of, then we begin to lose our confidence. Our peace goes, and in this state of double-mindedness our thoughts are thrown into turmoil. Being *"tossed to and fro"* like the wave of the sea has a very unsettling effect upon our spiritual vitality. Not only do we become, as the Bible says, *"unstable in all our ways"* (James 1:8), we find ourselves being weary through anxiety and fear. Negative thoughts then occupy our thinking and torment our minds.

God has promised never to fail or forsake us and to provide for our every need. However, the torment of doubt can frequently make us feel distant from God. In losing our assurance, we become aware of going through a dry period, where little seems to be happening in terms of answered prayer or fruitful, productive service. It is in these 'wilderness' experiences, we need to remember the clear commitment of God to continually lead and fulfil our lives. The prophet Isaiah brings this assurance when he declares,

"And the Lord will guide you continually, and satisfy your desire with good things, and make your bones strong; and you shall be like a watered garden, like a spring of water, whose waters fail not" (Isaiah 58:11).

· Each of these areas: Disconnection, Discouragement, Distraction, Deception and Doubt are potential door-openers to the enemy! The devil will come in to oppress and build strongholds in our lives through any one of these things, if we allow him to. It doesn't matter how long we've been a Christian, whatever experiences we've had with God, or what position we may hold in our church, we can all find ourselves falling prey in some way.

There are many examples of this that come to mind, which, during the course of ministry I've met, one instance was a woman who sent me an e-mail from Cambridgeshire. She was the worship leader of a lively church that I'd been to speak at. This charismatic, vivacious woman had a tremendous gift to lead others in worship. Her enthusiasm and passion so naturally inspired the congregation to respond to the Lord. How things appeared outwardly though were quite different to what was going on inside. She shared with me how she felt spiritually dry and distant from God and in her e-mail she wrote:

"Yan I can honestly say that I didn't feel I was going to make it. I had literally lost the will to live and no amount of preaching or worship could penetrate my heart – I didn't even believe it anymore, I was ready to leave everything behind. It wasn't as if I was rebelling against God or had turned my back on Him, I hadn't; I did however feel very empty and was convinced that God had left me and I was on the

21

scrap heap. As much as I cried out to Him to take
the pain away I felt nothing from Him."

This was a major problem in her life, but praise God she
did go on in her e-mail to say how the Lord had brought her
through, setting her completely free! This does however
illustrate how we can't always tell where a person is in their
relationship with Christ. There are many in the Church I
believe, who battle with the same feelings of barrenness,
and simply struggle on quietly alone, without anyone
noticing.

Another case in point was a leader I was speaking to
from the Midlands, who had been in the ministry for over
forty years. This man felt so dry and discouraged that he
had decided to commit suicide. He told me of how he'd
been sitting in his front room, with a mug of coffee on the
table and a bottle of sleeping tablets beside his drink. He
was just a moment away from taking the tablets and killing
himself.

As he was thinking about this, there came a noise
behind him, the postman had just delivered a parcel
which had dropped onto the mat in the hallway, so he
got up from his chair to have a look at what this was. In
opening the parcel he saw it was one of my books entitled
'Answering Today's Problems', which he had ordered a
month previously. He sat back down in the chair and
started reading through some of the scriptures. As he
did so, something stirred within his heart; faith began
to rise in his despair and with great emotion he told me
that this incident saved him from killing himself - Glory
to God!

One other example was a man that I met recently while
speaking in Yorkshire, he was part of the leadership team

of his church. I shared in the meeting the previous two incidents of those I've mentioned who had been struggling, and after the service he came forward for prayer. He told me how downcast and weary he was feeling and that he too was planning to commit suicide. Sadly, this man hadn't been able to speak of his problem with anyone else for fear of what they might have thought of him. That day he was encouraged and set free!

The simple point in mentioning each of these situations is that even those who are spiritually mature, and in a place of significant responsibility, still battle with this problem. They can have influence and pastoral care for others, and yet still be feeling spiritually dry themselves. This really shouldn't come as a surprise to us, because throughout the scriptures we can find similar examples. Let me mention three of them:

Firstly, there's the prophet Elijah in 1 Kings 19:1-10. Here we have a remarkable man of outstanding faith and power! He could call fire down from heaven and had seen the prophets of Baal slain under his ministry. Many mighty miracles were brought about through him, yet literally just a few moments after the greatest victory of his life, we find him running away in fear. He hid in a cave, became overwhelmed by despair and felt suicidal, even to the point of saying 'I've had enough; I don't want to live any longer, take my life from me!'

Then we have the Psalmist David. There was no doubt that he loved the Lord with an intense passion; this was the man who wrote, *"As the deer pants for streams of water, so my soul pants for you, O God"* (Psalm 42:1, NIV). He was set apart as God's chosen, anointed king, and yet he came to the place of feeling desperately dry.

In his case it was because of unconfessed sin that he was hiding in his life. Because David was not living in reality and was trying to hide his sin it had a dramatic effect upon him spiritually and physically. The Bible describes the consequence of this in Psalm 32:3-4. Here he says,

"When I declared not my sin, my body wasted away through my groaning all day long. For day and night your hand was heavy upon me; my strength was dried up as by the heat of summer."

The third person to consider is Moses who was such an outstanding man of God. He led nearly two million people out of the bondage of Egypt and through the wilderness. This man saw the intervention of God in miraculous, spectacular ways, as plagues came upon the land to bring about Israel's deliverance. He was the only person recorded in the Bible to actually converse with God *"face to face, as a man speaks to his friend"* (Exodus 33:11). Also, in a dramatic act of faith he stood at the edge of the Red Sea, raised his rod with great confidence and the sea actually parted in two. In doing this the children of Israel were able to walk through on dry land, to safety on the other side.

Moses was directed by God in all his ways during his time of leadership in the wilderness, being led by a pillar of fire by night and a cloud by day. Even though he had experienced this supernaturally unique and amazing relationship, he too came to the place of feeling tired and spiritually dry. The weariness that overwhelmed Moses was the result of all the grumbling and complaining of Israel against him. This despair is referred to in Numbers 11:14 where he says,

"I cannot carry all these people by myself; the burden is too heavy for me. If this is how you are going to treat me, put me to death right now...." (NIV).

As we can see from what has been said so far, the problem we are looking at is a major issue that affects a great deal of people from all walks of life. This is why I have felt motivated to write such a book, and in the following chapters we shall consider some important steps to maintaining spiritual freshness.

Before looking at these though, let me emphasise that unless we take responsibility to 'do' something, we will grow dry and become another casualty in the Christian Church. Let us never think that such a problem couldn't affect us. We are all vulnerable, particularly if pride or complacency tells us otherwise. Therefore we need to be proactive and take some specific, scriptural and practical steps; we can't take anything for granted! The Bible's directive is, *"...work out your own salvation with fear and trembling"* (Philippians 2:12b). Also the apostle Peter says in 2 Peter 1:5, *"...make every effort to supplement your faith..."* He then explains why in verse 8 and 10,

"If these things are yours and abound, they keep you from being ineffective and unfruitful ... for if you do this you will never fall."

Chapter 2

Maintain A Close Relationship With God

The first and most important step to staying spiritually fresh is developing an intimacy with the Lord. We need to be rightly connected to the one who is the source of our life. The Psalmist refers to the enthusiastic dynamic of that connection in Psalm 37:4 when he says, *"Take delight in the Lord, and he will give you the desires of your heart."* This active relationship is vital to the well-being of every area of our lives, yet it is often easily neglected. Daniel, who faced enormous challenges, the like of which few people have ever been confronted with, understood the importance of God being the strength of his life. He declared, *"The people who do know their God shall be strong, and do exploits"* (Daniel 11:32, AV).

Intimacy in any relationship is something we neglect at the cost of losing the precious fulfilment we value the most. We should always be pressing into a greater revelation and experience of the Lord in our daily lives, taking care to guard against any complacency.

Jesus said, *"Blessed are those that hunger and thirst for righteousness, for they shall be satisfied"* (Matthew 5:6). There can be no doubt that spiritual fulfilment is found in proportion to the intensity of our desire. The reality is though; very often people just do not have a deep degree of hunger, thirst and longing. Paul knew how vital this was for him when he expressed his heart's desire in Philippians 3:10a. His all consuming passion was, *"that I may know him and the power of his resurrection..."* There were surely few people that knew the Lord better than Paul, nor many that had a greater experience of His power, than this outstanding apostle. Yet, with an intensity of emotion, he expresses the deepest hunger of his life – to know Jesus even more intimately than he knew Him at that present time.

During the course of preaching overseas, this intensity of desire is something that I found very evident, particularly in Africa and India; sadly though, rarely is it apparent in the U.K. One such occasion, indelibly impressed on my mind, was the first ministry trip I made to S. India. Having left Heathrow in the freezing snow I arrived weary, after a 10 hr flight, in the humid atmosphere of Chennai airport, in the early hours of the following day. From there I was taken to my accommodation located above a church where I fell into bed at 3.00 a.m. Just 2 hrs later I was woken by the thunderous sound of fervent prayer and praise ascending from beneath me as the church gathered for their morning prayer meeting!

This hunger for God marked the start of what was to come during my stay, as in each place I spoke there was a passionate spirit of joy, faith and expectancy. At every service the attentiveness of people in the meetings, which often lasted 4 hrs in very hot temperatures, was remarkable. Their alertness and sharpness of mind in turning with amazing speed to every scripture quoted was extraordinary! Each individual took detailed notes, listening with intense interest, from the youngest at 7 yrs to some who were in their 90's! The experience was certainly a revelation to me of what heartfelt love for God really meant, especially as they were all from extremely poor backgrounds and living in exceptionally difficult conditions.

Although we can learn and be inspired by the example of others, we cannot live off the revelation and experience of someone else. Nor can we substitute our responsibility to seek God with merely attending conferences, or avid viewing of Christian television channels. The words of David speak of an individual responsibility to develop a personal relationship. Essentially this is a D.I.Y. job; no one else can do it for us and we cannot do it for anyone else. He says in Psalm 16:8a, *"I keep the Lord always before me..."* David then goes on to explain, in verse 9, it was this priority that resulted in a spiritual freshness permeating every part of his being: *"Therefore my heart is glad, and my soul rejoices, my body also dwells secure."*

In Acts 3:19b, we read that, *"... times of refreshing shall come from the presence of the Lord."* As important as holidays undoubtedly are, 'times of refreshing' do not come simply from relaxing in a deck chair on a two-week Mediterranean cruise. They are not experienced just by enjoying a couple of hours on the golf course, nor are they found merely by sitting on the riverbank with our fishing rods, enjoying the peace and solitude of being away from the pressures of life. No, true times of spiritual refreshing can only come from spending time in God's presence.

This guarantee of refreshing is not automatic, just by being a believer. Not every Christian will experience the energising and revitalising life that God wants them to have. It is the minority rather than the majority who will receive what they so desperately need to stay spiritually fresh. The fact that it is only a few is because not everyone is prepared to pay the cost of what is required. Isaiah 40:31 speaks of a very specific category of people who will experience this: *"they that wait for the Lord shall renew their strength..."* Only those who take the time, and make the sacrifice to be with God, will discover renewal; those who are prepared to discipline themselves, come aside and seek Him – they are the ones who will know the refreshing promised in God's Word.

Some people can sound extremely 'spiritual', and talk very enthusiastically about how much they want to spend time with God, to know a deeper relationship. They convince others and perhaps even themselves that this is their greatest goal in life. However, for one reason or another it never materialises into anything of substance, rather it remains empty words, and an elusive dream. Sincere as their desire may be, they are deceiving themselves. The renowned American author and Bible teacher A.W. Tozer once said, "Every one of us have as much of God as we want, nothing more, and nothing less!" This is the stark reality! We need to stop allowing ourselves to be robbed by our own deception. If we truly want this intimacy with God then let us move beyond the delusion of words and into decisive action!

We must make time to wait upon God and not let the busyness of the day take priority. Herein is found the secret simplicity to a fresh and flourishing Christian life - how difficult it is though for us just to be still in the presence of the Lord! We often feel we have so much to do that there is little time to read the scriptures, pray, or wait upon God. The fact is however, we cannot afford to do anything other than put Him first, if we want to live in the full benefits of all He promises.

In Psalm 103:2a, having said, *"... forget not all his benefits,"* David goes on to speak of God in verse 5 as being the one, *"who satisfies you with good as long as you live so that your youth is renewed like the eagles."* Also in Psalm 27:14 we are instructed,

"Wait for the Lord; be strong and let your heart take courage..."
Every Christian certainly needs to heed this command, if they
are to find the vitality and courage required, to accomplish
God's will.

An example of someone who proved this in his own life
was evangelist George Muller. His life is both a challenge and
encouragement for all believers. With regards to faith and
prayer, he stood head and shoulders above people of his time,
and he still does to this day. He was both a spiritual giant and
also a person of incredible busyness, yet he always took time
to wait for the Lord and put Him first. His words are an
inspiration to us all; he said:

> 'I look upon it as a lost day when I have not had a good
> time over the word of God. Friends say, "I have so much
> to do, so many people to see, I cannot find time for
> scripture study". Perhaps there are not many who have
> more to do than I. For more than half a century I have
> never known one day when I had not more business
> than I could get through. For four years I have had
> annually about thirty thousand letters, and most of these
> have passed through my own hands. Then, as pastor of
> a church with twelve hundred believers, great has been
> my care. Besides, I have had charge of five immense
> orphanages; also, at my publishing depot, the printing
> and circulating of millions of tracts, books and Bibles;
> but I have always made it a rule never to begin work
> until I have had a good season with God and His word.'

God is not interested in merely informing our minds, He
wants to transform our lives that we might more effectively
represent Him. This is only possible when we are prepared to
make the commitment of really getting to know Him.

31

Developing intimacy with God essentially means spending time with Him, not simply studying with our intellect but being in a place of stillness so that He can speak into our lives and bring the change that is necessary. Paul wrote to the believers in Corinth about this process of transformation when he said, *"... we are being changed into his likeness from one degree of glory to another"* (2 Corinthians 3:18).

One of the major keys to staying in a close relationship with God, and thus remaining spiritually fresh, is for us to SET OUR HEART ON A SINGLE PURPOSE. We are most energised when we are investing our strengths and talents into a God-given purpose. It is impossible for any Christian to fully accomplish God's will and to fulfil their destiny without doing this. The heart of the issue is without question the state of our own hearts. Jesus taught His disciples in Matthew 6:21, *"For where your treasure is, there will your heart be also."* It is vital therefore to establish clearly where our treasure is. A person's treasure is that which is of the greatest importance to them; it catches their attention; occupies their thoughts, and motivates their lives.

The reason why many Christians are often frustrated, dissatisfied and distant from God is basically because their treasure is not 'Spiritual'. Today, in the 21st Century, very often people are more concerned to get ahead, be successful, make a good impression and improve their standard of living rather than to be captivated by the value of a 'Godly Obsession!' With the pressure of difficult circumstances, the pursuit of material security and the priority of personal fulfilment, people's lives become too stressed and much too complicated. This ultimately results in three major dangers to our relationship with the Lord:

(a) A Divided Heart
(b) A Distracted Mind

(c) A Deluded Commitment

Any one of these things inevitably has the consequence of bringing a spiritual dryness into our lives. If we are to cultivate a close relationship with Christ the King we must appreciate what it means to be a citizen of His Kingdom; living as a person with 'One Thing' in mind. Jesus made clear in Matthew 6:33 what our foremost priority should be when saying we were to, *"Seek first his kingdom and his righteousness..."*. The worth we place on this will determine its influence on our entire life.

Living with the mindset of a godly obsession was illustrated by Jesus when He spoke about the parable of a businessman in search of costly pearls. Addressing His disciples Jesus said, *"The kingdom of heaven is like a merchant in search of fine pearls, who, on finding one pearl of great value, went and sold all that he had and bought it"* (Matthew 13:45-46). This 'one pearl' and 'single treasure' was such an obsession, and meant so much to the merchant that he was prepared to give everything he had to have it! For this man there was no holding back. He knew it meant all or nothing, and until our value system is changed in such a radical way we can't begin to experience the full benefits of kingdom living. The hymn writer, John H. Sammis, when speaking about the reward of giving our all to Christ, put it so well when, in 1887, he penned the words:

> "But we never can prove the delights of His love
> Until all on the altar we lay;
> For the favour He shows and the joy He bestows,
> Are for them who will trust and obey."

Looking at the significance of this 'One Thing', let us consider three examples that bring a warning to the believer, teaching some important lessons about our relationship with God. These are: **(a)** Ministering Martha and the danger of a divided heart; **(b)** Devoted David and the danger of a distracted mind; and **(c)** Passionate Paul and the danger of a deluded commitment.

Firstly, MINISTERING MARTHA

- The Danger Of A Divided Heart

On a positive note, the encouraging thing we see about Martha in Luke 10:38-42 is that she started well; she opened her home to Jesus! This is the best and wisest decision we will ever make in life; to open the door to Christ; to swing wide the gates and let the King of Glory come in!' However, it is not merely how we begin our relationship with the Lord that matters, it is also how we continue and ultimately finish that really counts.

When Jesus comes into Martha's home, her sister Mary demonstrates what it means to be a person with 'One thing in mind'. Captivated by a godly obsession, Mary sits at the feet of Jesus, enthralled with His presence and soaking in His every word. In contrast to this Martha is preoccupied with the busyness of serving and working hard to impress, or at least meet the needs of others, at the cost of not listening to Christ. She was seeking to do what in her mind was more important – the practical responsibility of 'catering'.

Because of her divided heart Martha puts herself under unnecessary pressure, wearing herself out, and in so doing starts to get irritable, snappy and even bossy towards Jesus. She says in verse 40, *"Lord, do you not care that my sister has left me to serve alone? Tell her then to help me."* The response of Jesus to this comes with compassion, but also

with the intention to correct her wrong values and to
emphasise the 'One Thing' she should have set her heart
upon. In verse 41 and 42 Jesus said,

> *"Martha, Martha, you are anxious and troubled about
> many things;* **one thing** *is needful. Mary has chosen
> the good portion, which shall not be taken away from
> her."*

Within these few verses is the greatest and most
important principle necessary to learn if we are to stay in a
close and vibrant relationship with the Lord. Having a
'Martha Ministry' in terms of serving is good and necessary.
After all someone has to be practical! In Martha's case she
had a very important guest in her home; someone had to
look after the hospitality. Just imagine what her neighbours
would have thought if she wasn't providing in the way that
culturally would have been expected. Having accepted this
though, we must never let our busyness get in the way of
meeting with Christ.

Serving is a gift that can be a tremendous benefit to
others, particularly in terms of administration, manual
labour, hospitality etc. The 'behind the scenes' supportive
roles, that aren't glamorous and few ever get to see, can be
a wonderful God-given ministry. However, if like Martha,
it causes a person to be stressed out, frustrated and irritable
with those around them – if it causes someone to lose
perspective of the greater importance of spending time with
God, then this is a problem that must be addressed.

It is not our activity but always our undivided attention
that is of primary concern to the Lord. He knows that our
need of spiritual refreshment can only come from out of the
position of stillness in His presence. This is why we must

understand Psalm 46:10a as a commandment and not an invitation, or a kindly option:*"Be still, and know that I am God."* Hearing God's voice may mean you have to sacrifice lesser things and tune out other voices, but it must be done if progress in the goal of greater intimacy with God is to be achieved. Nothing is more important than learning to be still and giving priority to listening to the Lord.

Even though we can easily rationalise and justify our busyness, our *'Doing'* is never more important than our *'Being'*; we are human 'beings', not human 'doings!' This is something that needs to be kept in mind for anyone involved in any sort of ministry, not just the Pastor, Deacon, the music ministry, Sunday school teacher etc., but every member of the body of Christ. Being still is certainly not the 'easy option'. It is much harder to stop and come aside that we might hear from God than it is to remain on the treadmill of activities. This is difficult for several reasons:

(a) A person's sense of importance, security and identity can often be in the busyness of what they do, and in the position they hold. It can be the means of feeding a person's ego and meets a desire within them to be needed.

(b) In our society today busyness and responsibility equals status and success. Therefore people can allow themselves to come under unnecessary pressure and stress simply to conform and do what others expect, so they will be accepted and respected.

(c) Some use their busyness to hide behind, as a means of avoiding issues they would rather not face. Often this can be issues of intimacy, either with God or with other people. The thinking, whether consciously or subconsciously, is that if they immerse themselves in work then it will be understood that they haven't time to get involved on a deeper level in relationships.

While the world's estimation of a person's worth may be in what they can produce, contribute and do, it certainly is not God's; He teaches us to be still and to be secure in the knowledge of His love and acceptance of us. In staying spiritually fresh we need to learn the important lesson that our ministry must always come out of our relationship, and this is a decision we all have to make. Jesus said to Martha, *"Mary has chosen what is better..."* (Luke 10:42, NIV). It is a choice, as with Mary, that may well be misinterpreted by others, and at times criticised, but one that will always enrich our lives and be rewarded by the refreshing of the Lord's presence.

Secondly, DEVOTED DAVID

- The Danger Of A Distracted Mind

Throughout David's writings in the Psalms we see someone whose longing was to consistently please and honour God. He had a remarkable relationship, one that was highlighted as unique from other people when God said of him, *"I have found in David the son of Jesse a man after my own heart..."* (Acts 13:22). As a result of his devotion to God and God's favour upon him, David was chosen to rule over Israel and to accomplish remarkable things in his generation. This was his destiny and the extent of his potential was awesome! However, the solemn lesson we learn from David's moral failure is that distraction leads to temptation, which has the power to ruin our lives. No matter how great a person's prospects may be, their character must be consistent with their calling; otherwise, ultimately they are heading for ruin. David demonstrates to us that, once distracted, the strongest and most spiritual can fall into sin!

When we are not consistently single-minded in our 'high calling' then we become vulnerable to temptation. Integrity, privately *before* God is the basis for public ministry *for* God. David discovered the tragic cost of getting distracted and the consequence of losing sight of a single purpose. This is recorded for our benefit in 2 Samuel 11:1-17. Here we find him in his palace relaxing, and as he looks out of the window he sees Bathsheba bathing. Allowing himself to get distracted by lust David goes on to commit adultery with her. Then on hearing that she is pregnant with his child he manipulates the death of the woman's husband, Uriah. This mighty man of God fell to such depth of sin, and all because of distraction!

Potential danger stalks every child of God, particularly those whom the Lord has raised up and set apart to serve Him in some outstanding way. We hear too often today of the collapse of large and powerful ministries because of some moral weakness on the part of the leader; great men of God that once were household names and who had the respect of literally millions of Christians, have found themselves ensnared in an aspect of poor judgement, or lack of integrity. The result has been not only the disgrace to themselves and the damage to the faith of their supporters, but also the dishonouring of the name and testimony of Christ. In every case the problem can be traced back to distractions, in one form or another, from their original devotion to Christ.

We have been created to live for the praise of God's glory; our personal integrity and single minded devotion is the major key to unlocking a vibrant relationship and victorious walk with the Lord. Once we get distracted from this position then, just like Peter in the New Testament, who enthusiastically stepped out of his fishing boat to walk on water, we soon get into trouble. He moved from the ordinary to the extraordinary in following the example of his Lord, but, because his faith became preoccupied with 'the crisis', rather than 'The Christ', he quickly began to sink!

David, at a more 'enlightened' time in his life, speaks of the most important and foundational principle of any relationship with God. Expressing his single-minded devotion, he says in Psalm 27:4: *"One thing have I asked of the Lord, that will I seek after; that I may dwell in the house of the Lord all the days of my life, to behold the beauty of the Lord, and to enquire in his temple."* This man could have asked for many things, but the one thing he prized most was the value of his relationship with God. To dwell in His presence, appreciate His beauty and to stay in that place of unbroken communion was worth more than anything life could offer. He continues to affirm this when he says, *"Better is one day in your courts than a thousand elsewhere"* (Psalm 84:10, NIV).

In terms of a relationship, to 'dwell' or to 'abide' speaks of a lifestyle of living in a position of intimacy. Everything of lasting value and true fulfilment blossoms out of this one thing – *'abiding in Christ.'* In John 15:1-8, we find this vivid imagery of the branch, you and me, abiding in the vine, being the Lord. The branch draws from the vine all it needs for growth and presents a picture of absolute dependence. From this position verse 5 shows us that without any effort it naturally blossoms out, full of life and with a bountiful supply of fruit.

Again, the same principle of this one thing – 'dwelling', or 'abiding' in God – causing vibrant life, is found in Psalm

1:1-3, but here David introduces the word, 'delight' when referring to our relationship:

> *"Blessed is the man who walks not in the counsel of the wicked, nor stands in the way of sinners, nor sits in the seats of scoffers; but his delight is in the law of the Lord, and on his law he meditates day and night. He is like a tree planted by streams of water, that yields its fruit in its season, and its leaf does not wither. In all that he does, he prospers."*

In these verses, God is clearly promising that those who make such a single-minded commitment will prosper in all they do. This prosperity will be made manifest in that they will be fruitful in the due season of God's timing. They will be consistent as the leaf of their testimony does not wither under the heat of adversity. Also, there will be a continual freshness in their lives as the roots of their faith go deep down into the living waters of God's provision.

The prophet Jeremiah uses the same thought, of how spiritual refreshment flows from an un-distracted, single-minded trust, even in tough and dry periods of discouragement. His words come out of personal experience. They strengthen the faith of all who seek to persevere in what God has called them to do, irrespective of whether other people are willing to believe. In Jeremiah 17:7-8 he declares,

> *"Blessed is the man who trusts in the Lord, whose trust is the Lord. He is like a tree planted by water, that sends out its roots by the stream, and does not fear when heat comes, for its leaves remain green and is not anxious in the year of drought, for it does not cease to bear fruit."*

This servant of God never really witnessed the vindication of his life's work, but he faithfully committed himself to fulfilling his destiny. He had the wearisome task of proclaiming the message of the Lord to a very hardened and rebellious people, at a particularly difficult time in Israel's history. However, even in the most dry periods of his life, when he was persecuted and beset by controversy, his leaves remained green. Jeremiah persisted, determined not to be distracted from his calling, and he was able to do so because he planted his spiritual roots where they would find renewal and refreshment - near to the heart of God.

Satan, knowing the importance of this 'one thing', is always seeking to destroy its potential just as he was determined to do so at the beginning of creation, in Genesis 3. The one thing Adam and Eve had to do was simply obey God's Word. In considering this point we learn a very important truth that is often overlooked: God's will is not something that is complicated to understand, nor is it restrictive and narrow. In actual fact this single purpose we are to live by is wonderfully broad and liberating! God had provided in the garden everything to meet the need of man; He had said that Adam and Eve could eat from all of the trees that were there; everything in the garden had been provided to bring fulfilment. God was saying, 'it is all yours' - what liberty! The only condition and restriction was that they should not touch one tree; the knowledge of good and evil.

The fall of man always begins with distraction from God's will; it is followed by a distortion of God's Word and ultimately results in a departure from God's way. Still today Satan makes the 'forbidden fruit' seem appealing to the eye by stirring the desire of man to have what has been placed 'out of bounds'. He achieves this by sowing doubt into the mind of man. Once a person's mind has been distracted by the whisper, *"Has God said?"* -*"You will not die"* he has undermined what God has clearly stated, causing man to question within his heart. From this distraction and doubt, the third part of the satanic strategy is discontent.

Restlessness comes in because of the feeling that God is withholding something, for whatever reason. This is reinforced as Satan whispers, "God doesn't want you to touch the fruit on that tree, because He doesn't want you to have the same knowledge He has got, He doesn't want you to be like Him and have the knowledge of good and evil." This then results in disobedience, causing our communion with God to be broken, and in disobeying His commandment the final outcome is death – the death of our intimacy with God!

God's way is always the best and it is founded on the simplicity of 'one thing' – gladly walking in obedience to His will. He is not withholding anything from us, in fact His Word says in Psalm 84:11b, *"No good thing does the Lord withhold from those who walk uprightly."* When our delight is to please Him, all that we ever need in life will be given to us. We do not need to grab and take and make ourselves satisfied and secure, we just need to trust in Him.

Thirdly, PASSIONATE PAUL

- The Danger Of A Deluded Commitment

Delusion is never very far from any religious experience. Therefore our relationship with God must not only begin with an encounter with Christ, it must also be expressed in a consistently Christ-centred lifestyle. In considering the example of Paul, thinking specifically of his earlier days as Saul of Tarsus, we are reminded of the danger of a deluded commitment. Paul, as a young man, shows us how we can passionately pursue a single purpose, but if Christ is not our dominant motivation and primary focus, then our religious zeal can lead us down the wrong path. We learn from Paul's pre-conversion days that a person can be totally persuaded they are 'right' and others are wrong. They can be convinced about being active in God's work and walking in His will, but in actual fact find themselves doing the very opposite.

Thank God for passion, may we all be fired up with more fervour; with a greater intensity; an unreserved enthusiasm, uninhibited emotion, and unrestrained commitment. The danger is though, in our zeal we can become blinkered by legalism, dogmatic, narrow-minded and intolerant of other people's views. We are then in danger of being blinded to the mistake of pursuing the wrong goals, following the wrong objectives and fighting the wrong battles.

There was no-one more passionate than this young hot-headed zealot, Saul of Tarsus; no-one more knowledgeable about God's requirements; he was a leading teacher of the law. However, misguided or 'unenlightened zeal' can bring many regrets and be the cause of a great deal of damage to the Church, just as was the case with this proud Pharisee. When Jesus isn't the centre of our lives we eventually, by degrees, become opinionated and unbalanced. No longer seeing things clearly we start to go off at a tangent, majoring on minor issues. Even in things that are important we become fixated to the extent that our attitude undermines our argument. We get enthusiastically zealous about some matter, but more often than not it isn't what God wants us to be throwing our lives into.

In 2 Thessalonians 2 we read of a great deal of religious fervour and speculation taking place that was only causing confusion and division. God's warning to the Church in verse 2 was for them not to be *"...quickly shaken in mind or excited, either by spirit or by word, or by letter purporting to be from us..."* Also in verse 3 we read, *"Let no one deceive you in any way."* Furthermore, the believers at Thessalonica were being warned in verse 11, that such individuals would be blinded by a *"Strong delusion."* Deception will be wide-spread in the last days with people convinced that what they stand for, and are doing is right, but who like Saul will be completely deceived.

There are many 'religious' people who are totally deluded today. They fight over doctrinal matters, fall out over minor issues of Bible translations; overemphasise aspects of truth; uphold their own interpretation of scripture and defend with fierce and strong conviction their personal theories. Some are able to do this with great persuasiveness but have no grace or love. When there is no close relationship with Christ they are just as deluded as Saul of Tarsus, and equally as dangerous!

Thank God though for His amazing mercy! The outcome of this religious person's deluded commitment is quite different after his conversion to Jesus as Lord. Following his surrender to Christ, we find a man passionate about the one and only thing that mattered to him and that was dying to himself, that he might live fully for Jesus! He expresses his single-minded devotion when writing to the Corinthian Christians. Here he says, *"For I determined not to know anything among you, except Jesus Christ and him crucified"* (1 Corinthians 2:2, NKJ).

In addressing the Church in Philippi, Paul's single-minded resolve was clear: *"One thing I do, forgetting what lies behind and straining forward to what lies ahead"* (Philippians 3:13b). A person can only effectively pursue this one goal when they have dealt with the matter of their own past regrets. Enthusiastically serving God and staying spiritually fresh becomes impossible while struggling with condemning memories. Allowing regrets to remain drags down the individual and destroys their relationship with God. Regrets eat away at us and will bring a barren weariness to our spiritual vitality.

We've all made mistakes and have done things we wish we hadn't. There are foolish choices we've made that have had negative consequences, but God doesn't want us to live tormented and overshadowed by our past. Just as was the case with Paul, there is forgiveness, restoration and release from all condemnation and sense of failure as we determine to make Jesus Lord of our lives. We see from Paul's story that as he brings Christ into the centre of his life, everything begins to take on a whole new perspective. He has a new passion and purpose, one that gives him the desire to be fully active in the work of the Lord.

Having made the necessary point earlier about the danger of being too busy to spend time with Jesus, it does need to be stated that God doesn't want us sitting around in passive inactivity either, as we 'wait upon Him'. Some Christians today should be a lot busier in the work of God than they are. Jesus said in John 9:4, *"We must work the works of him who sent me, while it is day; night comes, when no one can work."* Paul himself instructed the Church at Corinth to be, *"... steadfast, immovable, always abounding in the work of the Lord..."* (1 Corinthians 15:58).

There's a job for Jesus every one of us can do. He has got a plan and a purpose for our lives. We should use every opportunity to serve the Lord as much as we can, and as often as we can. Paul was a man of many talents,

45

demonstrating a variety of gifts and ministries. He was certainly a man of much activity in teaching the Church and evangelising the lost. One thing though held everything in balance and that was his priority to stay in a close relationship with Christ. When we have this right then all is well, however, if this principle isn't motivating our lives, we just strive in our own strength, struggle in our own ability, and wear ourselves out in the process!

In making sure our most important purpose and highest calling is living for Christ, we will always experience a peace, even in the busyness of life. There can be no such thing as 'burn out' when we are truly walking together with the Lord. Those who speak of their Christian life being so difficult and full of stress, to the point of being drained, clearly haven't understood the words of Jesus. He said, *"My yoke is easy, and my burden is light"* (Matthew 11:30). Anytime we find ourselves under unreasonable pressure and have little joy or peace in our lives, it is because we are working in our own strength and not the Lord's. God's work done in God's way may cause tiredness spiritually and physically, nonetheless, rest, restoration, refreshing and renewal will ultimately be the outcome. For this reason He is constantly calling us to a closer walk and partnership with Him.

Having looked at 'Ministering Martha', we've thought of how busyness can rob people of coming before the Lord and listening to His voice. With 'Devoted David', we've considered how distraction can lead Christians into temptation and cause even the strongest to fall into sin. And from 'Passionate Paul' we've seen that zeal, not centred on Christ, no matter how ardent or sincere, can bring delusion, causing people to be narrow-minded, blinded to the truth and leaving them with deep regrets.

As we finish this chapter let us briefly consider how to set our hearts on a single purpose:

1. Reaffirm Your Commitment To Walk In God's Will

Discovering God's purpose for our lives and remaining there is of utmost importance for every one of us. In Matthew 7:21-23 we read of people engaged in much busyness and being involved in dynamic, impressive activities, all of which are carried out in the Name of Jesus. This is one of the most challenging passages in the whole of the Bible and there is no easy way around what it is saying. Jesus states:

> *"Not everyone who says to me, 'Lord, Lord,' shall enter the kingdom of heaven, but he that does the will of my Father who is in heaven. On that day many will say to me, 'Lord, did we not prophesy in your name, and cast out demons in your name, and do many mighty works in your name?' And then I will declare to them, 'I never knew you; depart from me, you evil doers.'"*

It is not our ceaseless activity that matters, but being in the centre of God's will is what ultimately counts, and therefore this must always be our prayer and commitment.

2. Re-evaluate Your Present Priorities

To do what we should be doing we have to stop doing what we shouldn't. One of the clever tactics of Satan is to minimise our effectiveness by overloading our schedule with 'good works'. We must ask ourselves, 'Is the way I am spending my time, talents, energy, and my resources strengthening or weakening God's purpose for my life?' He does have a plan for all of us. He has a destiny for each one of us to fulfil, but we must regularly review the way we are using what He has given. We need to consider if how we are living is helping or hindering that God-given objective.

It was William Gladstone, Britain's oldest Prime Minister, who said, "To comprehend a man's life, it is necessary to know not merely what he does but also what he purposely leaves undone. There is a limit to the work that can be got out of a human body or a human brain, and he is a wise man who wastes no energy on pursuits for which he is not fitted; and he is still wiser who, from among the things he can do well, chooses and resolutely follows the best."

3. Eliminate Anything Hindering Your Life

Having identified anything that might be a hindrance in our life we must determine to be personally ruthless with ourselves. Here is where the call of living a consecrated life to God gets costly and painful. Enthusiastically pursuing what we know He has given us to do and maintaining that vigour will demand sacrifice. Sometimes people are spiritually depleted simply because of the 'excess baggage' they are clinging to, or at times are allowing to cling to them. This maybe sinful habits or just things unnecessary for them in the season and for the particular part of the Christian race they are in at the moment.

The writer to the Hebrew believers put it like this: *"Let us lay aside every weight, and sin which clings so closely, and let us run with perseverance..."* (Hebrews 12:1). Laying aside every weight is not just about always choosing between the 'bad' and the 'good'; it's about choosing between the 'good' and the 'best'. As far as specific sin is concerned though, this is a different matter. In Matthew 5:29-30 Jesus speaks of how ruthless He expects us to be when eliminating any sinful hindrances. Although of course this isn't instructing people to literally dismember or maim their bodies, but it is a command to radically deal with all sin. Jesus says,

> *"If your right eye causes you to sin, pluck it out and throw it away; ... if your right hand causes you to sin, cut it off and throw it away; it is better that you lose one of your members than that your whole body go into hell."*

4. Redefine Your Future Objectives

Where do you want to be twelve months from now? We need a clear vision and to set specific goals to give our life specific direction. Unless we have divine objectives to pray into and work towards, we will just go round in circles, wearing ourselves out. Just like the children of Israel whose journey from Egypt to the Promised Land should only have taken 11 days, yet took 40 years, we will be in the same position in twelve months from now as we are today. Also like the Israelites, we will find ourselves continually grumbling and complaining at God, when in actual fact, the confusion and delay is due to our own lack of focus.

If there are no goals, objectives and vision that motivate our lives, we grow tired and stagnate rather than developing a vibrant life. We need clarity of purpose to move us beyond where we are at the moment, so that we are pressing forward and running with eternity in view. The Apostle Paul understood this when he said in 1 Corinthians 9:26, *"I do not run aimlessly, I do not box as one beating the air."*

5. Re-establish The Principle Of Being Still

The reason why we must re-establish this is quite simply because every single day things crowd in and push Jesus out! Every day we get overwhelmed with people wanting our attention and demanding our time. Problems suddenly crop up that need to be fixed and we find our time with the Lord gets relegated, and Jesus gets marginalised. Therefore we must be decisive about the daily routine in our lives and develop the habit of waiting upon Him.

In Matt 6:6, Jesus spoke about the fact that there is something very simple and practical we have to do, He said *"... go into your room and shut the door..."* We must get away from everyone else and spend time alone, uninterrupted and unhurried with God, even if this requires taking the phone off the hook and shutting ourselves away. If Jesus is the most important person in our lives and time spent with Him is of utmost value to us, we will do whatever it takes. We can all make excuses and think of reasons why it cannot happen, but when we get this right, everything else begins to fall into place.

Therefore, where our lives have become too complicated and stressed out and we find ourselves chasing around with too many activities, resulting in weariness, we must recognise the Lord's call to be still. Let us choose to be people of *'one thing in mind'* and allow everything else to flow from that singleness of purpose. Our commitment needs to be affirmed as we declare 'I refuse to allow my heart to be **Divided,** my mind to be **Distracted**, or my spirit to be **Deluded**'. When we do this, the enemy will not be able to rob us of the time we must spend, and the action we must take, to stay in a close relationship with God.

Chapter 3

Seek Out Meaningful Fellowship

While the Lord Himself is the direct source of our life, He has provided the stimulation, strength and encouragement of other people for our wellbeing. Therefore to stay spiritually fresh we must not only be rightly connected to God, we need to be rightly connected to one another. An eternal truth, declared from the beginning of creation, is found in Genesis 2:18: *"... it is not good for the man to be alone."* One helpful definition of loneliness is **'The lack of any deep meaningful relationship with anyone'.** We were never created to live in isolation, but to be in fellowship with others of like mind; those made in God's image and who are 'carriers of His glory'. Being in a positive, productive relationship with our fellow believer reflects the reality of our intimacy with God.

Every born again believer needs Christian friendships; people they can trust; those who love them unconditionally and with whom they can share their lives. It is others we have a common purpose with, and to whom we are accountable, that will help keep us resilient, refreshed and renewed in life's battles. There is no doubt we are stronger together than we are on our own. The Bible says, *"A three-fold cord is not quickly broken"* (Ecclesiastes 4:12).

Using a different analogy, the red hot burning coal, falling out of the main blazing fire is very relevant here. As the coal falls out and is isolated from the whole, it grows dim, gets cold, and is no longer able to serve its original purpose. This is the case when meaningful fellowship is not part of our lives; we grow dim in the light of our testimony, cold in our love for God and unable therefore to fulfil the great destiny He has placed within us.

Christian fellowship is best understood from the Greek word *Koinonia*. This is an important word; one never used simply in a secular sense like a social club, or merely having a common interest with others in their hobbies etc. The idea of an earthly fellowship founded upon just human nature, or physical ties like in a family, or purely church affiliations, or solely on self-centred interests was a completely alien concept in the New Testament Church. To the Disciples of Christ, fellowship always had a **spiritual foundation**, a **spiritual orientation**, and a **spiritual purpose**. It became part of their everyday life and was expressed in everything they did.

The Basis for Meaningful Fellowship

Establishing a clear understanding here is essential in thinking about meaningful fellowship because the devil can so easily rob us of our spiritual freshness simply by keeping us busy with religious activity. There are therefore fundamentally three primary principles that form the basis for true Christian fellowship:

(a) The most important starting place is the centrality of Jesus Christ as Lord, in all aspects of life. Paul makes this apparent when saying, *"... in everything he should be pre-eminent"* (Colossians 1:18b). At a time when the Church is so fragmented and squabbling over minor issues, we must be united in Christ, not divided by doctrine. With all the different denominations and diverse interpretation of scripture that prevails, there are many things that we could find to disagree and fall out over. However, we need to major on the things we can find agreement in –*"For no-one can lay any foundation other than the one already laid, which is Jesus Christ"* (1 Corinthians 3:11, NIV).

True Christian fellowship is always based on a personal experience of who Jesus is. Without this revelation there can be no meaningful fellowship. In Matthew 16, the direct and personal question that Jesus challenged His disciples with, in verse 15, did not revolve around debate or discussion, it was, *"..but who do you say that I am?"* This gave Peter the opportunity to nail his colours to the mast and respond unequivocally in verse 16 with the declaration, *"You are the Christ, the Son of the living God."* It was upon this absolute and non-negotiable truth that the Lord replies, *"... on this rock I will build my Church"* (verse 18). That 'rock' of course was not Peter himself, as some religious people would claim, but the God-given revelation of who Jesus is.

(b) Another primary factor that establishes the basis for meaningful fellowship is an openness, integrity and honesty with one another. The apostle John emphasises the importance of there always being a transparency and sincerity with each other when he writes, *"If we walk, in the light as he is in the light, we have fellowship with one another..."* (1 John 1:7).

There can be no darkness of selfishness, pride or arrogance; no unrighteous attitudes nor shadow of mistrust and suspicion of one another. To benefit mutually from our lives together we must walk in the light with each other. Notice that the radiance of that standard is not our own estimation of what light may be; it is living our lives in the same degree of truthfulness and purity as God, who is The Light. This, of course, is in stark contrast to the ungodly that are spoken of in John 3:19b when we read, *"... men loved darkness rather than light, because their deeds were evil."*

(c) Servant-hood is the third foundational characteristic of genuine fellowship; it is the practical outworking of genuine love that holds all things together. The command of Jesus was that we should not only wholeheartedly love God, but also, *"You shall love your neighbour as yourself"* (Mark 12:31). In fact the reality of our claim to love God is demonstrated in how we unconditionally relate to others. This is something clearly implied in 1 John 4:20, which says, *"Anyone who does not love his brother, whom he has seen, cannot love God, whom he has not seen"* (NIV). Through the attitude of servant-hood we express, in meaningful and practical acts of kindness, our compassion for the needs of others.

Jesus lived among us as 'The Servant King' and by His example demonstrated how we are to sacrificially serve one another. He spoke in a parable to the religious leaders of the day about the practical actions of the Good Samaritan, concluding with the challenge, *"Go and do likewise"* (Luke 10:37). Ultimately, Christ himself took this to the extent of giving His life to be rejected, humiliated, abused, tortured and put to death, that we might be healed emotionally, physically and spiritually. He looked beyond His own needs and with compassion and commitment lived and died to serve others.

A fundamental outworking of true fellowship is our regular corporate gathering with one another, and therefore God's instruction is, *"Let us not give up meeting together, as some are in the habit of doing"* (Hebrews 10:25a, NIV). The devil knows that he will wear Christians down and rob them of vibrant spiritual power if he, **(a)** delays them from finding meaningful fellowship, **(b)** disconnects them from such relationships, or **(c)** devalues the importance of this to their lives.

According to Greek scholar Kenneth Wuest, the word *'forsake'* is a compound of three Greek words which translated has the meaning of rejection, defeat and helplessness. They describe someone who feels left out and helpless; spiritually and emotionally down; far behind everyone else. The moment a person feels like that, Satan can begin to drain their strength by causing them to focus on their negative thoughts of discouragement, disillusionment and resentment. This in turn soon affects their motivation to want to meet together. It is during this process that the alternative of staying home becomes much more attractive and the progression of lethargy slowly begins to set in, resulting in a spiritual inertia.

If Satan can isolate you from other believers at the very time when you need them most, he will steal God's blessing from you! Over the course of 34 years in full-time ministry I've frequently come across those who decided not to come to a church meeting because of tiredness, or just feeling they'd had a 'hard day'. In doing so they missed the very message that would have been perfect for their situation. By giving way to their feelings they allowed themselves to be robbed of what could have been a means of encouragement and restoration. Also, something becoming more common today is people who think they can just stay home and read their Bibles; turn on Christian radio and watch Christian television. In both cases this is a grave deception of the enemy. It is a strategy designed to rob people of their divine calling, restrict their great potential and bring increasing weariness and weakness into their lives.

To grow and stay spiritually fresh we need to find the best possible environment to make this happen. Ideally we must seek to be in a church that is not only sincerely loving but also Bible-based, Christ-centred, Spirit-led, prayer-reliant, evangelistically-motivated and, socially-active. Surrounded by such a company of believers you'll get answers to life's difficulties, experience meaningful joy, and receive counsel and prayer that you just won't find anywhere else. It is not God's will that we should be independent of other Christians. When the Bible speaks about the collective Christian faith it is best understood in terms of a corporate body, a community, an army, a family etc. The impact of this on a fragmented, dysfunctional and unbelieving society is profound and seen in the words of Jesus when He said, *"By this all men will know that you are my disciples, if you have love for one another"* (John 13:35).

Jesus is building His Church! - Not of bricks and mortar, but the united lives of those who love Him and also one another. The local Church therefore is the last thing the devil wants you to be a part of, especially when you're feeling low. He knows he can never prevail against the unified force of meaningful fellowship. It is within this environment we can be comforted by the **People of God**, encouraged by the **Presence of God**, reassured by the **Peace of God**, strengthened by the **Power of God**, enlightened by the **Perspective of God** and motivated by the **Purpose of God**. Having said that, no Church is perfect, and probably we will never find one that ticks all the boxes of our preferences. However, I do believe that there is a spiritual home for all who are willing to find one, wherever they may be.

There is no doubt also that Christians do disappoint and let us down. We may have been deeply hurt by the insensitivity of certain people, in fact some of the worst treatment we've received and many of our deepest wounds might well have been caused by fellow believers. Even though the command of Jesus in John 13:34 is uncompromisingly direct - *"... love one another; even as I have loved you,"* it never ceases to amaze me the appalling damage that one Christian will do to another. I've lost count of the ministers who've shared with me how they had almost been destroyed by the treatment of their congregation; the church members who've been spiritually and emotionally abused by their Pastor, and the number of Christians severely wounded by one another through gossip, criticism or ridiculous squabbles of one kind or another.

A similar problem was seriously affecting the spiritual health of the Church at Galatia; they were in danger of destroying themselves from within. Such ungodly behaviour fosters bitterness and hatred among people and robs a congregation of their enthusiasm. Paul addresses this concern in Galatians 5:15, warning the church, *"But if you bite and devour one another take heed that you are not consumed by one another."* The Greek scholar Robertson in his book, "Word Pictures", says that the verbs here were commonly used to describe the actions of wild animals tearing and destroying each other. The words biting and devouring are obviously used figuratively. *"Biting"* refers to the aggressive and incisive action of gnashing on one another through words and actions. It is little wonder therefore that James, when speaking about the evil of the tongue exclaims with exasperation, *"... My brethren, this ought not to be so"* (James 3:10b).

Regardless of the frustration we may have about a particular church, and in spite of the pain others have caused us, we must never let the devil take advantage here. Refuse to allow him to use your bad experiences of imperfect fellowship to rob you of what can be a tremendous source of help and restoration to your life. This is why the principle of humility and forgiveness is essential if we are to stay spiritually fresh. Harbouring wrong attitudes, no matter how justified we think we may be to hold them, can only damage our own lives and leave us wearied and weakened by feelings of bitterness and anger. The Bible's clear instructions therefore, in Mark 11:25 are, *"forgive, if you have anything against any one..."* and in Ephesians 4:32, *"Be kind to one another, tender-hearted, forgiving one another, as God in Christ forgave you."*

The Danger Of Rebellious Christians

In the same way that we draw power from God, we also draw energy and life from each other. While the good of *"Iron sharpening iron"* (Proverbs 27:17) can be a great strength and help to us, the opposite becomes true when there are carnal, independent, rebellious Christians who are a law unto themselves and have no submission to any specific local Church. They sap the life and energy of those they attach themselves to and can blunt the sharp cutting edge of dynamic believers.

'Butterfly Christians' flit from place to place with no intention, or inclination, to do anything but enjoy the benefits of fellowship, while staying elusive from responsibility. They can become subtle agents of the enemy bringing disharmony and distraction. These dangerous, idle people, go from church to church with no thought of sacrificing themselves or strengthening others; they are simply motivated by self-centred aims. They neither give of their time, talent, tithe or resources, nor are willing to submit to any kind of authority over them. These transient individuals weaken the strength of the Church and invariably become divisive to its unity. The Bible warns us in Romans 16:17-18 to, *"... take note of those..."* and also in 2 Thessalonians 3:6 to, *"... keep away from..."* such people.

We've had personal experience of this menace becoming a drain on the strength of our ministry in the Leicester Open-Air witness that we hold twice a month. For nineteen years a team has joined me to preach in the town centre and this has proven very fruitful, with the group growing, and many people making decisions for Christ. More recently though, we found ourselves under great spiritual oppression which left us completely exhausted after each meeting, and it became clear that this was a subtle attack of the enemy. Very quickly we discerned there were several 'floating Christians', who had no commitment to any church, coming along and engaging team members in pointless conversation, being a distraction and giving the appearance that they were part of our team. This was not only creating heaviness upon the meeting, but also significantly weakening its unity and fruitfulness.

In recognising this to be a spiritual battle we took immediate action; firstly, going straight to God in prayer and fasting, then alerting others by circulating the need for prayer among our Trustees, the team, and two intercessory networks throughout the country. Having done this we then confronted one of the main trouble makers responsible. His rebellious, independent attitude was instantly exposed as he aggressively refused to abide by the guidelines we'd laid down, and was unwilling to be submissive in any way. However, the united prayers and intercession of our friends both in Leicester and around the country soon prevailed. The problem was dealt with and it resulted in the heaviness lifting. A stronger unity was established amongst the team to witness with even greater effectiveness, and also the individual concerned came under conviction and eventually apologised for his attitude!

Committed Relationships, Not Comfortable Religion

Meaningful fellowship is not simply attending church meetings, looking at the back of people's heads, going through a predictable routine of hymns, prayers and preaching, then saying to people 'How are you?', and 'goodbye'. Nor is it established merely by enjoying tea and cakes after the service, or being caught up in endless social events to foster a happy, pleasant atmosphere. It can only come out of committed relationships that are based on a deep love for Christ and His call to active service together – characteristics far removed from comfortable religion!

The powerful principle of committed relationships is seen throughout the book of Acts, as we look at the dynamic life of the New Testament Church. These early Christians gladly yielded themselves, not only to God, but also to one another. The Bible says in Acts 2:42b they did not just *have* fellowship, but they *"devoted themselves to fellowship."* Moreover, we read that for them, this was a joy to express and something they practiced on a regular basis:

> *"And day by day, attending the temple together and breaking bread in their homes, they partook of food with glad and generous hearts"* (Acts 2:46).

A radical change of mindset is therefore necessary, so we can benefit from what God intended true fellowship to be. The distinctive characteristics must be a commitment to be together, serve, and show genuine concern – a willingness to look beyond our own problems and be a part of meeting the need of others. It is taking time to listen to another person's circumstances; to show interest in them, their family, work, joys, sorrows etc. Simply expressing encouragement, speaking a kind word, extending a warm embrace, or just communicating a smile goes a long way to ensure that someone feels valued and important. A selfless approach to life is fundamental, so that we move the focus away from our own needs, and are prepared to pour out our lives for others. Paul's instruction to the Church at Philippi, had this in mind when he wrote,

"Let each of you look not only to his own interests, but also to the interests of others" (Philippians 2:4).

To stay spiritually fresh, it is without doubt vital that we personally have regular input into our lives, and receive all the help we can ourselves. We must see though, of equal importance, the willingness to enthusiastically give out also. We need to move beyond passively receiving, to active, practical giving. Rather than just having the attitude of coming together to be blessed and refreshed, we ought to be sacrificing ourselves for others. Luke 6:38 is a principle that applies not merely in its immediate context to giving financially, but the sacrificial giving of our entire lives. We see from this verse how it enables us to be replenished and remain full of the blessing of God's resources:

*"Give, and it will be given unto you; good measure,
pressed down, shaken together, running over, will
be put into your lap. For the measure you give will
be the measure you get back."*

If someone comes along to church merely to discover
what they can 'get out' of the service, with the attitude of
sitting in judgement on the style of the meeting, the
eloquence of the sermon, the quality of worship and
assessing how many people spoke to them, then they are
going to be disappointed. This is because not only have
they come with the wrong motive, but by the measure they
have given, they have received – hence their lives are left
spiritually barren and dry.

On the other hand if a person's attitude is to come as a
worshipper, to give their best to God and also to contribute
in whatever way they can to build others up, the outcome
will be completely different. In seeking to move in the
gifts of the spirit, to pray out in the meeting, to speak well
of all they can, they will come away refreshed and filled
with God because; by the measure they have given will they
receive. The benefit of this truth is also seen in the wisdom
of Solomon when he writes, *"... he who refreshes others,
will himself be refreshed"* (Proverbs 11:25).

Looking further than our own circumstances, and
wanting our lives to be a source of refreshing to others,
unlocks one of the major secrets to staying spiritually fresh.
It cannot be emphasised enough that true Christian
fellowship, if it is to be meaningful, must of necessity be
practical! The key factor to the strength of the New
Testament Church was their practical commitment to one
another. These people not only had an amazing unity, but
we read this was followed through significantly, by their

willingness to personally share the burden of each others needs:

> *"Now the company of those who believed were of one heart and soul, and no one said that any of the things which he possessed was his own, but they had everything in common...there was not a needy person among them, for as many as were possessors of lands or houses sold them, and brought the proceeds of what was sold and laid it at the apostles' feet; and distribution was made to each as any had need"* (Acts 4:32 and 34).

For the New Testament Christians, meeting together was not out of a sense of religious duty, but the reality of delight in their common faith – they had an absolute dependence on one another. This is especially important to staying spiritually fresh because one of the other major tactics the enemy can use to wear people down, besides the emotional wounds inflicted upon them, and the infiltration and influence of rebellious Christians, is the opposition of persecution. The early Church was only too aware of how much they needed each other. They were acutely conscious of their vulnerability, due to the continual threat against their lives of harassment as they uncompromisingly preached the gospel. Their united, committed fellowship was of absolute necessity to keeping the vibrancy and vitality of their new lives in Christ burning brightly.

Reliance on one another and the fact that we can accomplish more together than by ourselves is powerfully illustrated in a wonderful story told about Jimmy Durante, one of the truly great American entertainers of the 1920's, through to the 70's. He was asked by the famous TV host,

Ed Sulivan, to accompany him to entertain some of the wounded and disabled veterans of World War II.

The comedian said he'd be delighted to do this, but because of his busy schedule he could only do one short monologue, then he'd need to leave immediately after, for his next appointment. This was understood and agreed, but when Jimmy got on stage he not only went through the short monologue, but stayed much longer than he'd planned. Soon he'd been on stage for over 30 minutes! Finally he took a last bow and left to thunderous applause. Backstage someone stopped him and said 'I thought you had to go after a few minutes - what happened?' Jimmy answered, with tears brimming in his eyes, 'You can see for yourself if you look over there on the front row.' As the man looked, he saw two veterans, each of whom had lost an arm in the war. One had lost his right arm and the other had lost his left. Combining their efforts, they were able to join the rest of the audience by clapping enthusiastically their two remaining hands together.

The Body Of Christ

Such interdependence and supportive commitment is the practical outworking of Paul's teaching to the Roman Christians when he wrote saying, *"We, though many, are one body in Christ, and individually members of one another"* (Romans 12:5).

The well known African-American spiritual song, "Dem Bones, Dem Bones, Dem Dry Bones" was used, allegedly, to teach basic anatomy to children on how the bones in the human body connect to each other. *"The hip bone is connected to the thigh bone. The thigh bone is connected to the knee bone. The knee bone is connected to the leg bone. The leg bone is connected to the ankle bone"* – etc.

There are 206 bones in the human body. Every one of them is important, but not one of them can function without the physical body. We have approximately 640 skeletal muscles, depending on which expert you consult - all important, but useless without the body. There are over 50 billion white cells in the body - all vital to fighting off disease, but not one stays alive outside the body.

The Apostle uses the analogy of a physical body to illustrate the relevance and importance of each member of the Church. Jesus Christ is its head and every believer, connected to one another, makes up its members. At conversion we become part of the world-wide body of Christ, but to stay alive spiritually and develop, we also need to be more specifically involved in the local expression of that body; part of a church where we can grow and function. God's plan is for us to play an active role and see ourselves as an integral part of a local fellowship of believers. He intends His Church to be healthy places and for the members of those churches to be spiritually healthy as well. For this to happen, each member must contribute to the health and growth of the whole. We therefore need to find and fulfil our God-given roles in the body of Christ.

Frequently I am asked the question, "How long have you been in ministry?" While I know what is meant by the enquirer, it does, at times, reveal a misconception that is common amongst Christians. As far as the Church is concerned there are not two categories of believers – those 'in the ministry' and those without. Every born-again Christian is called to some role or other within the church. It is true that 1 Corinthians 12:29 does say that not all are Prophets, Pastors, Apostles, Evangelists etc, but Paul teaches that every member of the body is significant and plays a vital role. Everyone is unique and has a special gift or ability.

To stay spiritually fresh we all need to be actively involved in using our gifts for God's glory and the benefit of the church in which we are a part. The question we need to be asking is the same as Saul of Tarsus, who at the point of his conversion wanted to know, *"Lord, what do You want me to do?"* (Acts 9:6, NKJ).

One very common problem among Christians today is an uncertainty about their gift and ministry. This is something that should initially be identified, encouraged and nurtured, within the local church. However, it requires from the person first of all a commitment to that local body, and secondly a submission to its leadership; two qualities of character that some Christians, because of impatience or independence, are not too enthusiastic about working on.

It has to be said also that not all Ministers are as positive and helpful as they could be, to see individuals express themselves and grow in their particular ministry. Sometimes, because of insecurity on their part, they see other Christians with potential as a threat to themselves. It is not uncommon for the Pastor, by choice, to do everything within a church and therefore give little or no opportunity and room for others to develop. If people are stopped or stifled in their function several things start to happen that affects their spiritual freshness:

(a) They become anxious and insecure in so far as they feel unimportant, unrecognised and unwelcome; like a spare part in the church, with nothing much to offer. The feeling of rejection, insignificance and inadequacy can cause people to struggle and strive to fit in and therefore they lose confidence.

(b) Frustration and dissatisfaction begins to develop because their enthusiasm is being dampened and the sense of destiny within them denied. In feeling like a 'square peg in a round hole', people become discouraged and unfulfilled.

(c) Wrong attitudes then soon start to surface and result in people getting resentful, critical, and negative about the leadership's lack of recognition towards their personal situation. This in turn quickly spills over towards those around who do have a function in the church, and they become jealous and judgemental about the ability of others.

(d) Spiritual lethargy ultimately develops because as people feel overlooked, unappreciated, or squashed, they lose all motivation and interest. Becoming conditioned to inactivity is a dangerous threat to spiritual freshness. Where little is expected of people other than to turn up, listen and pay their tithe, eventually they will decide to sit back and leave everything for others to do, thinking, 'Why bother!'

The ultimate end product of this process can be seen in Billy Graham's perception of a church in spiritual decline. He illustrated the problem using the analogy of a football match where 90 thousand overweight and unfit people look on from the comfort of their stadium seats. Vigorously they shout out advice and express criticism towards the two teams playing, while the twenty-two players on the field are running around exhausted doing all the work! The crowd might well feel justified in their attitude, thinking, "It's their job; they get paid for it, and that's what they've been trained to do." However, while that might be so in terms of football, it certainly should never be the case as far as the Church is concerned. May God deliver us from the prevailing problem in most churches of too few doing too much! We are all, without exception, called, gifted and anointed to work together as one!

If every member of the Church isn't actively involved in some way, not only will the spiritual life of the individual suffer, but the strength and growth of the church will be affected also. A body with non-functioning or partially functioning parts will be handicapped, undeveloped and restricted in its great potential. This is obvious in the natural realm, but it is equally true on a spiritual dimension.

In 1 Corinthians 12:1, Paul says, *"Concerning spiritual gifts, I do not want you to be uninformed."* We must not get side-tracked here into thinking merely in terms of supernatural gifts, vital as these are to the believer's development. The underlying purpose in all of the Apostle's teaching was that people might be clear in their mind concerning the will of God for them in every aspect of their lives. This is why in praying for the Colossian Church he said,

> *"We have not ceased to pray for you, asking that you may be filled with the knowledge of his will, in all spiritual wisdom and understanding, to lead a life worthy of the Lord, fully pleasing to him, bearing fruit in every good work and increasing in the knowledge of God"* (Colossians 1:9-10).

The moment we are converted this area of knowing God's will is a crucial matter throughout our lives. Before we can be actively involved and function effectively in the body we need to be clear about our ministry. God's purpose for us should never be a secondary issue in our priorities, nor should we stumble along in the thinking that this is something only for a select special few to know. The will of God therefore is not something vague, mystical and unknowable. He doesn't hide it from us, but does reveal it to those who want to know and are prepared to seek Him with all their hearts.

The Involvement Of Every Believer

Even on a bad day every Christian has at least one gift! We may feel inept and inadequate at times, but God has gifted us all to do at least one thing well in His body. There is no such thing as an appendix in the body of Christ, each person has a vital function and a part to play that is important. No-one is unnecessary! Ephesians 4:15-16 says, *"... we are to grow up in every way into him who is the head, into Christ, from whom the whole body, joined and knit together by every joint with which it is supplied..."* When each part is working properly and every joint is supplying, it makes bodily growth possible and builds itself up in love. God's desire for every individual, and the goal for each believer, is maturity and growth, as seen in verse 13, *"... to mature manhood, to the stature of the fullness of Christ."*

Such growth is only possible in an environment of love and encouragement where people feel secure to take risks and to step out and see themselves stretched and developed. One of the major strategies of Satan is to destroy this environment of love and mutual respect, because then the body becomes damaged. This was a problem that Paul had to address in Corinth, because of the division, party spirit, cliques, criticism and resentments. In 1 Corinthian 12:15-16 he says,

"If the foot should say, "Because I am not a hand, I do not belong to the body," that would not make it

any less a part of the body. And if the ear should say, "Because I am not an eye, I do not belong to the body," that would not make it any less a part of the body."

Harmony within the body can only be experienced when every person feels valued in whatever role they have; no-one should feel insignificant if they haven't the same ministry as someone else. Paul goes on therefore in 1 Corinthians 12 to teach some foundational truths about the Church as the body of Christ:

Verse 18, "God has arranged the organs in the body, each of them, as he chose."

We have been chosen by God to serve in a particular way and in a specific place within the church. God knows where we will be fulfilled and function best and wants to place us there as we submit ourselves gladly to His will.

Verse 21, "The eye cannot say to the hand, "I have no need of you," nor again the head to the feet, "I have no need of you."

We cannot function independently of the body in isolation to the whole. An attitude of interdependence on one another is needed. Each person must see that they are in the body, not primarily to express themselves, though that is important, they are there to serve the whole.

Verse 24-25, "God has so composed the body, giving the greater honour to the inferior part, that there may be no discord in the body."

God gives greater honour to those parts that might 'appear' less important, attractive or visible. In His sight their role is just as valuable. God sees our worth and honours us. Because of this we must have the same attitude of respect and esteem towards one another.

Verse 26, *"If one member suffers, all suffer together; if one member is honoured, all rejoice together."*

We see here an attitude of deep care and sensitivity to each other. What affects one part of the body is felt by the whole. This is why God's Word says in Romans 12:15 that we are to, *"Rejoice with those who rejoice and weep with those that weep."* Every single Christian is like a living cell in the body and for the body to be fit and strong every cell must live in harmony with the other cells. In Romans 15:5-6 Paul speaks of this unity of purpose when he writes,

"May the God of steadfastness and encouragement grant you to live in such harmony with one another, in accord with Christ Jesus, that together you may with one voice glorify the God and Father of our Lord Jesus Christ."

Identifying Our Ministry And Function

In bringing this chapter to a close let me just conclude with some simple, practical points that will help people find their place and function in the local church. These steps must of course be accompanied with prayer and much patience because of any potential barriers that might be encountered on the way. This is particularly so if a person is in a church that gives little encouragement and recognition to the members being involved. In such situations let us remember that if God has led us to that church then ultimately He will make a way for us to be used as we follow these steps:

1. Start on the basis of a wholehearted commitment, motivated by faith that believes God has a role for you to function in. It is out of this submission to fulfil God's will and your enthusiasm to see His purpose worked out in your life that you can discover what He has planned for you. Solomon said in Proverbs 3:6, *"In all your ways acknowledge him, and he will make straight your path."*

2. Maintain a servant attitude and approach to life that is willing and available to do whatever can be done. This will involve being alert and responsive to situations of need that may arise, without waiting to be asked to volunteer. We won't get a verse of scripture saying "Cleaning rota", "Welcoming people at the door", "Hymn book distribution", "Coffee/tea, Crèche or Flower rota", "Sunday School work", "Visiting the sick", or "Gardening" etc. Therefore our attitude of heart must be that we want to serve wherever and whenever there is a need.

3. Be faithful in the small things so that whatever we do we carry out with a spirit of excellence, to the best of our ability. Our motive in everything we involve ourselves with is to honour God and not to be seen by others. Luke 16:10 says, *"He who is faithful in very little is faithful also in much."* Also in Ecclesiastes 9:10 we read, *"Whatever your hand finds to do, do it with all of your might..."*

4. Do something practical to discover your gift, not just praying and asking the Lord. For example diligently search the scriptures and see the wide variety of things that can be done.

We find in God's Word three distinctive streams, or areas of gifting – Romans 12:6-8 – Ephesians 4:11-14 – 1 Corinthians 12:8-10. These are clearly defined roles, but also there are many other areas, besides those previously mentioned, that aren't so obviously stated, such as counselling, administration, singing ministry, drama group, intercession etc.

5. Consider the natural talents that you have been given; things you enjoy being involved with and what you feel comfortable doing. Ask yourself how you can use these abilities for the Lord. Our natural abilities and talents are often a good clue to the area of ministry that God wants to use us in. If we are artistic, musical, practical with our hands, good at figures, enjoy giving hospitality, find communication naturally easy etc. then these are areas we could blossom out in as we use our gifts within the Church context.

6. In humility and with a teachable spirit seek the counsel and confirmation from those in leadership, so you can discuss and pray through the areas that are on your heart together. Often other people will see in us a gift or ability long before we ourselves are made aware of it. This was so in my own life; before I went into full-time ministry it was one of the leadership in my local Brethren church who recognised the call of God on me. He said he believed I should take the step of faith and asked if I would pray about it. Solomon saw the importance of other people's guidance when he wrote in Proverbs 11:14b, "... *in an abundance of counsellors there is safety.*"

7. When you know your ministry you can confidently ask God to make a way, even where there seems to be no way. Trust Him to create the opportunities that you need to develop. Your faith must be in Christ who said, *"I have set before you an open door, which no man is able to shut"* (Revelation 3:8). Furthermore, the added assurance we have is that we will not need to force the situation or manipulate people because the Bible says, *"A man's gift makes room for him and brings him before great men"* (Proverbs 18:16). Also, Peter writing from his own personal experience, to encourage the believer, instructs them saying,

> *"Humble yourselves therefore under the mighty hand of God, that in due time he may exalt you"* (1 Peter 5:6).

Chapter 4

Thirst For The Fullness
Of The Holy Spirit

To stay spiritually fresh and in a position to be effectively used by the Lord we must continually be filled with the Holy Spirit; living lives infused by the dynamic energy of God. Our total dependence on His anointing, indwelling and transforming power is essential if we are to maintain the quality of living which made Christians, throughout Church history, so extraordinary.

Charles Finney is an outstanding example of what God can do through the life of someone dependent on the person of the Holy Spirit and wholly yielded to Him. Born on August 29, 1792 he became an important figure in the second 'Great Awakening' that swept across America at the end of the 18th Century and into the 19th Century. His influence during this period was so significant that he has been called "The Father of Modern Revivalism." Referring to the fullness and impact of the Holy Spirit upon his life he wrote:

"God gave me mighty infillings of the Holy Spirit that went through me, as it seemed, body and soul. I immediately found myself endued with such power from on high that a few words dropped here and there to individuals were the means of their immediate conversion. My words seemed to fasten like barbed arrows in the souls of men. They cut like a sword. They broke the heart like a hammer. Multitudes can attest to this. Sometimes I would find myself in a great measure empty of this power. I would go and visit, and find that I made no saving impression. I would exhort and pray with the same results. I would then set apart a day for private fasting and prayer, after humbling myself and crying out for help, the power would return upon me with all its freshness. This has been the experience of my life."

In the early days of Dwight L. Moody there was not much that caused him to stand out as someone who would later become a world famous preacher, and regarded by many as the greatest evangelist of the 19th Century. Born February 5th 1837, he grew up in a poor family, as one among eight other siblings, and whose father died an alcoholic at the age of 41, when he was only four years of age. His spiritual journey did not get off to a very auspicious start. The first application he made for membership at the local Congregational Church was rejected and his teacher, Edward Kimball, said of him:

"I can truly say, and in saying it I magnify the infinite grace of God that has been bestowed upon him, I have seen few minds that were spiritually darker than was his when he came into my Sunday School class. Also I think that the committee of the church had seldom met an applicant for membership more unlikely ever to become a Christian of clear and decided views of

gospel truth, still less fill any sphere of public usefulness."

Though initially this unremarkable young man showed little promise, eventually he left his mark upon history, not only by the grace of God, but also, notably, because of his complete surrender to the Holy Spirit. In one instance when he was about to have a large campaign in England an elderly pastor protested, "Why do we need this 'Mr. Moody?' He's uneducated and inexperienced. Who does he think he is anyway? Does he suppose he has a monopoly on the Holy Spirit?" A younger, wiser pastor rose and responded, "No sir, but the Holy Spirit has a monopoly on Mr. Moody!"

Here is where we find the secret to every great servant of the Lord; a willingness to unreservedly yield all to God so that the power of the Holy Spirit might take control. This was also very much the case with Kathryn Kuhlman, born on May 14th 1907, who arguably was one of the greatest healing evangelists of the 20th Century. God used her in an extraordinary way to bring miraculous healing to many who were totally incurable. She had no doubt about the importance of the Holy Spirit in her life and frequently referred to His abiding presence with her as, *'My best friend and greatest teacher.'*

There are various symbols of the Holy Spirit in Scripture, each of which express some distinctive attribute of His character and work, such as:

(a) **Wind** or **Breath** – as an activating force, imparting the life, strength and power of God (Genesis 2:7, Ezekiel 37:9-10, John 3:8, John 20:22, and Acts 2:1-2). This, as with every aspect of the Holy Spirit's operation, is dependent on His sovereign initiative, but we can benefit from positioning ourselves accordingly. It was Charles Spurgeon who said, "Although we can't make the wind blow, we can put up our sails."

(b)   **Wine** – representing a life where the ordinary is transformed to the extraordinary (John 2:1-11) bringing confidence and joyful freedom from inhibitions (Acts 2:15 and Ephesians 5:18). This imagery can also refer to a new work of God's Spirit that can't be restricted by old and inflexible structures (Luke 5:36-39).

(c)   **Oil** – speaking of divine anointing for service: Kings, Priests and Prophets were anointed with oil (Exodus 29:7, 1 Kings 19:15-16, Leviticus 8:10-12 and Psalm 133:2). Jesus Himself was anointed by a woman with an Alabaster box of oil, as an expression of her worship for who He was, and what He had come to accomplish (Matthew 26:6-13). Oil was also used as a symbol of the Holy Spirit bringing healing, (James 5:14-15) and the substance of energy that causes our lives to shine, (Psalm 104:15).

(d)   **Fire** – an enabling supernatural power (Matthew 3:11, and Acts 2:3-4); a sign of God's approval and intervention on behalf of His people to overcome their enemies (1 Kings 18:24-39). This is also understood as a picture of the Holy Spirit expressing judgement and purification, to illuminate and purge our lives from sin (Zechariah 13:9).

(e)   **A Dove** – expressing peace and sacrifice, reflecting His gentleness, purity and mercy (Mark 1:9-11, and John 1:32-34).

(f) **A Cloud** – an evidence of the manifest presence of God's glory among His people, indicating His guidance, protection and abiding faithfulness (Exodus 13:21-22, and 1 Corinthians 10:1-2).

Each of these images are important aspects of the Holy Spirit that we would benefit from seeking a greater revelation of. For the purpose of this book though, it is the symbol of 'Water', bringing refreshing and renewal that our main focus will be upon. Water is an integral source of life and without it the world would be a dry and desolate wasteland. One of the most memorable incidents of God speaking to me relates to this symbol and came during a sabbatical trip to Canada, while visiting Niagara Falls. The experience was amazing and the sight quite spectacular, particularly as our approach by boat took us right into the very mouth of the falls.

Although all on board were given protective raincoats, we found ourselves quickly drenched, because of the enormous amount of spray coming from the deluge of cascading water. The powerful, thunderous sound was almost deafening as we stood on the boat looking up, watching in awe, the vast and endless supply which was pouring down. God reminded me of how the river of His Holy Spirit is sweeping powerfully across the world today and of His promise in Joel 2:28, *"... I will pour out my Spirit on all flesh..."*. This is something that all, in every generation, who set their hearts on seeking, can receive, for God has said,

"I will pour water on the thirsty land, and streams on the dry ground; I will pour my Spirit upon your descendants, and my blessing on your offspring. They shall spring up like grass amid waters, like willows by flowing streams" (Isaiah 44:3-4).

79

This incident at Niagara was particularly significant because prior to flying to Toronto, a leader from one of the churches I'd spoken at, shared a vision God had given him for me. He knew nothing about my sabbatical, or where I was going but the voice of the Lord could not have been clearer. This man said he saw me standing under a waterfall, being refreshed and renewed, and as a result I would be more effective in bringing the power of God's life to others. It was a word that immediately came alive to me as I gazed up at the waters giving thanks to the Lord for what I was privileged to be experiencing.

God's River Of Life

The picture of water in the form of a river bringing the life and blessing of God is one that can be traced right through the Bible, from the beginning in Genesis 2:10, to the end in Revelation 22:1-2. As Christians we can be assured that in every phase of our walk with God, from life's first breath to our last, the Holy Spirit is brooding over us, working within, and enabling us to fulfil our destiny.

This is particularly so in the unsettling experiences of life; those turbulent times people go through that have the potential of causing weariness, wearing them down. For some Christians such dark seasons of the soul can bring them to a place of despair and spiritual barrenness. In Psalm 46 though, we find even during these difficult periods of adversity, the Lord has made provision to keep His people refreshed, strong and in a place of rejoicing. In this chapter, amidst all the tumult and instability going on, we see the supply of a supernatural river in verse 4: *"There is a river whose streams make glad the City of God..."* There will never be a crisis, or a calamity that will stifle the joy of the Lord in our lives, as long as we are filled with His Holy Spirit.

It is interesting to note in verse 4, the Psalmist speaks of one river, the Holy Spirit, but various streams that flow out from its source, bringing refreshing and gladness to the people of God. Here we see the miracle of the Lord's provision to refresh us in times of need. He sends His grace, sometimes directly, and on other occasions through anointed, Spirit-filled people who bring to us hope, healing, deliverance, renewal, guidance, encouragement, comfort, joy etc. God's intention in doing this, is that we are brought to the place of living in the flow of His Spirit, and that these living waters then issue out from our lives to meet the needs of others.

The early Church was filled with the power of God and brought that dynamic life wherever they went. We too will carry the same blessing to people, if we are prepared to be led deeper into the realm of the Holy Spirit. In Ezekiel 47 we see a wonderful picture of this 'River of Life', symbolising the Spirit and power of the Lord working in our world today. Notice in verse 1, the source of the river comes out from the Temple, signifying the location of God's presence. The river then flows past the altar, which refers to the place of our surrender and sacrifice. It begins as a small trickle but grows into a mighty river, too deep to stand in. We then see in verse 3-5 the servant of the Lord willingly being led, gradually, in measured degrees; first to ankle depth, then to the knees, further still to the loins and eventually to where the river is deep enough to swim in.

Gently the Lord takes us forward to the place of experiencing liberty in the fullness of the Holy Spirit. To know this freedom though, ultimately we must be prepared to take our feet off the bottom. By doing this, we let go of being in control and abandon ourselves to the flow of His direction. From the position of having been in the river we are then able to see the effect it has on all it touches.

Not until we have yielded ourselves to the fullness of the Holy Spirit and He has changed our lives can we perceive the supernatural significance of what is happening all around us. This is why the Bible says,

> *"The unspiritual man does not receive the gifts of the Spirit of God, for they are folly to him, and he is not able to understand them because they are spiritually discerned"* (1 Corinthians 2:14).

Ezekiel is prophetically teaching that, after the experience of our new found freedom, our eyes will be opened to see the wider work of what the Lord is doing. When the Holy Spirit flows from God to man it will result in a transformation both personally and generally in the earth around:

(a) Verse 7 and 12: Here we see lining the river banks, fruitful life-sustaining trees with leaves that bring healing. This symbolism speaks of mature people being raised up who remain close to the river and whose roots go deep down into its life giving flow. These then become a source of healing to others.

(b) Verse 8: Ezekiel writes of how the River of God flows into the Dead Sea and turns its salty, stagnant waters into fresh water. Only God's Spirit can accomplish this; with Him lifeless situations are miraculously transformed and stagnant circumstances that seem beyond change supernaturally come alive!

(c) Verse 9-10: Shows us that wherever the river goes it brings life. This results in so many fish in the Dead Sea that fishermen line up on its banks ready for a catch of multitudes! What we have here is an encouraging reference to a new motivation for effective evangelism occurring! Almost effortlessly remarkable results are seen; even in areas that previously have shown no response at all there will be an unusual and large catch!

The Dependence Of Jesus On The Holy Spirit

One of the great titles given to Jesus in scripture is, 'The Christ', meaning the Anointed One sent by God. Although Jesus was conceived of the Holy Spirit we read in Luke 3:21-22 that at the age of about thirty years, after Jesus was baptised, the Holy Spirit *"..descended upon Him in the form of a dove."* Further on in Luke 4:1 we see that He returned from His baptism in the Jordon, *"Full of the Holy Spirit and was led by the Spirit for forty days in the wilderness, to be tempted by the devil."* After this time of fasting and resisting the enemy He must have been extremely tired, but verse 14 tells us, *"Jesus returned in the power of the Spirit into Galilee..".* Then in verse 18-19 He declares,

> *"The Spirit of the Lord is upon me, because he has anointed me to preach good news to the poor. He has sent me to proclaim release to the captives, and recovering of sight to the blind, to set at liberty those who are oppressed, to proclaim the acceptable year of the Lord."*

From this point on there were immense demands made upon the ministry and work of Jesus that could have left Him exhausted. Tremendous pressures spiritually, physically, and emotionally were consistently confronting Him due to the multitude of needs He was surrounded by. Success was only possible because of the continual presence of the Holy Spirit that daily refreshed, filled and sustained His soul. The same is true of ourselves as His disciples; we need to depend on the fullness of His Spirit to remain spiritually alert and fresh at all times.

Whatever God has assigned us to do, and all that He has called us to be, can only ever be accomplished effectively and fruitfully in the fullness of the Holy Spirit. Without doubt there is no quicker way of feeling weary and dry than struggling and striving in our own strength to complete any task. Success in accomplishing our assignment in life is achieved by the power of God, which is why He said, *"Not by might, nor by power, but by my Spirit, says the Lord of hosts"* (Zechariah 4:6).

The Promise Of Jesus To His Disciples

The simple fact is that we never need to be in a position of relying on our own resources. The promise of Jesus to His disciples in John 7:37 is direct, clear and one we can all claim today: *"... If any one thirsts, let him come to me and drink. He who believes in me, as the scripture has said, 'Out of his heart shall flow rivers of living water."* Jesus does not speak about a trickle, a dribble, or even one river – His promise is that 'rivers' shall flow out of our lives! Therefore we become a blessing everywhere we go! When meeting people, they then go from our presence refreshed, rather than depressed, built up and strengthened, instead of drained!

Water is the most essential element next to air, to our survival and without it we would die in just a few days. The human brain is made up of approximately 80% water molecules; blood is 85% and our lungs around 82%. A mere 2% drop in our body's water supply can trigger signs of dehydration: fuzzy short-term memory, trouble with basic maths, and difficulty focussing on smaller print, such as a computer screen.

Health experts tell us that our physical bodies benefit greatly from drinking eight glasses of water a day. Apparently this is extremely good for us, and the same is true spiritually. When we are regularly thirsting for and drinking of the Holy Spirit, it enables us to enjoy vibrant healthy living. Therefore, Ephesians 5:18 says that we are to, *"... be filled with the Spirit."* This must be a constant and continual filling in our lives, not simply an initial 'one off' experience.

We are all, at times, 'leaky buckets'; one moment we can be full of the Holy Spirit, then because of sin, offence, and wrong attitudes, we can quench or grieve the Spirit of God, and find ourselves parched and empty! Great care needs to be taken that our lives never dry up, particularly amidst the various conflicts, temptations and pressures of life. Regardless of the difficulties we face, we are able to draw upon His full and limitless provision. To do this, we must have an expectant, faith-filled attitude: *"With joy you shall draw water from the wells of salvation"* (Isaiah 12:3).

In gathering together as the Church, we ought to take time to personally prepare spiritually and drink of the Holy Spirit before setting out, rather than coming to the meeting to drink. Imagine how different Church would be if every member took the time to be filled with the Holy Spirit before they came to any service. They would arrive with the anointing of God upon them and with the power of His presence in their lives. In that position they could, right from the start of the service, not only worship the Lord in a meaningful way, but also be a tremendous encouragement to others.

Interestingly, people have an understandable expectation that the minister or visiting preacher has taken the time to prepare himself, prior to each service. Congregations would not be too happy if the Pastor just turned up to preach, without making sure he was full of the Holy Spirit and had the anointing of God upon his life, before he came. They would consider it an affront to God and a sign of disrespect towards them if he wasn't prepared. This being true, why shouldn't the congregation show the same diligence and consideration towards God and each other, so they too are spiritually prepared? Whether it is the deacon welcoming people at the door, the Sunday school teacher, youth leader, worship group, or individual church member – all need to be filled with the Holy Spirit for effective service.

When we come together we are all ministers and priests before the Lord and as such ought to prepare accordingly. It is no good complaining about the dryness or dullness of the church we go to if we are not willing to make a difference! If we want spiritually healthy churches we must be spiritually healthy believers – those that have a dependence on the Holy Spirit and who seek to be continually filled with His presence. With such an attitude God promises to ensure our lives flourish; in fact an important part of our destiny is to thrive and remain spiritually fresh. Isaiah speaks of this when he says,

> *"And the Lord will guide you always; he will satisfy your needs in a sun-scorched land and will strengthen your frame. You will be like a well-watered garden, like a spring whose waters never fail"* (Isaiah 58:11, NIV).

The significant difference the Holy Spirit makes to our lives is seen in the words of Paul when he writes to the Christians at Ephesus. His prayer for them is that they might be, *"... strengthened with might through his Spirit in the inner man"* (Ephesians 3:16). There is the outer man that we want everyone to love and be impressed by, and then there is also the inner man – that spiritual part of our being which very often nobody else but God truly sees. Most people spend a great deal of concern, cost and care, making sure that the outer man is presentable and acceptable to others, but we ought to be far more concerned that our inner man is strong and pleasing to the Lord.

The New Testament Church

It was the author and pastor Dr. A. W. Tozer who said, "If the Holy Spirit was withdrawn from the Church today, 95 percent of what we do would go on, and no one would know the difference. However, if the Holy Spirit had been withdrawn from the New Testament church, 95 percent of what they did would stop, and everybody would know the difference!"

Those whose lives are dependent on the Holy Spirit and who are being regularly refreshed and renewed by His presence, display an obvious enthusiasm in living for Christ – a vigour that is unmistakeable in all they do. Wherever people are continually thirsting for the fullness of God's Spirit then not only is growth accelerated, but also there is an anticipation, excitement and freedom in their living as well. The Bible tells us, *"... where the Spirit of the Lord is, there is freedom"* (2 Corinthians 3:17). Because New Testament Christians walked in the power of the Holy Spirit their liberty was something that no demon from hell, or power on earth could contain – they became unstoppable history makers!

In a culture today, largely preoccupied with success, image and performance, Church growth is often only thought of in terms of strategy, organisational skills, special outreach meetings and endeavours of great effort. The actual need though is much more fundamental than this. What should be of greater concern is the importance of developing spiritually healthy believers, who live in the fullness of the Holy Spirit. Such people, by the very nature of the Spirit within them, will always be increasing in strength and in the influence they have on others.

Without doubt the early Church, while not without its faults, was vibrant and healthy as long as it walked in the power of God. They influenced multitudes and *"... the Lord added to their number day by day..."* (Acts 2:47). They grew and made a tremendous difference in their society, so much so that they couldn't be ignored! The Church became what Jesus declared it would be: *"A City set on a hill that could not be hid"* (Matthew 5:14) – not a hamlet, or a village but a City! It was impossible not to notice their presence; in fact great concern was caused to the Jews by them. Anxiously they said, *"These men who have turned the world upside down have come here also"* (Acts17:6).

The astonishing thing is that their vibrant, dynamic spiritual health was developed against a background of serious spiritual sickness all around them. Diverse pagan religions, dark occult practice, degrading temple prostitution, dogmatic vain traditions, the demands of Emperor worship and the dangers of fierce persecution were widespread. However, in spite of this we see Christian believers exuding radiant vitality, radical commitment and remarkable growth. Early Christianity was attractive, exciting and effective – certainly a stark contrast to the bland religion of its day and the blatant depravity of the society in which it lived. Without doubt it was the presence of the Holy Spirit among them that transformed their lives and made the difference.

Jesus had previously said to His disciples, *"You shall receive power when the Holy Spirit has come upon you; and you shall be my witnesses..."* (Acts 1:8). The fulfilment of this and other such related promises came to pass in the lives of the first Christians, and are still to be fully realised today in the Church. The distinctive evidence of such vivacious life is seen in four characteristics that express positive spiritual health. These are:

(1) A Purpose That Is Irrepressible

To be a witness for Christ and see others changed by the gospel was their main purpose for living. The early Church was thoroughly and unashamedly evangelical! They were united in the priority of sharing the gospel; it was their heartbeat and their life blood! Materialism and personal comfort meant nothing to them. Self-advancement and popularity held little attraction. Entanglement in secular pursuits was of no interest. They did not exist for their own end, but were gripped by a heavenly calling.

There was no confusion or vagueness, their mission was clear; they were purpose-driven believers. The religious leaders could not stifle them, the Roman powers could not squash them, and the demonic hosts could not subdue them. This selfless commitment of purpose is needed from every 'Spirit-Filled' believer, who desires to make a difference. Paul spoke about it when writing to the Church at Corinth. Using the example of Jesus he says,

"He died for all, that those who live should live no longer for themselves but for him who died for them and was raised again" (2 Corinthians 5:15, NIV).

Living for Jesus is the greatest purpose we can have in life. It is possible to have achieved a great deal in the eyes of man, but if Christ is not at the centre of our accomplishments, then whatever we've done amounts to very little in the light of eternity.

This could be said of the world famous British philosopher and intellectual Bertrand Russell. He was born into a Christian home, in Wales on May 18th 1872, and taught to believe in God, but he rejected this and became an outspoken atheist. He was awarded the Nobel Prize in literature in 1950 and received many titles, honours and accolades. However, his daughter said of him, "Somewhere at the bottom of his heart, in the depth of his soul, there was an empty space that once had been filled by God, and he never found anything else to put in it."

The tragedy of such wasted potential is summed up by the well known American baseball player Billy Sunday. He was born November 19th 1862 into poverty and at the age of ten spent several years in an orphanage. In spite of his difficult and disadvantaged childhood he committed his life to serving Christ. Leaving his successful professional sporting career, he eventually became one of the nation's greatest and most irrepressible evangelists during the first two decades of the 20th century. With profound insight Billy Sunday declared, "More men fail through lack of purpose than lack of talent."

When God's Word says in 1 Corinthians 1:26, *"Consider your call..."*, it is clear that He does not look for **Ability**, but **Availability**; those who will give themselves unreservedly to His purpose for their lives. God does not necessarily call the qualified, He qualifies the called! It is then, just as with the New Testament Church, He will pour out His Holy Spirit upon the most unlikely people, often from the most humble and difficult backgrounds, and enable them to be used in an outstanding way for His Glory. There can be found plenty of talent in the Church today, but what is needed more than this are those who have a clear God-given purpose through whom the Holy Spirit can work.

(2) A Passion That Is Inextinguishable

Someone can have a clear purpose, but unless they also have a passion to keep their objective alive then it becomes dry, empty and mere routine. Every great movement and denomination starts with a purpose, however once the passion is lost, then the purpose becomes meaningless and irrelevant.

In Revelation 12:11 we see the New Testament Christians had this passion which compelled them to make the ultimate commitment: *"..they loved not their lives even unto death."* There was no way that anyone could dampen the fire of the early church. We see how inextinguishable their passion was in Acts 4:1-3 and verse 18. Here, they had been arrested and threatened because of preaching the gospel. As soon as they were released though, verse 29 shows us they went to God in prayer saying, *"Lord, look upon their threats, and grant to thy servants to speak thy word with great boldness."* This prayer was immediately followed by them going out once more, proclaiming Christ. Then in Acts 5:17-18 we see the consequences of their action resulted in them being arrested again, and imprisoned. This time they were supernaturally released by the angel of the Lord and they immediately resumed preaching the gospel, (verse 25).

The outcome of their passionate enthusiasm is then seen in verse 26; they were arrested for a third time! By now the authorities were at a loss what to do, and Gamaliel, a Pharisee and teacher of the law; a man honoured by all the people, offered his counsel. He concluded in verse 36-39 that if what they were doing was not of God then it would just fizzle out. The apostles, in verse 40, were therefore beaten and warned not to speak in the name of Jesus. Confident that this would be an end of the matter, the authorities released them. The remarkable thing is that verse 41 tells us,

> *"They left the presence of the council, rejoicing that they were counted worthy to suffer dishonour for the name."*

then in verse 42 we read,

> *"And every day in the temple and at home they did not cease teaching and preaching Jesus as the Christ."*

When the Apostle Paul stood amongst all the idols and false gods in Athens, he reacted to the situation with a strong passionate conviction:*"His spirit was provoked within him as he saw that the City was full of idols. So he argued in the synagogue...and in the market place..."* (Acts 17:16-17). Imagine that sort of reaction from the 21st Century Church today. In our 'politically correct' society it would be unthinkable! The Church has remained silent out of fear of 'rocking the boat', and so we find ourselves overwhelmed by the same darkness that filled Athens. We are saturated by different religions, and idols, as well as the occult, and have learnt to co-exist with those things that are anti-Christ, rather than having the courage to take a stand and speak out against them.

Where are the so called 'Spirit-filled' believers today, who like Paul at Athens, preached against the religious idols that surrounded him with such passion that in Acts 17:5-6, he caused a riot - the City was in uproar! Today such passion is associated more with those fanatics that are Political Anarchists, Animal Rights Campaigners,

Environmentalists or Gay Rights activists – certainly not with the Church!

Due to compromise, we are reaping the inaction we have sown, and now we have what we deserve! We need to get down on our knees and repent for the lack of passion we have shown and the apathy that has overtaken us. Only a return to our 'first love' and seeking for the power of the Holy Spirit to be faithful, fearless witnesses will turn our society around – if it is not too late already!

William Booth was a man with an inextinguishable passion. Born 10th April 1829 in Nottingham, he founded the Salvation Army. Starting his ministry as a Methodist preacher he was largely self-educated, penniless, and practically friendless, but had a great passion to win the world for Christ. His particular burden was to reach out to the poorest and most needy of society, including alcoholics, criminals and prostitutes. "Go for souls and go for the worst!" was his constant cry. He was committed to his mission of reaching such people, not merely through preaching, but by also helping their plight in practical ways, to alleviate their suffering and thus enable them to be able to receive the gospel. He asserts his resolve to this goal when saying:

"I have no intention to depart in the smallest degree from the main principles on which I have acted in the past. My only hope for the permanent deliverance of mankind from misery, either in this world or the next, is the regeneration or remaking of the individual by the power of the Holy Ghost through Jesus Christ. But in providing for the relief of temporal misery, I reckon that I am only making it easier where it is now difficult and possible where it is now all but impossible, for men and women to find their way to the Cross of our Lord Jesus Christ."

The General was wholly reliant on the power of the Holy Spirit and during his lifetime he established the work of the Salvation Army in 58 countries and colonies, where his followers numbered millions. He would often come home from preaching bloodied and bruised, with his clothes torn having been attacked by those he was seeking to reach. In spite of all the opposition though, the passion that burned in his heart could never be dampened. He died at the age of 83 and such was the respect he had gained that 65,000 mourners passed by his coffin, with over 35,000 people attending his memorial service at London's Olympia. Among those present were Queen Alexandria and representatives of King George V and Queen Mary.

One of the great hymns written by this man in 1884, to celebrate the 50th anniversary of his conversion, was originally entitled 'The Fire.' Its words express the intention of God for His ministers to be *"Flames of fire"*, (Hebrews 1:7). They show clearly William Booth's belief that we all need the fullness of the Holy Spirit to fulfill our calling and bring a passion in our lives to serve Christ:

'Thou Christ of burning, cleansing flame,
Send the fire, send the fire, send the fire!
Thy blood bought gift today we claim,
Send the fire, send the fire, send the fire!
Look down and see this waiting host,
Give us the promised Holy Ghost;
We want another Pentecost,
Send the fire, send the fire, send the fire!'

(3) A Purity That Is Irreproachable

One of the clearest indicators of our spiritual freshness is the perception and pursuit we have of purity within our own lives. Worldliness has crept in to modern day Church life, as well as the 'froth and bubble' of subjective, experience-based Christianity. We therefore need reminding that to thirst for the *Holy* Spirit is to thirst for Holiness of life. In terms of our motives, attitudes and methods, we need to be beyond reproach. Tragically though, some of the things that go on in the name of Christ today, particularly by some 'Christian' TV prosperity/faith preachers is nothing less than scandalous!

There are many charlatans employing the most outrageous and manipulative techniques to build their own empires and bank balances, preying on the vulnerable and gullible, and all under the guise of Christianity! Such *'wolves in sheep's clothing'* will be exposed and judged for what they truly are, as will the television stations that give them the opportunity, at a lucrative fee, to continue with their corrupt practices.

With deceptive cunning these self appointed 'evangelists and teachers' offer *'Free* Green prayer Cloths, *'Free* Anointed Stones of David', *'Free* Miracle Water' and *'Free* Blood of Jesus anointing oil' to all that will contact them. Persuasive rhetoric is used speaking of how such items will bring salvation, deliverance, prosperity and healing to them and their loved ones. This is also reinforced by the testimonies of those deluded by 'results' they say they have experienced. Even though these may appear to be genuine signs, the Bible warns us that the devil will bring counterfeit miracles to deceive people (2 Thessalonians 2 verses 3 and 9).

Recently having watched one of these broadcasts, I phoned the number on the screen and requested one of the '*Free*' items, simply to confirm my suspicions. This duly arrived, accompanied by an extremely clever and carefully constructed personalised letter. My Christian name was frequently used; important points were underlined in red ink and given emphasis with asterisks. The letter was full of well chosen scriptures, all leading to the point of getting me to part with a substantial amount of money to guarantee my desired results. This was followed soon after by further, regular and increasingly cunning correspondence, each time inviting me to send a specific donation for even 'Greater Blessing!'

For all of us, purity and integrity must be part of our every day life, in all we do. We can easily find ourselves feeling outraged by the deceitfulness of some television evangelist and at the same time be living a life of compromise ourselves. For this reason the Bible says, *"Therefore let any one who thinks that he stands take heed lest he fall"* (1 Corinthians 10:12).

It was the poet and playwright Lord Tennyson who said "My strength is as the strength of ten because my heart is pure." The Bible teaches us in Joshua 23:6-10 that there is strength in purity. Here it says when we are careful to obey God and are not bowing down to idols; when we are not mixing with those people or their practices, then, *"One of you puts to flight a thousand ..."* (verse 10).

New Testament believers learnt very early on the importance of holiness and the need to walk in the fear of the Lord as they preached the gospel. In Acts 2:43 the Bible says, *"Fear came upon every soul..."* This was particularly the case with the account of Ananias and Sapphira, who, because of their sin of lying to the Holy Spirit in Acts 5:1-10, were both severely judged by God and dropped down dead! The result of such swift retribution is seen in verse 11 when it says, *"And great fear came upon the whole church, and upon all who heard of these things."*

The lesson to respect God's holiness and not to treat lightly the Holy Spirit had been learnt, and so they continued to practice what they preached. This soon strengthened their testimony, in the sense that not only did they find favour with all those they lived amongst (Acts 2:47), but also we read in Acts 5:13, *"..the people held them in high honour."*

Paul was very conscious of the need to be irreproachable in his own life; he not only preached Christ, but lived as a demonstration of the difference his 'High Calling' demanded. When he gathered the leaders of Ephesus together he was able to say to them in Acts 20:18b, *"You yourselves know how I lived among you all the time from the first day that I set foot in Asia."* It is a tremendous challenge for us to reflect on whether we could say the same thing about the consistency of our integrity to our work colleagues, next door neighbours or unsaved family members!

The Bible teaches in Galatians 5:9, *"A little leaven leavens the whole lump."* What starts off as perhaps a small issue of compromise soon grows and takes over to destroy the strength and value of a person's testimony. This point is made so clear in a poignant illustration that I read recently:

> "After a violent storm one night a large tree, which over the years had become a stately giant, was found lying across the road. Nothing but a splintered stump was left from something that had previously stood so proudly. On closer inspection it was discovered to be rotten at the core because thousands of insects had eaten away at its heart. The

weakness of the tree was not brought about by the
sudden storm, it began the very moment the first insect
nested in its bark".

The downfall, dishonour and damage of many a leader,
ministry and church will be brought about in the same
way, unless personal responsibility is taken to pursue
holiness. This is why the Bible says in 2 Corinthians 7:1,

> *"Since we have these promises, beloved, let us
> cleanse ourselves from every defilement of body
> and spirit, and make holiness perfect in the fear
> of God."*

To have a manner of life worthy of the gospel was the
calling of the New Testament Church and is still the same
today. Compromise and hypocrisy is never an option for
those that love and serve God. The benefits of such living
are peace, strength, encouragement and growth, as expressed
by Luke when he writes,

> *"So the church throughout all Judea and Galilee and
> Samaria had peace and was built up; and walking in
> the fear of the Lord and in the comfort of the Holy
> Spirit, it was multiplied"* (Acts 9:31).

(4) A Power That Is Indisputable

The Church in the book of Acts stood out from every
other religion and cult because of the miraculous power it
possessed: *"And with great power the apostles gave their
testimony to the resurrection of the Lord Jesus..."* (Acts
4:33). Clearly this was not their own ability, but God's.
Church life was characterised by miraculous 'signs and

wonders,' all of which pointed to the indisputable fact that the Lord was *"... working with them and confirming the word with signs following"* (Mark 16:20, AV).

The miraculous in terms of healing, deliverance and changed lives is able to silence the critics in a way that mere rational argument cannot. This was the result when pressure came upon the early Church - a man who'd been lame from birth was healed. The religious authorities, who'd been a 'thorn in the side' of the Church for a long time, were left speechless by the power of God. The Bible states,

"But seeing the man that had been healed standing beside them, they had nothing to say in opposition" (Acts 4:14).

This was also the case in Acts 15:4-5, with some legalistic believers at Jerusalem, when the apostles returned from their missionary work to give an account to the Church. Peter spoke of what the Lord had been doing through their lives and how the Gentiles had received the Holy Spirit, but some were not happy. Rather than rejoicing and giving thanks to God there was a group, from the party of the Pharisees, who were more concerned with majoring on minor points of the Law.

The same of course is going on in many churches today. There are people within the assembly of believers, who are more interested in making sure their doctrine is preserved, than in seeking the dynamic power of God for themselves. However, we read,

"And all the assembly kept silence; and they listened to Barnabas and Paul as they related what signs and wonders God had done through them among the Gentiles" (Acts 15:12).

In my various overseas ministry trips the miraculous power of God is commonly seen, transforming peoples lives. The people have an expectation that there is nothing too difficult for God who made the heavens and earth. Miracles happen in a way that attracts and impacts the masses. Certainly in this country there would appear to be a stark contrast in that expectation! We must rediscover our confidence in the miraculous, but this will only ever happen when we seek to live lives that are full of the Holy Spirit. Some today are more preoccupied with discussion regarding side issues, rather than the central importance of what God's Kingdom should reflect. Such people need reminding of Paul's words to the Church at Corinth when he said, *"For the kingdom of God is not a matter of talk but of power"* (1 Corinthians 4:20, NIV).

The Welsh revival of 1904 was a mighty invasion and demonstration of the Spirit; God's Kingdom became manifested on earth in an indisputable way. Rather than squandering money on drink and vice, the earnings of workmen were bringing great joy to their families. Outstanding debts were being paid by thousands of young converts. The gambling and alcohol houses lost their trade and theatres closed down due to a fall in business. Football during this time was forgotten by both players and fans, though nothing was mentioned from the pulpits about it. The people had been so radically changed that they had new lives and new interests. Political meetings were cancelled or abandoned. They seemed completely out of the question since spiritual priorities were more important. Even the political leaders from Parliament abandoned themselves to the revival meetings.

Wherever the Church today neglects the important role of the Holy Spirit, then vital qualities in its spiritual health will always deteriorate and its demise is certain. For this reason Paul's admonishment in Galatians 5:1 is imperative: *"For freedom Christ has set us free, stand fast therefore, and do not submit again to a yoke of slavery."* We must all be alert, taking responsibility not only to safeguard the new life we have received, but also to seek the fullness of God's Holy Spirit each day. Unless each Christian remains firm in this resolve we will be infected by the malaise of spiritual sickness that is widespread, and our presence will become irrelevant.

How To Receive The Fullness Of The Spirit

There is nothing difficult or complicated about experiencing any of God's gifts, though sometimes we make it more complex than we need. All that is necessary is that we believe God says what He means, means what He says, and will do what He says He will do! King Solomon's instructions are basic and very clear on this point. He writes, *"Trust in the Lord with all your heart, and do not rely on your own insight"* (Proverbs 3:5).

Child-like faith is the key, so that we don't let our logical minds rob us of what is promised by the Lord, and so desperately needed by all Christians. To illustrate the simplicity of receiving the Holy Spirit, Jesus, in Matthew 18:2-3, placed a child in front of the disciples saying, *"... unless you turn and become like children, you will never enter the Kingdom of Heaven."*

The wonderful characteristic of children is their absolute and straightforward trust in those that they love, and whom they know love them. There is no hesitancy, no convoluted thought process, no suspicion or fear; they just accept in an open and simple way. If we always took this same approach with God, we would have no problem living in the fullness of all Jesus died and rose from the grave to give us.

The following steps on how to receive the fullness of the Holy Spirit should make the process for everyone seeking this gift much easier:

(a) Don't Worry About Terminology

Very often our religious upbringing, traditions and denominational bias, condition us to accept the significance of truth only one way. We can find ourselves automatically accepting what we've been told by man, rather than being open to hear God and interpret the Bible for ourselves. One person's way of understanding the activity of the Holy Spirit might be completely different to another's. Let us not be overly concerned about words like 'Baptism in the Spirit,' 'Second Blessing,' 'Spirit-Filled' etc. Terminology really isn't the important thing. What is vital though is, have we got the scriptural evidence of being full of the Spirit of God, in terms of fruit, power and an effective Christ-like life?

(b) Recognise Your Personal Need

One of the metaphors describing the Bible is of a mirror that we look into, seeing ourselves as we truly are and what we can become (James 1:23-25). The Psalmist said about God, *"Surely you desire truth in the inner parts..."* (Psalm 51:6, NIV). Simply taking a look at our own hearts, with the mirror of the Bible, and being honest about what we see is vital, as the Holy Spirit cannot co-exist with sin. David therefore goes on in the same Psalm to pray: *"Create in me a clean heart, O God, and put a new and right spirit within me"* (verse 10). Honesty also about spiritual dryness and lack of boldness is something that, at first, might be uncomfortable to acknowledge, but absolutely necessary. Pride is the major problem that prevents many Christians from experiencing the full blessing of God.

(c) Search The Scriptures

Other people's experience alone is not something we can build our faith and expectancy upon, no matter how real it might be to them. Our final authority on all matters must be the Word of God. If what we are talking about is **firstly**, promised in the scriptures, and **secondly**, the Old and New Testament show examples of people who received the Holy Spirit's power, then that is our starting point. Simply getting out a Bible concordance and doing our own study, or using the internet to search out the specific promises relating to the Holy Spirit, will yield sufficient evidence to meditate upon. We must be like the Beareans of whom it was said,

> "...they received the message with great eagerness and examined the Scriptures every day to see if what Paul said was true" (Acts 17:11, NIV).

(d) Believe The Promises

There are so many promises in the scriptures to encourage us in our search, the basis of which is found in Mark 13:31 and speaks of their eternal relevance to us today. Here Jesus says, "Heaven and earth will pass away, but my words will not pass away." Also when Peter was referring to the first time the fullness of the Holy Spirit was poured out, he gives an assurance that we too are included as recipients. Peter said, "For this promise is to you and to your children and to all that are far off, every one whom the Lord our God calls to him" (Acts 2:39). The promises of God always strengthens our faith, but only when we believe them. Therefore we must feed our faith and our doubts will starve to death! In believing, let us be just as childlike as Smith Wigglesworth who lived by the adage, "God said it, I believe it, and that settles it!"

(e) Ask, Expecting To Receive

Having come to the place of clarity and conviction about what the Bible says, we only need now to be convinced regarding God's willingness to give. This motivates us to ask, expecting to receive. Such anticipation was taught by the writer to the Hebrew Christians when he wrote about God saying, *"... He rewards those who earnestly seek him"* (Hebrews 11:6, NIV). Taking this principle of God's willingness and our expectation, Jesus explained how straightforward our approach in asking for the Holy Spirit should be. He does this using the example again of a child, saying,

> *"What father among you, if his son asks for a fish, will instead of a fish give him a serpent; or if he asks for an egg, will give him a scorpion? If you then, who are evil, know how to give good gifts to your children, how much more will the heavenly Father give the Holy Spirit to those who ask him!"* (Luke 11:12-13).

Chapter 5

Be Alert In Your Thought Life

There are few things more invigorating to us spiritually than to know that our God given thoughts and ideas have made a difference to the lives of other people. Through God-inspired creative thinking, multitudes can be helped and blessed. I was encouraged by some interesting examples of this when reading Bob Gass's excellent daily devotional booklet 'The Word For Today' recently. Before a Scottish doctor named James Young Simpson came up with the idea of what he called 'artificial sleep', people would be operated on in excruciating pain. As a result of reading in Genesis 2:21, "So the Lord caused a deep sleep to fall upon the man...", Simpson thought that chloroform might be the answer. He first experimented on himself in 1847, and eventually it was used to greatly ease pain in childbirth and ultimately, to eliminate it during surgery.

Initially, Simpson encountered opposition. Some considered it a sin to interfere with nature. "Hand me the Bible," said Dr Simpson. "This is how God operated on Adam." Though there were some setbacks along the way, his idea was finally accepted when Queen Victoria gave birth to her eighth child, Prince Leopold in 1853 under chloroform, and declared she was "greatly pleased with its effect."

In 1824, Louis Braille, a blind Christian from a poor family background, invented a world-wide system of raised dots on paper so that blind people could read. He created a combination of 63 ways to use a six-dot cell in an area no larger than a fingertip. The position of the various dots would represent the different letters of the alphabet, and so God's Word was placed into the hands of the visually impaired for the first time.

As far as communications are concerned, in part we owe our modern interactions today to a Christian named Samuel Morse, who came up with the idea of what became known as Morse Code. A friend said to him, "When you were experimenting did you ever come to an absolute deadlock, not knowing what to do?" Morse replied, "More than once; what I did then was get down on my knees and pray for light, and light came. When my inventions were acknowledged by flattery and honours from America and Europe, I said, "Not unto me, O Lord, not unto me, but unto thy Name be the glory." That's why Morse's first telegraphic message, from Washington DC to Baltimore in 1844 read, 'What hath God wrought!'

Another Christian whose ideas made a difference to millions is Louis Pasteur, the French scientist, born December 27th 1822, who showed us that infection is the result of germs and viruses we cannot see. He introduced sterilisation methods that eventually saved the lives of countless multitudes.

Whether we are a scientist, inventor, doctor or would consider ourselves an ordinary person in the street, we need to be alert in our thought life to God-given ideas. Each one of us has the most wonderful capacity to see the potential of our minds expand, and be used in the greatest of ways for the glory of God and the good of others.

The Potential Of The Mind

At any particular moment in time we only use a small percentage of our mind's capacity. The brain is far more sophisticated than any computer mankind has ever made; it influences everything about us and is the command centre of our lives. It is able to process millions of pieces of information simultaneously, and is involved in controlling absolutely all we do. Being alert in our thought life therefore, is essential if we are to develop into the success we were created by God to be. Our brain determines how we think, feel, and act. It reasons, broods, remembers, classifies, describes, solves problems and also dreams – not just at night when we are asleep, but throughout the day as well!

Everything that goes on in our lives is filtered and processed through our thought life. Our minds consist of values, attitudes, fears, hopes, ambitions, patterns of behaviour, prejudices and perceptions. The mind is developed by procedures which stimulate thought, supply information, analyse experience, and place human events into patterns of meaning; its potential is extraordinary! For us to stay spiritually fresh, and avoid burn out, the area of our mind is one of the most significant factors for every Christian to protect. Because of its potential it is also one of the major targets that the enemy will attempt to attack and exploit, with the objective of wearing us down.

King Solomon speaks of the power of the mind when stating, *"For as he thinks in his heart, so is he..."* (Proverbs 23:7, NKJV). To a large extent a person is literally what they think, or are persuaded to think; their character being the sum total of all their thoughts. Therefore if our thoughts are not consistent with God's Word but are being shaped by external ungodly influences, or internal negative pressures, then we will never grow into all we are capable of being. Furthermore, the frustration, dissatisfaction and disappointment brought about by this tension of aspiration will have a draining effect upon us, particularly in the area of our motivation.

While the capacity of our minds to be creative, productive and constructive is outstanding, this potential is immensely increased when we are spiritually alert in our thinking. In his letters to the Corinthian Church, Paul deals with a variety of practical issues which were badly affecting their spiritual health. In addressing these problems what he was saying in essence was, the only way to truly live life to the full is for our minds to be captivated by the mind of Christ.

Paul teaches these early believers, and indeed ourselves, that part of the miracle of our conversion is, right now *"... we have the mind of Christ"* (1 Corinthians 2:16). Also in Philippians 4:7 we learn that God enables us to maintain that privileged position when we read, *"... the peace of God, which passes all understanding, will keep your hearts and your minds in Christ Jesus."* While this is wonderfully true, our co-operation and willingness to take responsibility for our thought life is fundamental, if we are to live in the refreshing experience of this peace.

In his letter to the Church at Philippi Paul says, *"Let this mind be in you, which was also in Christ Jesus"* (Philippians 2:5, AV). What we notice from this instruction is, we can help or hinder the process of our development by our daily choice to think and live as Jesus did. From verses 6-8 we see that to express the mind of Christ we must live in humility, obedience and sacrifice; three areas that are totally contrary to our former way of thinking. Without this mindset though, friction between our God-given destiny and a self-centred lifestyle will inevitably become a strain to us.

Things That Bring Weariness To The Mind

An important part of staying spiritually fresh and being alert in our thought life is having an understanding of the different things that bring weariness to our lives. We must look at these with the knowledge that we are to, *"..serve him with a whole heart and a willing mind; for the Lord searches all hearts, and understands every plan and thought"* (1 Chronicles 28:9). There are many areas that will adversely affect us, let me mention just a few:

(a) Conflict

Any form of conflict is a major source of stress to the mind and results in weariness. This is so whether it's conflict in our marriage, family, work-place, or within the Church. The Bible says, *"If possible, so far as it depends upon you, live peaceably with all"* (Romans 12:18). Unresolved conflict often results in bitterness and resentment and this can be the cause of a great deal of spiritual fatigue and barrenness in our lives. We need to do all we can to live in harmony with other people. To function at our best we must be at peace, therefore any agitation is an enormous drain upon our vitality. This is why when the apostle Paul was describing a wide range of relational conflicts in the Church at Colossae, such as anger, rage, malice, slander, greed, filthy language and lying, he wrote,

"Let the peace of Christ rule in your hearts, since as members of one body you were called to peace" (Colossians 3:15, NIV).

(b) Compromise

Our natural, rational mind and the philosophy of the world would say that compromise is 'A middle way between two extremes.' This is all very well in terms of logical negotiations aimed at reaching agreement and a resolution. However, in terms of the Kingdom of God, our thinking must be governed by spiritual and moral absolutes and not the pressure of appeasement, otherwise we have a false peace. Matthew 11:12 challenges us to think radically when it says,

> *"From the days of John the Baptist until now the kingdom of heaven has suffered violence, and men of violence take it by force."*

God's Word gives no room for liberal concessions, rather Jesus said, *"Man shall not live by bread alone, but by every word that proceeds from the mouth of God"* (Matthew 4:4). To compromise and live in any way at variance with His Word, will create turmoil and tension within us. Compromise at the very least brings restlessness, but also can result in spiritual and mental exhaustion because in our disobedience we are actually resisting God Himself!

(c) Complacency

Settling for mediocrity, and being unwilling to embrace change, causes people to lose their sensitivity to the Holy Spirit's leading. It wearies their enthusiasm for anything new that God wants to initiate, and blinds them to the danger of spiritual dryness slowly creeping in. It is a malady that depletes energy, distorts perception, dulls attitudes, and causes a drain on the brain! The first symptom is satisfaction with things as they are, and the second is rejection of things as they might be. "Good enough" is the mentality that becomes today's watchword and tomorrow's standard. Complacency makes people fear the unknown, mistrust the untried, and despise the new. Ultimately, it is a mindset that leads to indifference, apathy and idleness. This is a serious matter because Proverbs 1:32 says, *"... the complacency of fools will destroy them"* (NKJ).

(d) Clutter

In today's fast-moving technological age, we are inundated with information, bombarded with images, and confronted with a myriad of choices, so much so that people's minds can become totally chaotic. With all sorts of different discordant thoughts running back and forth, people's minds are literally becoming overloaded and weary! Having a cluttered mind makes it a struggle to be productive. Such a person will have a hard time simply starting projects, or getting round to finishing them. Even making plans, being reliable and showing consistency, will result in empty words and an emotionally exhausted life.

The consequences of those with cluttered or scattered thoughts will be they pay little attention to detail, or give entirely too much attention to it, and so lose perspective. We shall be looking in closer detail at how to de-clutter the mind in chapter nine. However, for now it is sufficient to say that the principle of Isaiah 26:3 is of paramount importance in staying spiritually fresh: *"You will keep him in perfect peace, whose mind is stayed on You. Because he trusts in You"* (NKJ).

(e) Cares Of The World

If the Word of God becomes choked in our lives, it will always cut off the spiritual energy that we need to remain alive and vibrant. Jesus made it clear that this is exactly what happens when we get unduly concerned and anxious about material interests. Worrying about such things causes us to lose our peace, as we allow ourselves to be deceived into thinking that security and fulfillment is found in the possessions around us, rather than pursuing eternal values. Jesus said in Matthew 13:22, *"... the cares of the world and the delight in riches choke the word, and it proves unfruitful."*

We are not to be preoccupied with worldly concerns. Our chief pursuit, or even slightest thought, should not be fame, fortune, a career, a house, a car, a hobby, a fashionable wardrobe etc. These cares will suffocate the Word in our lives; instead we are instructed in Colossians 3:2 to, *"Set your minds on things that are above, not on things that are on earth."* The author C.S. Lewis expressed this point when he said, "Aim at heaven and you will get earth thrown in. Aim at earth and you'll get neither!"

(f) Criticism

Corrective words that enable us to see areas where we need to make adjustments are essential for us all, providing they are constructive. However, criticism that is only negative is a common cause of people feeling discouraged and tired, to the point of wanting to give up. Disparaging words can be the means of not only troubling our confidence, but also tormenting our minds. This is so, particularly if we feel our best efforts are not appreciated, and the only time people express something about what we've done is to pull us down, then we become very disheartened and wearied.

Many a person has reached breaking point and spiritual collapse because of the draining effect of such criticism.

The Bible teaches us to be sensitive and careful about the power of negative words when it says, *"Let no evil talk come out of your mouths, but only such as is good for edifying.."* (Ephesians 4:29). Also we are told, *"Encourage one another daily, as long as it is called Today"* (Hebrews 3:13, NIV).

(g) Compulsion

2 Timothy 1:7 states that, *"...God has given us a sound mind"* (NKJ). This is the birthright of every Christian. Any form of compulsive behaviour that makes people nervously anxious if they are not engaged in a particular activity, or they feel irrationally forced to act in a certain way, brings mental exhaustion. Intrusive thoughts, that seem to take control and produce anxiety, is especially common in people who are meticulously anxious about detail, or those absorbed in a cause, or otherwise fixated on something or someone.

This can be so, not only with obvious compulsions such as repetitive hand washing or turning off light switches etc, but also eating disorders, religious mania, the workaholic, or those who feel compelled to exercise and are frequently at the gym working out excessively. Anything that we have little or no control over soon becomes our master and will result in the agitation of restlessness, rather than a life of peace.

No matter how great the potential of our mind is, unless we are actively seeking to be alert to these dangers in our thought-life, then we will be extremely vulnerable to weariness and our lives will always be limited. Our strength will be significantly diminished and we will find ourselves quickly worn down and overpowered. There are, therefore, three fundamental actions necessary relating to our thinking, if we are to stay spiritually fresh; these are: **(1)** Reclaim Your Brain, **(2)** Restrain Your Brain, and **(3)** Retrain Your Brain.

Firstly, Reclaim Your Brain

Jesus said in Matthew 22:37 that we are to love God not only with all our heart and with all our soul, but we are to love Him also with our entire mind. The magnificent and complex creation of our mind belongs to God and we need to re-claim it for His glory. The battleground of the mind is a major war zone causing problems for many people, resulting in them being drained and defeated by **(a)** The World **(b)** The Flesh and **(c)** The Devil. Our goal therefore must be to take back what has been relinquished so we live in the benefit of what the Bible speaks of when it says, "... *to be spiritually minded is life and peace*" (Romans 8:6b, NKJ).

(a) The World

When Jesus was praying for His disciples in John 17 about being *in* the world, but not *of* the world He was referring to the world system ruled by Satan; a society independent of God. Therefore although ungodly influences are all around us, if we are to be spiritually minded we must be distinctively different in our values, priorities and lifestyle.

Paul teaches that the only way this is possible is when we have reclaimed our thought life from worldly thinking: *"Do not be conformed to this world but be transformed by the renewal of your mind"* (Romans 12:2). The New Living Translation puts it in an even clearer way, *"Don't copy the behaviour and customs of this world, but let God transform you into a new person by changing the way you think."* A mind conformed to the world is a shallow, weary mind, but a mind being renewed by God's Word and God's Spirit, will be progressively restored until it is conformed to the image of Christ.

Separation from the world in our thinking is essential because the Bible says, *"... friendship with the world is enmity with God"* (James 4:4). We cannot straddle the fence between God and the world. To be fruitful and effective our lives must be uniquely different. This will inevitably cause a disruption to the view of the status quo, and at times will make us unpopular. Jesus had this in mind when He said, *"If you were of the world, the world would love its own; but because you are not of the world, but I chose you out of the world, therefore the world hates you"* (John 15:19). While we are to be distinct in what we think and believe, we are not to be objectionable. Jesus was known in Luke 7:34 as, *"... a friend of tax collectors and sinners!"* While being different, we also must maintain a mind that expresses friendliness and compassion, so we may win people to Christ.

(b) The Flesh

The Bible tells us that one of the signs of the 'Last Days' will be that people are, *"...lovers of pleasure, rather than lovers of God"* (2 Timothy 3:4b). This is the primary characteristic of the carnal mind; it is set upon gratifying the 'Flesh' rather than the 'Spirit'. Our struggle with sin and temptation will be determined by which of these two natures we favour and feed. The flesh's appetite is fed by ungodly thought patterns that lead to fleshly actions and sin. If we choose to satisfy our carnal nature it will not only ensnare us, but will dramatically dampen our enthusiasm for spiritual things, drain spiritual life from us and ultimately deaden our relationship with God. The seriousness of this is seen in Romans 8:6 when Paul says, *"To set the mind on the flesh is death..."* and also in verse 7-8,

> *"For the mind that is set on the flesh is hostile to God; it does not submit to God's law, indeed cannot; and those who are in the flesh cannot please God."*

The perception of our mind is darkened and it is dulled, not only by yielding to sinful pleasure, but also by having an outlook that is not spiritual. This is manifested in low expectation, fearfulness, selfish attitudes, defeatist-talk, small-mindedness, indecision, laziness, indiscipline, unbelief etc. To reclaim our minds from the flesh we must ask ourselves the question, 'Is my thinking ruled by my sinful nature, or is it under the control of the Holy Spirit? As we live according to God's Word it exposes our mindset because it is, *"... sharper than any two-edged sword, piercing to the division of soul and spirit"* (Hebrews 4:12).

(c) The Devil

Our greatest enemy is Satan. He very effectively manages to blind people's minds by bringing confusion, fear and uncertainty about God's love for them. This is achieved as he sows doubts, suggests things that are going to go wrong, whispers lies and undermines people's confidence. Unless we are alert in the area of our thought-life, then we will become extremely vulnerable to his attack which is always aimed at unsettling our faith.

We must be of the same mind as King David in 1 Samuel 30:1-8. On returning home to Ziklag he found the Amalekites had burned down the village and taken captive all its inhabitants, including his wives and the wives of those in the army. He therefore enquired of the Lord as to whether he should go after them and reclaim what had been stolen by the enemy. God's reply was decisive: *"Pursue; for you shall surely overtake and you shall surely rescue."* Likewise, with strong confidence, and with the same determination, we must take back what the devil has stolen from us in terms of having a sanctified mind.

Jesus warned Peter of the devil's desire to oppress and shake his confidence when He said, *"Satan demanded to have you, that he might sift you like wheat, but I have prayed for you that your faith may not fail..."* (Luke 22:31-32). How wonderful to know, and something we must always keep in mind, especially when the enemy's attack has left us battered, intimidated and exhausted, Jesus is praying for us! He is interceding on our behalf that we will not let defeat, fear or despair torment our thoughts. He is praying that we will settle in our minds to rise up again, reclaim our authority and ultimately stand firm in victory.

The Power Of Prayer And Fasting

It seems superfluous to say how vital prayer is to reclaiming the mind and staying spiritually fresh. However, the obvious does need to be stated because meaningful prayer is a weakness with most Christians, as indeed it is in many churches. The least attended meeting in almost every church throughout our country today is the prayer meeting - if they have one at all!

Some wonder why the impact of the Church within society is negligible and its relevance unrecognised, yet we need look no further than the priority it gives to prayer. Put on a praise concert or social event for the 'Saints' and you'll have the building full, call for a prayer meeting and you do well to get a dozen to come along! We cannot know the vibrancy of a dynamic relationship with the Lord until prayer becomes a priority, in the same way it was for the Old Testament patriarchs, Christ Himself, and the early Church. Prayer is as essential as the air we breathe! That said; it is not only prayer, but prayer and fasting that becomes life-changing and where we find strength to recover a spiritual mindset.

One of the most effective and powerful means of reclaiming the brain from *The World, The Flesh* and *The Devil* is the spiritual discipline of fasting. Regular occasions when we abstain from food, for the purpose of giving ourselves to specific prayer, brings us into a new depth and dimension with God. These two aspects of our relationship with the Lord should be seen as inseparable from each other. It has to be said though, often fasting is merely adopted as a last resort, in a time of crisis, or as a special need comes up in our lives. In actual fact it should characterise the life of every believer, particularly those seeking to stay spiritually fresh.

You don't find much enthusiasm for fasting in these days, when microwave foods and take-away meals are readily available, and so attractive to the flesh. Dazzling advertisements entice the mind and the easy option of convenience takes preference to sacrifice. The Bible though has plenty to say about fasting, and we can see throughout scripture that it was a common practice. A few, among the many reference are, Judges 20:26, Ezra 8:21-23, Psalm 35:13, and Psalm 69:10. Other Old Testament individuals who fasted were Moses the lawgiver (Exodus 34:28), David the king (2 Samuel 12:16), Esther the queen (Esther 4:16), Isaiah the prophet (Isaiah 58:6-9), and Daniel the seer (Daniel 9:3).

In coming to the New Testament we find the Lord taught more on fasting than on repentance, water baptism and Communion! Jesus Himself fasted in Luke 4:1-2 and clearly expected His disciples to do so, as twice He said to them in Matthew 6:16-17, *"...When you fast."*- not *"if you fast."* Furthermore, in Matthew 9:15 the Lord spoke of the time He would no longer be with them and He said, *"..then they will fast."* Fasting was also very much part of the life of the early Church in Acts 13:1-3, Acts 14:21-23, and 1 Corinthians 7:5.

This Biblical practice contributes to our spiritual and mental alertness. When we fast, our minds and perception get sharper because we are focusing less on secular, transient things and more on eternal realities. We are not rushing through our prayers, but are taking time to be sensitive to the Holy Spirit, praying things through in a more concentrated way. Our soul is alerted as our mind is disciplined, which in turn brings into subjection our emotions and releases our spirit to pursue God. This discipline is fundamentally an act of obedience to His Word and causes us to humble ourselves before Him. It crucifies the flesh and subdues our desires so that we are saying, 'God, you are more important than everything else to me.'

Moreover, fasting also teaches us to be less selfish as we intercede for others who have needs. This is particularly so when confronted by what seems an immovable problem. It creates within us expectancy for answered prayer, as we centre more intently on God as the only answer, rather than letting our minds be overwhelmed by any difficulty. This is illustrated in Mark 9:14-29 where a boy was gripped by evil forces and the disciples found they were powerless to break the hold of

119

the enemy. As they ask Jesus why they weren't able to deal with the situation He says to them in verse 29, *"This kind can come out by nothing but prayer and fasting"* (NKJ).

Not only are both the Old and New Testament full of scriptures about this remarkable principle, more recent examples encourage us to recognise the importance of fasting and prayer. Throughout Church history we can find many illustrations of mighty men of God who regularly fasted, and we see powerful ministries being born out of and sustained because of this practice: In the 18th Century George Whitefield and John Wesley were firm believers in fasting. In the 19th Century Charles Finney the great American revivalist regularly fasted. It is estimated that during the year 1857-58, over a hundred thousand people were led to Christ as the direct or indirect result of his ministry. In the 20th Century, Arthur Wallis, affectionately know as the 'Father of The Charismatic Movement' that swept the United Kingdom in the 1960's preached, practiced and wrote about fasting.

Andrew Murray, born in South Africa in 1828 was an influential minister and author of over 240 books which greatly impacted this country. He said,

> "Prayer is the one hand with which we grasp the invisible; fasting, the other, with which we let loose and cast away the visible. In nothing is man more closely connected with the world of sense than in his need of food, and his enjoyment of it. It was the fruit, good for food, with which man was tempted and fell in Paradise. It was with bread to be made of stones that Jesus, when He was hungry, was tempted in the wilderness, and in fasting that He triumphed."

Several forms of fasting can be found in the Bible and various periods of time to fast, all of which will strengthen us in reclaiming our minds to love and serve God. The topic though is far greater than we have space to go into in this short section. However, there are a wide variety of books giving clear and helpful teaching on the subject which would be invaluable for study; for example: 'Shaping History through Prayer and Fasting' by Derek Prince; 'Fasting for Spiritual Breakthrough' by Elmer L. Towns, and 'The Hidden Power of Prayer and Fasting' by Mahesh Chavda.

Secondly, Restrain Your Brain

We all know how destructive viruses on our computer can be, and how important it is to have virus protection installed. However, we're not so careful when it comes to protecting our own minds, with the often devastating effects random thoughts can have on it. The American essayist, philosopher and poet, Ralph Waldo Emerson, once said, "Your mind is a sacred enclosure into which nothing harmful can enter except by your permission."

There are many harmful things that can influence our minds today, which is why we should always be alert and on our guard. As Christians we must cast away our care but not our responsibility to protect our minds. This is why Paul taught, *"... take every thought captive to obey Christ"* (2 Corinthians 10:5). Our mind is filled with thought-patterns, habits and attitudes that we have not only permitted to enter, but also have entertained and allowed to develop. Ungodly thoughts are those processes that we are not simply bombarded with, but that we actively engage in. To maintain a spiritual freshness we must be alert to the danger of these, and refuse to give room to them in any way. In 1 Peter 1:13 we read,

121

"Therefore, prepare your minds for action; be self-controlled; set your hope fully on the grace to be given you when Jesus Christ is revealed." (NIV).

Before we can prepare our minds for action we must be self-controlled. It is one of the fruits of the Holy Spirit and without this discipline the Bible says a person is defenceless, *"... like a city broken down, without walls"* (Proverbs 25:28, NKJ). Some of the areas where we must exercise restraint in our minds are:

(a) Lustful Thinking

The thought life is where all sexual immorality in our actions begins. Great restraint is needed therefore, particularly in the light of Mathew 5:28. Here Jesus taught that to even lust after a woman in our thoughts, means we have already committed adultery with her in our hearts. The area of unholy thoughts will always drag us down and never lift us to the heights that God wants us to experience. Holiness is not a part-time pursuit or an optional extra for an elite few; it is an essential requirement for all that would ascend to a higher realm in their relationship with God. This is exactly what David meant when he wrote in Psalm 24:3-4,

"Who shall ascend the hill of the Lord? And who shall stand in His holy place? He who has clean hands and a pure heart, who does not lift up his soul to what is false, and does not swear deceitfully."

Jesus addressed the issue of lust in Matthew 5 because it is a common problem to every person, and to show that our thoughts are important to a Holy God. While it is a fact that we can't live in this society without being confronted with sexual images and messages, we don't however have to stare! The sin is not in the initial flash-thought, common to every person, but in playing out that thought in the theatre of our minds. Here is where we must immediately take action, exercise restraint and refuse to dwell upon the thought. This is important, not only with pornographic magazines and television programmes, but also provocative dress fashions, and posters on buses and awnings etc. Added to this is the internet, where access is so easily available at all times to all ages, bringing a flood of temptation.

It is a crucial area to staying vibrant and spiritually alive because Jesus taught, *"Blessed are the pure in heart, for they shall see God"* (Matthew 5:8). Lusts create confusion and spiritual blindness preventing us from seeing God's glory and power. His will and plan for our life then becomes distorted and we fail to see our prayers being answered. If our hearts condemn us, or we feel ashamed in any way, we lose the peace we need between ourselves and God. Lust is a cancer to the soul that will eat away at our spiritual health. It is a deception promising much but providing nothing of lasting value. As someone once said, "Lust is like craving for salt by a man who is dying of thirst."

(b) Anxious Thinking

In restraining our brain it is helpful to remind ourselves that Jesus said in John 14:1 *"Let not your heart be troubled."* This means we do not have to let our minds be troubled nor allow our thoughts to be tormented; there is something we can do about the situation! We have complete control over our thought-life. Though we can't restrain what goes on around us, we can regulate what goes on inside us. Worrying wears us down and will dry us up.

123

Instead of worrying, we need to turn to God, rather than trying to solve problems ourselves. David said in Psalm 55:22, *"Cast your burden upon the Lord, and he will sustain you; he will never permit the righteous to be moved."* Notice here that as far as our spiritual well-being is concerned, God's promise is, He will not only sustain us, but He will also never allow us to be moved by any adverse circumstance. If God will not permit us to be moved, there is not a demon in hell, or person on earth, that can possibly do so!

We must take responsibility to be in charge of our minds so that we do not allow our thought life to run away with itself. An undisciplined mind will produce an exhausted life that is incapable of functioning at its full capacity. We must restrain over-active thinking, particularly just before going to bed. Replaying in our mind the events that have taken place during the day, or trying to sort out possible future difficulties, can become a problem. Jesus taught in Matthew 6:34, *"Therefore do not be anxious about tomorrow,... Let the day's own trouble be sufficient for the day."* Unless we restrain our minds it will be a sure way to rob ourselves of the sleep we need, resulting in restlessness throughout the night, and weariness in the morning. It was C.H. Spurgeon who said, "Our anxiety does not empty tomorrow of its sorrow, but only empties today of its strength."

(c) Negative Thinking

We unintentionally create limitations, suffering and weariness for ourselves by unconscious negative and often illogical thoughts that we listen to within our minds. There is an endless stream of chatter drifting through our consciousness and most of it does not issue from faith. 'Self-talk' isn't constructive thinking; it is just a commentary going on inside us all the time that continually undermines our confidence. It is like background noise while we engage in other activities. Yet behind everything we do is a thought, and each individual thought contributes to our character, achievements, and quality of life. How our minds work dictates how much joy we experience, how successful we feel, and how we interact with other people. Our habitual thinking patterns either encourage us towards success, or nudge us into failure.

The incessant babble of 'self-talk' and our negative thinking, is inseparable from our self-esteem; the view we have about our worth and ability. This is shaped by a whole variety of memories both good and bad: the kind of nurture we received from our parents; the interaction between our family members, childhood experiences, and life-changing events that have occurred throughout our lives. These all create our inner-self and form the opinion we hold about who we are and what we think we are able to do.

High self-esteem comes from positive thinking, and low self-esteem comes from negative thoughts. Our old nature, where Christ isn't given pre-eminence as Lord, feeds off negative memories and these reverberate within us dictating the conclusions we come to about our potential and worth. This is why we must become alert to the need to restrain our mind and bring our thoughts into line with what God says about us. The Holy Spirit will lead us into all truth, but we must respond to His voice and come into agreement with the Bible which says, *"Let the word of Christ dwell in you richly..."* (Colossians 3:16). As we read and study the Word of God, His Word becomes part of our thoughts and will be expressed through our speech and actions.

(d) Rational Thinking

One of the major things that will always rob us of God's provision to stay spiritually fresh is our own understanding, and the tendency we have to rationalise spiritual experiences. So often if what we read in the Bible or see in the lives of others doesn't make sense to the analytical mind, then we hold it in suspicion and fail to receive what God is so willing to give. He wants to take us to a place that is beyond the natural and into the supernatural, for it is only *'in the Spirit'* that we can experience the refreshing life of God. Paul says,

> *"Eye has not seen, nor ear heard, nor have entered into the heart of man the things which God has prepared for those who love Him. But God has revealed them to us through His Spirit"* (1 Corinthians 2:9-10, NKJ).

A few verses later the apostle goes on to explain that merely having a logical approach to life will block spiritual development: *"But the natural man does not receive the things of the Spirit of God, for they are foolishness to him; nor can he know them, because they are spiritually discerned"* (1 Corinthians 2:14, NKJ). In Isaiah 55:8: God says, *"For my thoughts are not your thoughts, neither are your ways my ways.."*. It is very hard to restrain our minds from rational thinking, because throughout our lives we have learnt the habit of living and thinking according to our natural senses, as well as other people's opinions and influences. However, if we are to live in the fullness of God's promises and experience everything He wants us to, restraint is vital. We need to discipline ourselves not to reject or neglect what we don't understand, and live by faith, not just by sight.

Strange as it might sound for someone with a scientific mind, Albert Einstein stated, "I never came upon any of my discoveries through the process of rational thinking." This man was not only a genius in physics and mathematics, he could see the importance of being creative, imaginative, and open to thinking 'outside of the box.' Unless we acknowledge the importance of this, then we will not only be held back and miss discoveries ourselves, but we may be a hindrance to others also – even to the Holy Spirit!

This can be illustrated by an incident that happened in the life of minister and author Andrew Murray. There was an occasion in Worcester, S. Africa when the Holy Spirit unexpectedly fell in revival power during a meeting at his church. People were crying out noisily in emotional prayer to God, and being offended, he determined unsuccessfully to control what he did not understand.

He walked down the aisle for some distance and called out as loudly as he could, "People, silence!" This had no effect so he shouted forcefully again, "People, I am your minister, sent from God – Silence!" But there was no stopping the noise. Mr. Murray then tried to start a hymn to squash the outburst, but the emotions were not quieted, and the people went right on fervently praying. Indignantly he shouted, "God is a God of order and here everything is confusion!" With that he stormed out of the church and left. As impertinent as this may seem, the same thing goes on every week in some churches, as both ministers and some members of the congregation try to rationalise and control the moving of the Holy Spirit.

(e) Inferiority Thinking

Someone once amusingly said, "I have an inferiority complex, but it isn't a very good one!" While this seems like a harmless joke we must be alert to the subtle way in which our lives can be influenced by inferiority thinking. You'll never hear of a baby, who felt inferior to other babies, and so didn't want to play because of feeling it wasn't as good as them. No one is born inferior, but it's our culture and past life experiences that teach us to think of ourselves as inferior. Society worships success, money and beauty. This inevitably programmes the mind to constantly compare ourselves to other people who have these things, and then results in us feeling inferior if we find we are different.

Throughout the Bible we find several instances of people who initially thought of themselves as inferior. If these individuals had not been moved by God beyond that mindset, they would have been unable to effectively fulfil His call upon their lives. After Moses spent forty years being raised in the courts of Pharaoh, and forty years in the wilderness looking after sheep, God came to him. The Lord intended to use this man to bring deliverance to the people of Israel who were being held as slaves in Egypt. He almost missed the opportunity of a lifetime though, because of thinking he was inferior to others and not qualified. His response was,

> "Who am I that I should go to Pharaoh, and bring the sons of Israel out of Egypt?" (Exodus 3:11).

Gideon was someone who displayed little courage when faced with the prospect of being a great warrior for the

Lord. He was very unsure of himself, and certainly wouldn't have been the choice of any Army General who knew much about him. However, this was the man God wanted to defeat Israel's enemies and tear down their foreign gods and idols. Inferiority could easily have prevented this happening when anxiously he responded to God saying,

> *"O my Lord, how can I save Israel? Indeed my clan is the weakest in Manasseh, and I am the least in my father's house"* (Judges 6:15, NKJ).

Another example of inferiority thinking is seen in the life of Jeremiah. God's plan was to use this man to be a Prophet, and speak against Judah and Jerusalem of impending disaster. He was given the task of proclaiming God's judgement on the people because of their disobedience, and had the assurance that the Lord would be with him. However, when he received this directive from God, his first reaction was to think of his inadequacy rather than God's strength. He responded saying, *"Ah, Lord God! Behold, I do not know how to speak, for I am only a youth"* (Jeremiah 1:6).

Through insecurity and self-doubt, fear can quickly seize our minds, and we must restrain our thoughts from the tendency to feel inadequate in any way. This is especially so when faced with tasks that seem overwhelming, or a crisis suddenly takes us by surprise. God has a tremendous plan for our lives and if we are to see and accomplish great things for Him then we must be alert to the danger of inferiority thinking. Our thoughts must be controlled by believing in our worth to God and in His Word, which teaches us to declare, *"I can do all things through Christ who strengthens me"* (Philippians 4:13, NKJ).

129

(f) Victim Thinking

Throughout our lives there will be many occasions when unkind, thoughtless, hurtful and unjust things are said and done to us. We therefore need to be very careful and alert in our minds that we don't develop a victim mentality, as this will inevitably wear us down. It will rob us of the joy and enthusiasm we need to stay spiritually fresh. Bad things do happen, even to good people, and yet, in every circumstance of life, the Bible teaches, *"... we are more than conquerors through him who loved us"* (Romans 8:37).

With some people when difficulties occur, they feel, walk and talk like a victim and in doing so bring heaviness upon themselves. This only drains them of strength. God's will for us all is that we live as victors and not victims. This is impossible unless victim-thinking is restrained and an overcoming mind-set is established. Such a change can only be accomplished when we move away from the tendency to turn in on ourselves, thinking 'Why me?' Instead our focus must be Christ, who became the ultimate victim for us, yet triumphed gloriously over the injustice of rejection, abuse, humiliation, betrayal and death.

A young woman called Immaculee Ilibagiza, who is regarded by many as one of the world's leading speakers on peace, is an inspiration and example of not thinking as a victim. She lost most of her family in the 1994 Rwandan genocide, and yet has focused her efforts on working for the United Nations and writing her moving autobiography, 'Left to Tell – *Discovering God Amidst the Rwandan Holocaust.*' She's had every reason to be bitter, and live as a victim, but instead has chosen the path of being a victor, asking "What can I do to improve this situation?" and "How can I forgive those who killed my family, and spread a message of survival and hope?"

130

It will always be counter-productive to dwell on injustice done to us. When I pause for a moment and think of the many different wrongs that have been done to me, particularly from other Christians, and especially leaders, it is always something the enemy would try to use to drag me down. There is a choice for us every day that we have to make if we are to maintain our spiritual freshness, and that is to choose the path of forgiveness and move on victorious in our minds, so that we give no foothold to the enemy. We have the greatest example of all in Jesus to restrain our minds from victim-thinking. The writer to the Hebrew Christians says,

"Consider him who endured from sinners such hostility against himself, so that you may not grow weary or fainthearted" (Hebrews 12:3).

An amazing thing happens when we choose to move beyond victim thinking, rather than let it wear us down, and that is, God vindicates us in the end! This was so a few months ago when a leader introduced himself to me at a church in the North of England where I was preaching. It wasn't his congregation, but he came that night specifically to meet me. After the service he explained that he was the new pastor of a church nearby that, at one time, I used to minister in. He went on to say that he'd learnt his church had treated me badly years ago and God had told him to make right the injustice which had caused hurt. The pastor said he 'wanted to repent on behalf of his church and to ask my forgiveness!' This was readily given of course and after we prayed together, he warmly invited me back to preach again at the church.

131

Each of these areas we've looked at show us the need to restrain our minds from dwelling on things that will rob us of God's blessing. The Bible gives us a beautiful picture in the Song of Solomon, of His rich provision of grace to feed upon when it says, *"He brought me to the banqueting house, and his banner over me was love."* (Chapter 2:4). Figuratively speaking, everything we need to sustain our lives and to stay spiritually fresh is in His banqueting hall, laid out on the banqueting table. In fact the Psalmist says of the Lord, *"You prepare a table before me in the presence of my enemies"* (Psalm 23:5, NKJ).

Some Christians though, because they haven't exercised restraint in their thought-life, have not reached God's banqueting table of fellowship and communion. As a result of their mind not being restrained, their thoughts have strayed and taken them away from God's provision. Picture it like this; in a large house there are many corridors. On the way to the banqueting hall, some wander down corridors in their mind of lustful thinking, anxious thinking, negative thinking, rational thinking inferiority thinking and victim thinking. These corridors lead them away from the banqueting hall. The point of restraining our minds is that we must refuse to allow ourselves to go down any corridor in our thought life that takes us away from the presence and blessing of God. We must be vigilant to exercise restraint otherwise we will lose our way to the banqueting table.

Thirdly, Retrain Your Brain

Not only do we need to restrain our wandering thoughts, we must also purposely retrain our mind so we replace them with spiritually positive ones. A single positive thought can destroy an army of negative thoughts! This point was the premise for the inspirational writings of author James Allen. Born in Leicester, England on November 28, 1864 he became the author of 19 books that have impacted the lives of millions for good. Allen was a quiet unrewarded genius who wrote much about the power of positive thinking. His writings were influenced in some aspects by the Bible but there is no evidence that he ever committed his life to Christ. However, in one of his helpful insights he said:

> "A man's mind can be likened to a garden, which may be intelligently cultivated or allowed to run wild; but whether cultivated or neglected, it must, and will, *bring forth*. If no useful seeds are *put* into it, then an abundance of useless weed seeds will *fall* therein, and will continue to produce their kind."

While the philosophy of positive thinking can be good, we must be careful not to stray into the area of mere self-improvement and the power of 'Mind over Matter.' Ultimately it is only when Christ and the Holy Spirit become our inspiration, and our minds are being shaped by disciplines taught in scripture, that we can bring glory to God. As often is the case though, much of the wisdom man discovers is already in the Bible.

The spiritual outworking of Allen's words is best summed up in the teaching of Paul when 2,000 years ago he wrote, *"..whatever a man sows, that will he also reap"* (Galatians 6:7). Whether we are consciously and intentionally sowing good seed into the garden of our mind, or by neglect, sowing bad seed, we will always reap the consequences. It is therefore extremely important we take time, and much care, to cultivate a harvest glorifying to God.

In retraining the brain we need to learn not just to be alert and protective over our minds, but be pro-active in our thinking. To guard against all the evil and negativity that is around is important, but only the first step. We must reject anything ungodly and unscriptural, but more than reject the bad; we must feed upon the good if we are to maintain a spiritual freshness in living for God. The Bible's instruction is, *"Be renewed in the spirit of your minds"* (Ephesians 4:23).

Pro-active thinking was taught by Paul, and he was a man who spent a great deal of time experiencing negative circumstances, both inside and out of prison, yet he lived consistently in peace. If the peace of God is with us in our daily lives, no matter what we face and irrespective of whoever, or whatever may try to wear us down, then we will always stay spiritually fresh. This is how the apostle could write with clarity and conviction even from his prison cell and say,

> *"Whatever is true, whatever is honourable, whatever is just, whatever is pure, whatever is lovely, whatever is gracious, if there is any excellence, if there is anything worthy of praise, think about these things...and the God of peace will be with you"* (Philippians 4:8-9).

An important aspect of pro-active thinking is that we constantly remind ourselves of the goodness and faithfulness of God. King David said, *"Bless the Lord, O my soul, and forget not all his benefits..."* (Psalm 103:2). The reason why this is necessary is quite simply because we soon forget! We might have had a wonderful miracle or an amazing answer to prayer six months ago, yet it only takes a crisis to crop up and we find ourselves forgetting the occasions in the past when God proved Himself faithful to us.

We must think back and remind ourselves how good and faithful God has been in that never once has He let us down; never has He not been true to His Word; never has He failed in any crisis to make a way where there seemed to be no way. We need to take the same wise and firm stand that Jeremiah took when he was going through a particularly dry and low period in his life; he said in Lamentations 3:21-23,

> *"But this I call to mind, and therefore I have hope:*
> *The steadfast love of the Lord never ceases, his*
> *mercies never come to an end; they are new every*
> *morning; great is thy faithfulness."*

In our aim to retrain the brain by being pro-active in our thinking, there are specific things that will be an enormous help to us. When we are alert in our minds to these areas then they will make a significant difference in keeping us spiritually fresh; these are:

(a) Meditation

This is not sitting cross-legged, 'navel gazing'; emptying our minds and opening ourselves to anything that comes along, as eastern philosophy might teach. Meditation is taking time to reflect, dwell upon and absorb God's Word. In Joshua 1:8, God's command is to meditate on His word day and night, being careful to obey it. The Psalmist says that the blessed person is the one whose, *"... delight is in the law of the Lord, and on his law he meditates day and night"* (Psalm 1:2). This scripture-based reflection is a

135

powerful way of influencing our thought-life and nurturing our mind.

Through meditation we expand our perception of Christ. We increase our expectation and deepen our anticipation so our mind is trained to believe that *"God is able to do far more abundantly than all that we ask or think"* (Ephesians 3:20). It is through Christian meditation that our thoughts are raised to a higher plain – way beyond the natural realm of thinking.

Benjamin Disraeli was born in 1804 and grew up to be one of Britain's finest Statesmen and Prime Ministers. He once said, "Nurture your mind with great thoughts, for you will never go any higher than you think." Meditation helps us to do exactly that. It is a practice that keeps us refreshed as we reprogramme our mind to think beyond ourselves, and realign our thoughts to be obedient to God's Word. This is not 'brain washing', rather it is an effective means of adjusting all our distorted thinking. Through specific periods of restful contemplation, waiting upon God, and quietly practising the presence of God in our daily activities, we bring our minds to the place of focusing more clearly on Him.

(b) Revelation

The input of information to retrain our brain is important in terms of study, particularly of God's Word. Also reading spiritually minded writers and inspirational biographies of those who have accomplished great things in their lives is a tremendous help. We can though, discover and be changed more in a moment through the Spirit of revelation than a lifetime of academic learning. Revelation is where God steps into our understanding, reveals Himself and brings alive to us what previously we have been oblivious to. In Jeremiah 33:3 God issues this invitation,

"*Call to me, and I will answer you, and show you great and mighty things, which you do not know*" (NKJ).

There is a great deal we "*do not know*" and we will only ever see with a renewed mind. One such truth I've personally discovered is, '**In the revelation of God's greatness we find the restoration of our destiny.**'

This is seen in Psalm 8:1-6 (NKJ), where the Psalmist speaks of the greatness of God revealed in the wonder of His handiwork, which created the universe. In awe and wonder he looks at the heavens, the moon and stars and says in verse four, "*What is man that You are mindful of him, and the son of man that You should visit him?*" His revelation of how magnificent and mighty God is doesn't diminish him, rather in verses five and six it restores and establishes him in his destiny. He sees: **(1)** "*You have made him a little lower than the angels;* **(2)** *You have crowned him with glory and honour;* **(3)** *You made him to have dominion over the works of your hands;* **(4)** *You have put all things under his feet...*"

These four aspects of our destiny were originally given to man by God at the beginning of creation. We have though, drifted far from this in our thinking, and have let our minds be limited by the magnitude of our problems, rather than the majesty of God's power. Only revelation can open our eyes to see this changed, so that we are restored. The greater our concept of God is, the greater our thoughts of ourselves will be. For this reason we must join David in saying, "*O magnify the Lord with me, and let us exalt his name together!*" (Psalm 34:3).

Revelation always raises us up to fulfil our calling, irrespective of our problems. When the Spirit of revelation is shaping our thinking we always see that our destiny is greater than our difficulties. Joseph is a good example of this in Genesis chapter 37 to 45. He faced many problems that stood against his God-given destiny to be ruler over Egypt. Joseph went from the **Pit of Rejection**, to the **Prison of Injustice**, before he arrived at the **Palace of God's Favour**. This reminds us that life is about times and seasons. There are some seasons in our lives we'd rather not be going through and certain times we would prefer to avoid. However, by the Spirit of revelation we see that, whether we are in the **pit** or perhaps the **prison**, ultimately we are heading towards the **palace!**

(c) Aspiration

American business magnet and socialite Donald Trump once remarked, "As long as you're going to think anyway, think big!" This is the point about our aspirations; never be restricted by 'small-minded' thoughts, or small-minded people. We must aspire to be our very best for God. When Jesus taught His disciples about their potential, He sought to stretch their expectation, by encouraging them not to let their minds be limited, as to what they could accomplish. His message to them was, "... *Nothing will be impossible to you*" (Matthew 17:20b). We are capable of the most extraordinary things and, therefore, must refuse to yield to thinking that undermines our potential, or allows our minds to be belittled by anyone.

Somebody once said, "When you reach for the stars, you may not quite get them, but you won't come up with a handful of mud either!" Our minds need to be filled with a sense of purpose for without aspiration we are prone to discouragement and fatigue, because life seems futile. A person who has no vision for the future will always settle for mediocrity. Because the Apostle Paul's mind was filled with aspiration to live his life fully for Christ he was unshakeable and unstoppable. Even when he stood as a prisoner before King Agrippa, he made his defence with absolute confidence saying,

> "... I was not disobedient to the heavenly vision, but declared first to those at Damascus, then at Jerusalem and throughout all the country of Judea, and also to the Gentiles, that they should repent and turn to God and perform deeds worthy of their repentance" (Acts 26:19-20).

Our desire for advancement and accomplishment is strengthened by what the Bible calls 'hope.' Paul expressed his longing that the Church in Rome might be full of such aspiration when he wrote, *"May the God of hope fill you with all joy and peace in believing, so that by the power of the Holy Spirit you may **abound in hope**"* (Romans 15:13). Christian hope is a future certainty grounded in a present reality; the conviction that God is for us and has a plan and purpose for each of us to fulfil. Without this hope our lives become sluggish under the burden of despair. This is what the apostle meant when he said,

> "And we desire each one of you to show the same earnestness in realizing the full assurance of hope until the end, so that you may not be sluggish..." (Hebrews 6:11).

(d) Identification

If there is restlessness going on within our mind, emotions or will, then it becomes impossible to stay spiritually fresh. Rather than wearily struggling on by ourselves we must come to the only person who is able to bring us rest. Jesus, who knows our weaknesses and is fully aware of all our struggles, gives a wonderful invitation to be identified with Him:

"Come to me all who labour and are heavy laden, and I will give you rest. Take my yoke upon you, and learn from me, for I am gentle and lowly in heart, and you will find rest for your souls" (Matthew 11:28).

In being alert in our thinking our aim is to have a mind that is occupied with walking in close union with Christ. Fundamental to this is making sure that every area of our life is in complete agreement with His Word. The prophet Amos asks the rhetorical question, *"Can two walk together unless they be agreed?"* (Amos 3:3, NKJ). The answer, of course, is that it is impossible to do so; there must be on our part an absolute surrender and identification to His teaching. The rest that we long to find is not experienced merely in coming to Jesus with our problems, but by also taking His yoke upon us, walking together in harmony with His will, and seeking to learn who we are in Christ.

This daily walk requires a radical change in our thinking so that we retrain our minds to think in terms of identifying with His yoke, which He has designed specifically for our lives. We can only move in the direction of our destiny when we realise this has already been prepared for us to fit into. The yoke designed for us was shaped by Christ long ago; nothing else will fit and be comfortable until we understand this:

"For we are God's own handiwork, His workmanship, recreated in Christ Jesus, born anew, that we may do those good works which God predestined and planned beforehand for us, taking paths which He prepared ahead of time, that we should walk in them, living

*the good life which He prearranged and made ready
for us to live"* (Ephesians 2:10 Amp).

Another very important aspect of identification that
affects our spiritual freshness is the kind of people with
whom we associate and walk together with. We need to
connect and spend time with spiritually-minded people;
those that are like-minded and will have a godly influence
upon us. The Bible says, *"He who walks with wise men
becomes wise, but the companion of fools will suffer harm"*
(Proverbs 13:20). We must always remain friendly in our
manner to whoever we meet and look for the good in all
people. However, we must also be alert to the fact that God's
Word teaches we cannot be unequally yoked without it
having a detrimental affect on our lives: *"... Bad company
ruins good morals"* (1 Corinthians 15:33).

(e) Determination

On October 29, 1941 Prime Minister Winston Churchill
visited Harrow School, where he had been educated as a youth.
Part of what he said to inspire the students on that occasion
was, "Never give in – never give in, never; never; never; never
– in anything, great or small, large or petty – never give in
except to convictions of honour and good sense." This mindset
of determination is crucial to staying spiritually fresh and seeing
great victories in life. We must be on our guard to any thinking
contrary to this, because otherwise it will be the cause of
allowing ourselves to be worn down by frustration and
discouragement. When we could have conquered if we'd
remained steadfast, we will give in under the pressure of negative
thoughts.

We all have battles to fight and challenges to overcome
in life. The Bible however encourages us to steadfastly

believe for God's purpose to come to pass: *"If it seems slow, wait for it; it will surely come..."* (Habakkuk 2:3). This determination was most certainly the example Jesus demonstrated for us to follow. We read of Him, *"He steadfastly set His face to go to Jerusalem"* (Luke 9:51, NKJ). It is also an attitude we will always find in those who accomplish remarkable things with their lives, even against insurmountable obstacles. For instance:

In America, Rev Martin Luther King, winner of the Nobel Peace prize at the age of thirty five, was a prominent leader in the African-American civil rights movement. He had a God-given dream to end racial segregation and discrimination; for all men to be treated equally regardless of the colour of their skin. This man lived with danger all the time; his home was bombed on two occasions and he received hundreds of telephone calls and letters from people threatening to kill him. On 28th August 1963, at the Lincoln Memorial, Washington D.C., he delivered his memorable and most famous address – '**I Have a Dream**'. This struck a chord not only in America, but also around the world. In part of this speech he said,

> "I have been to the mountain top and I have looked over and seen the Promised Land. I may not get there with you, but I am not worried about anything. I am not afraid of any man. Mine eyes have seen the glory of the coming of the Lord."

His determination to be faithful to the vision that he'd been given cost him his life five years later, on 4th April 1968, when he was assassinated in the city of Memphis, Tennessee at the age of 39. Although he didn't personally see his vision fulfilled, his courage not to give up changed not only his generation, but generations to come.

In India, a young barrister by the name of Mahatma Gandhi won freedom for his people, from the oppression of British rule in 1947. This was because of his determination and courage to believe in the principle of resistance with non-violence. He was reviled, humiliated and severely beaten on many occasions. Eventually he was assassinated on January 30th 1948, at the age of 78, when he was shot dead on his way to a prayer meeting. This one man's determination changed a nation!

In South Africa, history was made and a nation changed by Nelson Mandela. He fought against the injustice and evil of apartheid in his country and he spent 27 years in prison, most of that time in a tiny cell on Robin Island. He eventually was released and came out with courage and dignity to become the first black President of South Africa on 10th May, 1994, and to win the Nobel Peace Prize.

We should never underestimate the difference a single individual can make when they are determined not to give in to thinking contrary to God's thoughts and ways. It only takes one person with a tenacity of mind to bring about major change, no matter how impossible it might seem. Therefore we should always be alert in our thought-life so we understand the potential of our mind. As those born again by the power of God, we have been given *'The mind of Christ.'* Our responsibility is to guard it against anything that would be harmful in any way and to take steps to **reclaim**, **restrain** and **retrain** our brain.

Chapter 6

Practice Dying Daily

If we are to maintain a spiritual freshness in our lives it is necessary that we die to everything in us which does not reflect the character and nature of Christ. Each day there will be plenty of occasions when our reaction to pressures, conflicts, temptations and problems will require a Christ-centred response, rather than a self-centred one. This is a process of learning; a response of which it can be said, 'Practice Makes Perfect', and one that is foundational to being a true disciple of Christ. There was no ambiguity in what Jesus expected when He called people to follow Him; He stated,

> *"If any man would come after me, let him deny himself and take up his cross daily, and follow me"* (Luke 9:23).

The 19th Century British Statesman and four times Prime Minister William E. Gladstone spoke about self-centredness as being, "The greatest curse of the human race." It is a blight we inflict upon ourselves and is always, without exception, counter-productive. This is because it is an attitude focused more on what affects us, before having any concern for other people, and it brings weariness into every aspect of our lives. Serious erosion slowly takes place in relationships, which eventually becomes evident in how it introduces coldness into marriages, friction into families, unrest into society and impotence into the Church!

Preoccupation with 'self' brings striving and futility, divine revelation however, awakens and refreshes our soul. Nothing can be more exhilarating than being introduced to the eternal purpose of God and His destiny for our lives. One of the most exciting truths we can discover is His amazing plan of salvation. Christ's death and resurrection was not simply that we should find forgiveness for our sins, be reconciled to God and ultimately be saved from going to a lost eternity in hell. Nor is it limited to just defeating and destroying the works of the devil. More broadly speaking, it is also for the purpose of achieving transformation, so we are conformed to the image of Christ, and restored back into an intimate relationship with God, reflecting His glory.

By restoration, it is His intent that through the Church the *"manifold wisdom of God might now be made known to the principalities and powers in heavenly places"* (Ephesians 3:10). His purpose is that we should be changed to live a 'Christ-centred' life, individually and corporately together. Paul explains this when writing to the believers at Corinth. He says of Jesus,

> *"He died for all, that those who live, might live no longer for themselves, but for him who for their sake died and was raised"* (2 Corinthians 5:15).

146

The self-life is very short-sighted and always protective of its own interests; preoccupied with thoughts, desires, and objectives that are contrary to a life consecrated to Christ. It is a lifestyle that centres primarily on pleasing oneself before anything else. A simple rhyme I came across recently expresses this serious point, amusingly:

> "I gave a little tea party this afternoon, at 3.
> 'Twas very small, 3 guests in all - I, myself, and me.
> Myself ate all the sandwiches while I drank all the tea.
> 'Twas also I, who ate the pie, and passed the cake to me."

In addressing such selfishness Paul spoke to the church at Philippi about the need for them to change when he wrote,

> *"Let each of you esteem, and look upon, and be concerned for not merely his own interests, but also each for the interests of others"* (Philippians 2:4, Amp).

The 'I', 'Me' and 'My' must be radically purged from our thinking and vocabulary, not only because it grieves the Holy Spirit and spoils the image of Christ in us, but also because it drains the power of God from our lives. This is only possible when we live according to the basic premise of genuine Christianity which Paul establishes in his assertion, *"... You are not your own; you were bought with a price..."* (1 Corinthians 6:19-20). We are to live as those who have been purchased at the cost of His blood, and enthusiastically allow Him to live His life through us.

This means living under His authority, and acknowledging His Lordship over all aspects of our lives.

In submitting to this change we relinquish our pride, our autonomy and our self-will so that we desire to please the Lord more than pleasing others or ourselves. It is only when death to self has become a reality that we will be able to live in the life-changing power of Christ's resurrection. Failing to accept this fact is why so many Christians do not experience the 'abundant' relationship Jesus promised in John 10:10. Although our salvation is not dependent upon how well we accomplish this, our peace, strength, and quality of life most certainly are.

Only Death Can Produce Resurrection Life

Every Christian can live in the exciting power of new life, in the 'here and now', but this is only possible to experience when death has first taken place. Nothing else we believe will help us as much as recognizing that whatever we give up, or put to death, God will resurrect into something far more constructive and valuable. Paul understood this principle and made a bold statement about himself which reveals to us the key to self-less, dynamic living; he said,

> *"I have been crucified with Christ; it is no longer I who live, but Christ who lives in me; and the life I now live in the flesh I live by faith in the Son of God, who loved me and gave himself for me"* (Galatians 2:20).

Here in the western world we take for granted the many privileges and comforts that surround us, and which the self-life revels in. In contrast to this, I well recall the cultural shock that confronted me on my first preaching trip to India. The stench of squalor and the sight of abject poverty was everywhere, with masses of people sleeping and making their home on the streets. In many places where I stayed, the accommodation and facilities were extremely basic. Provided for my 'convenience' was a hole in the ground for a toilet - that had no paper, and just a bucket of water to pour over my head for washing! In the first few days I can remember thinking to myself, "Whatever am I doing here!" However, the moment I made the decision to die to self, change my attitude and simply get on with living for Christ in the situation, it released an enthusiasm and vigour that previously had been wavering.

Jesus used a vivid illustration when talking about death producing resurrection life; He said, *"... unless a grain of wheat falls into the earth and dies, it remains alone; but if it dies, it bears much fruit"* (John 12:24). Consider what happens to the seed as it lays in the ground; **firstly,** the hard shell around the grain falls away, **secondly**, it takes on a new form, texture, colour, size, fragrance and usefulness – its whole appearance is completely transformed. **Thirdly,** as that which appeared dormant and unremarkable breaks out into life, its true destiny is realised. This is also the case with every Christian. When we are prepared to die to our own comfort, independence, opinions, pride, prejudice, passion and impulses, the hardness around our hearts begins to fall away. The result is that all the potential and beauty of the life of Christ within, then starts to emerge in resurrection power!

It is a work of grace that is accomplished, by the Holy Spirit, as we yield ourselves to Him. Speaking to the Church at Rome, Paul says, *If the Spirit of him that raised up Jesus from the dead dwells in you, he that raised up Christ from the dead shall also quicken your mortal bodies..."* (Romans 8:11, AV). There is no **'If'** as far as the believer is concerned; the Spirit of Him who raised Christ from the dead **does** dwell in us! We can therefore know a 'quickening' in our mortal flesh of faith, expectation and motivation every day of our lives, especially when weariness or heaviness tries to come upon us. It is this revelation that keeps us vibrant and strong in our walk with God.

Areas Where Dying To Self Is Essential

There are many aspects we could consider, where death to self is vital in releasing resurrection life. Let us look at some of the main areas which, if not taken to the cross daily, will be a major hindrance to our effectiveness:

(a) Self-Preservation

Every person has a disposition, intrinsic to their nature to preserve their being. We have a natural inclination to avoid suffering and pain; a drive within us to safeguard and to extend our lives. Such protectiveness is not wrong in itself, in fact the Bible says, *"For no man ever hates his own flesh, but nourishes and cherishes it..."* (Ephesians 5:29). This statement is true not only as common sense, but also in valuing ourselves as those purchased by Christ, and individuals who are, *"... a temple of the Holy Spirit"* (1 Corinthians 6:19).

We have a personal responsibility to respect and care for ourselves, also to make the most we can out of our lives. However, we must not confuse this with being anxious in our minds to the point that we become over-protective about our own importance, work, ministry, reputation, plans, opinions, preferences, material possessions etc. Those motivated by self-preservation believe these things alone represent their worth, and must be guarded at all cost. They are therefore often defensive and suspicious of other people's motives towards them. Also, they tend to have a very narrow view on life and an unspiritual approach to living. Dying to self is a necessity to this outlook because Jesus taught,

"For whoever would save his life will lose it, and whoever loses his life for my sake will find it" (Matthew 16:25).

Being motivated by self-preservation causes a person to be unspiritual because they are focused primarily on looking after themselves. One of the ways this becomes evident is when situations of dispute and conflict arise. They quickly become offended and defensive over minor matters; absorbed with justifying themselves and not losing face. By being preoccupied in protecting their image, 'territory', or sphere of responsibility; self-interest takes centre stage in the arena of their minds. Such self-preservation often results in people being stubborn in their point of view. Their attitude then causes unnecessary division and damage to relationships amongst family, neighbours, in the working environment and within the church.

By dying to self we choose not to take offence, in fact we shouldn't be surprised when we are criticised and our good is spoken of as evil; when the truth is twisted or we are unjustly treated and misrepresented. To become engrossed with defending or justifying ourselves drains us of an enormous amount of energy, eats away at our time, affects our appetite for food, and causes loss of sleep. In going over events in our mind, and replaying every detail, we can find ourselves continually talking about issues of contention; trying to understand why people have said or done what they have to us. All of this can leave us spiritually, physically and emotionally worn out!

We need to stay detached from personal offence and be objective so that we continue to love the person, even if we may disagree with them. This is made possible only when we have died to self and are applying the teaching of Christ, who said to His disciples: *"... Love your enemies and pray for those who persecute you"* (Matthew 5:44). Also in Romans 12:14-19 Paul teaches the same attitude of heart, but adds the important fact that we must live as those who believe God will ultimately vindicate the truth.

> *"Bless those who persecute you; bless and do not curse ... Do not repay anyone evil for evil. Be careful to do what is right in the eyes of everybody. If it is possible, as far as it depends on you, live at peace with everyone. Do not take revenge, my friends, but leave room for God's wrath, for it is written: "It is mine to avenge; I will repay," says the Lord"* (NIV).

The apostle Paul gave us a clear example of what it meant to die to self-preservation in his own life when speaking of the injustice and suffering he knew was going to be inflicted upon him. As he travelled towards Jerusalem he said,

> *"And see, now I go bound in the spirit to Jerusalem, not knowing the things that will happen to me there, except that the Holy Spirit testifies in every city, saying that chains and tribulations await me. But none of these things move me; nor do I count my life dear to myself, so that I may finish my race with joy, and the ministry which I received from the Lord Jesus, to testify to the gospel of the grace of God"* (Acts 20:22-24, NKJ).

(b) Self-Righteousness

A self-made businessman, well known for his success and ruthlessness, once proudly announced to American author and humorist Mark Twain, "Before *I* die *I* mean to make a pilgrimage to the Holy Land. *I* will ascend Mount Sinai and read the 10 Commandments aloud at the top." "I have a better idea," replied Twain. "You could stay in Boston and keep them!"

Self-righteousness comes in many guises, but fundamentally it is a form of pride and conceit that blinds people to the true state of their heart. One of the main forms it takes is improvement through self-effort. It promotes an alternative path to that of relying on God's grace and prescribed way of living. In the Old Testament Job recognised the delusion of this when he said, *"If I justify myself, mine own mouth shall condemn me: if I say I am perfect, it shall also prove me perverse"* (Job 9:20, AV).

The strongest words of condemnation spoken by Jesus were against some of the religious leaders of His day. They thought that through their own efforts they could make themselves acceptable to God. This of course is just as foolish as trying to pull yourself up by your own shoelaces! These leaders were laying upon people the burden of excessive man-made rules, aimed at gaining God's acceptance. It was a code of living that was impossible to keep and therefore brought only a sense of condemnation and failure. What provoked the anger of Jesus was that in their own blindness, they were leading those they were teaching away from God and into a lost eternity. These religious guides were living with a false security, thinking and acting as if they were morally superior to everyone else.

The attitude of self-righteousness is not merely a form of pride and conceit but also of hypocrisy; that is pretending to

153

be something we are not. Playing a role, or wearing a mask of pretence to impress others, is deeply offensive to God. It denies our true condition of sinfulness and rejects any need of repentance and faith in Christ. Jesus referred to this arrogance when He taught about two men - one a Pharisee and the other a tax collector. The tax collector humbled himself and acknowledged his need of help and forgiveness as he cried out for mercy. In contrast, the Pharisee stood up in the market place and prayed,

> *"God, I thank you that I am not like other men - extortioners, unjust, adulterers, or even as this tax collector. I fast twice a week; I give tithes of all I posses"* (Luke 18:11-12, NKJ).

Unless we are dying to self, in our own estimation of how important and good we are, we will drift away from experiencing an intimate relationship with God. There is no surer way of reaching the point of weariness and futility than trying to make our life meaningful and worthwhile through self-effort. In our own eyes we may have accomplished things we can be satisfied about but, in the light of eternity, they amount to nothing at all if we are not reliant on God. It was the great American evangelist Billy Graham who said, "The smallest package I ever saw was a man wrapped up wholly in himself."

The apostle Paul had the right attitude in Philippians 3:3b when he said, *"... I put no confidence in the flesh."* Summing up all the virtue and merit others might see in his life, he firstly spoke in verse 5a of his family tree, saying about his pedigree that he was, *"... of the people of Israel, of the tribe of Benjamin, a Hebrew, born of Hebrews."* Then he referred to his knowledge of the law and stated he was a *"Pharisee"* (verse

5b) - Paul was taught at a Pharisaic Rabbinical School headed up by Gamaliel, who the Jews considered to be one of the greatest teachers ever of Judaism. He therefore knew the letter of the law and, in fact, became one of the leading teachers of it himself. Furthermore, with regard to his moral integrity, he could confidently declare in verse 6, *"... as to righteousness under the law, I am blameless."*

Then as Paul reflects on all his self-righteousness he concludes:

> *"Indeed I count everything as loss because of the surpassing worth of knowing Christ Jesus my Lord... and count them as refuse, in order that I might gain Christ and be found in him, not having a righteousness of my own, based on law, but that which is through faith in Christ, the righteousness from God that depends on faith"* (verse 8-9).

What an inspiring example he is of someone who lived in the resurrection power of Christ because he was utterly dependent on what Jesus had done for him, rather than trying to find security in his own accomplishments. Paul did not seek fulfilment in the accolades that man could bestow upon him, nor was he secure merely in the impressiveness of his own ability. Rather he was committed to die daily to himself and say,

> *"But God forbid that I should boast except in the cross of our Lord Jesus Christ, by whom the world has been crucified to me, and I to the world"* (Galatians 6:14, NKJ).

True righteousness is imputed to us as God's gift, through the merit of Christ's finished work on the cross.

Claiming this as the result of our own efforts or abilities brings the greatest offence to what Jesus suffered to make possible for us. This is why the Bible says, that in the sight of God, *"... all our righteous acts are like filthy rags"* (Isaiah 64:6, NIV). The foolishness of pride will inevitably quench the Holy Spirit within us and be a major cause for spiritual barrenness and fatigue. It is a danger we must all continually be aware of and quickly put to death through repentance and faith.

The driving determination of accomplishment and self-effort to climb 'The greasy pole' of ambition and success is common in society today, and it has to be said, even in the Church. There is a proliferation of self-help books promoting how to get rich quick, how to be a success and how to maximize our potential etc. Charismatic, motivational speakers inspire people to achieve bigger and greater things. In the midst of all this, we have to be careful not to forget the absolute necessity of relying upon God. Jesus emphasises this point when teaching His disciples, saying, *"For apart from me you can do nothing"* (John 15:5b).

Another form of self-righteousness is observed with some Christians who act as though they are always in the right and can never be in error; they just find it inconceivable that they might be at fault in any way. Keeping short accounts with God, but also with our fellow man is important. This is particularly so in situations of misunderstanding and disagreement with others. We regularly need to check with God in prayer that we have not been in the wrong or need to admit any mistake on our part. Our humble prayer should be,

"Search me, O God, and know my heart! Try me and know my thoughts! And see if there be any wicked way in me..." (Psalm 139:23-24).

Self-righteousness can also be evident in the lives of Christians who are very opinionated, judgemental and critical. They will have a legalistic attitude that is harsh, devoid of compassion and be quick to condemn, jumping on anything they consider wrong in their eyes. They become self-appointed overseers of what is acceptable to God and act like the Pharisees Jesus spoke against who were, *"... blind guides, straining out a gnat and swallowing a camel"* (Matthew 23:24). Such people take pleasure in giving the impression they are spiritually better than anyone else and leave those they meet with a sense of condemnation and failure. They are quick to notice and point out the shortcomings of those around them, interpreting God's Word as always applying to others, yet are blind to their own sin. Jesus warned against this when He said,

"You hypocrite, first take the log out of your own eye, and then you will see clearly to take the speck out of your brother's eye" (Matthew 7:5).

Self-righteousness is therefore a form of deception which is why the Bible says, *"If we say we have no sin, we deceive ourselves, and the truth is not in us"* (I John 1:8). It causes us to think we can hide behind an image of good works and self-effort rather than living holy lives. Any true encounter with God will immediately strip this away, just as the prophet Isaiah discovered on the occasion he had a revelation of the Lord in the temple. His desperate cry of conviction was,

"Woe is me! For I am lost; for I am a man of unclean lips, and I dwell in the midst of a people of unclean lips; for my eyes have seen the King, the Lord of hosts!" (Isaiah 6:5).

157

The manifestation of God's presence, that we all need for spiritual refreshment, will inevitably bring conviction. Any self-righteousness is exposed and then no longer do people rely on themselves, but completely on God. As the Lord touches our lives He brings an awakening so that our swift and glad response is death to self, resulting in new vibrant life blossoming out in an unmistakeable way!

(c) Self-Pity

Dying to self-pity is something we all need to learn because it is a problem that, due to disappointment, hurt and set-backs, affects everyone at times. If this is left unchecked it will become a major cause of sapping our spiritual strength, and affect our general wellbeing. Self-pity is a crippling emotional disease that severely distorts our perception of reality, often blowing things up out of all proportion. It is a paralysis that hinders spiritual growth and motivation. By draining joy from our lives and keeping our minds preoccupied with personal problems, it stops us expecting the answer that we need from God.

Self-pity is always sin because it is an expression of unbelief, putting our self and our difficulties above God, ignoring His power and disregarding His intervention. No matter how we try to justify the issue, there is never any circumstance when it can be excused. This is because it extinguishes faith by pushing God out of the matter that is absorbing our time and attention. In effect we are saying, "God has forgotten me"; "He is not true to His promise"; "He can't be relied upon to watch over me"; "He has no plan for my life!"

Frequently self-pity will be expressed in negativity, grumbling and discontent. It shows an inability to see God as the 'Sovereign Lord'; someone who is at work in our lives, and able to bring good even out of evil. By being drawn into this indulgence we face the trap of self-pity becoming a habit, producing selfish short-term comfort, while not realizing it will smother and spoil everything good that is of long-term benefit. It can be used by people as a means of attention-seeking; an excuse for various deficiencies in their spiritual development; a tactic of escaping responsibility; and as a manoeuvre of blame-shifting by accusing others for the problems being experienced. We must recognise this as a weed which needs to be killed and rooted out of our lives, otherwise it will spread quickly.

It is a misconception to believe that life's troubles lead to self-pity. In actual fact it is always how we handle problems that result in our rising above, or going under in any situation. More often than not the issue is not *what* we face as much as it is *the way we choose to face it.* Choosing the right perspective can be half the battle in triumphing over life's stresses.

In looking at how the Lord led the Israelites out of Egypt, we see that self-pity still filled their lives despite their remarkable deliverance. God had saved them from the tyranny of bondage and had a wonderful plan for them, yet continually they expressed self-pity which exposed their unbelief. They complained about their thirst even though they had seen God miraculously make water come from a rock. They grumbled about their hunger even though He supernaturally had given them manna and quail to eat. They murmured about the leadership of Moses and Aaron, yet these two leaders were bringing them to the Promised Land. They complained about the hardships of their journey, yet previously they had been slaves in Egypt. They doubted they could conquer the Promised Land, in spite of the fact the Lord had parted the Red Sea and defeated the might of the Egyptian army before their very eyes!

It can be very difficult to be around or live with someone with this mind-set because their attitude and thinking of despair pollutes the atmosphere of faith. They bring tension and heaviness to everyone they come into contact with. If we are not careful, their pessimism can cause a gloom to come upon us, affecting our faith. An amusing tale illustrates the frustration of being with such a person: A marriage counsellor was asking a woman some questions about her disposition and attitude. He asked, "Did you wake up grumpy this morning?" "No," replied the woman, "I just let him sleep in!"

On one occasion German born Martin Luther, a leading Church reformer of the early 16th Century, became overwhelmed by self-pity and wouldn't eat. As a result his wife went to the bedroom and came out in a black mourning outfit. Luther asked her about it and she said she was going to a funeral. He asked whose? She said it was God's. He replied, "The Pope's trying to kill me, my friends have turned on me and now my wife is a heretic!" She said, "The only reason I thought God was dead was because of the way you are acting." Realising the sin of his depressing outlook Luther fell on his knees and cried out for his wife's and God's forgiveness.

One of the subtle and destructive things about self-pity is that it robs us of all hope. With some people, because it has become a lifestyle they have developed over the years, they live in a continual state of despondency. Our attitude of dying to self has a great deal to do with maintaining hope, especially in times of difficulty. We can only put this gloomy disposition to death and rid ourselves of this ungodly temperament, draining our spiritual freshness, when, as the Bible says, we, "... *hold our first confidence firm to the end*" (Hebrews 3:14).

There is a Welsh proverb that reads, "Bad news goes about in clogs, good news in stockinged feet." To die to self-pity we have to deliberately ignore the loud noises of doubt and fear which try to drown out God's Word, and choose to tune our ears to listen for the goodness of His still small voice. God's Word strengthens us to put to death all negativity, despondency and unbelief that finds its expression through self-pity, and gives us good cause for hope.

Irrespective of how strong the temptation may be to turn inward on ourselves, and regardless of any difficult circumstances overshadowing us, liberty and new life comes as we die to self-pity. This is possible when we firstly repent, then as we believe the truth of scripture which says,

> "*And God is able to make all grace abound to you, so that in all things at all times, having all that you need, you will abound in every good work*" (2 Corinthians 9:8, NIV).

(d) Self-Seeking

British actor Michael Wilding was once asked if actors had any traits which set them apart from other human beings. "Without a doubt," he replied. "You can pick out actors by the glazed look that comes into their eyes when the conversation wanders away from themselves." While this sounds mildly amusing it is sadly true of a lot of people today. Self-seeking is very much an attitude of being focused on personal advancement and how best they, and others, can strengthen their own position and goals. In the quest for achievement, fulfilment and recognition, much effort can be put into the improvement of people's own status and wellbeing, while having little or no genuine concern for others.

Giving negligible thought for people who cannot be useful to our own aims shows a disrespect that is anything other than Christ-like. If we do not learn to die daily to this attitude it will bring dryness and deadness into our spiritual lives. The hidden agendas behind some people's business and social 'networking' can be very subtle and questionable. Also the ulterior motives in their enquiries into aspects of another person's life, and some of the decisions and actions taken that appear to be sincere, may for a short while go unnoticed, but given time they are eventually exposed.

All motivation, that at its heart is self-seeking, is extremely shallow and is obvious to anyone with even a modicum of discernment. After Abraham Lincoln became President, before the days of civil service, 'office seekers' besieged him everywhere trying to get appointments to different jobs throughout the country. Once, confined to bed with typhoid fever, exasperated Lincoln declared to his secretary, "Bring on the office seekers; I now have something I can give to everybody!"

Using people for self-advancement and building personal kingdoms can occur with Christians, even in the lives of well known ministers who have an established ministry. This is true whether it is in terms of an evangelist manipulating the masses, the pastor neglecting or abusing his congregation, or individual Christians seeking to advance their own agenda. Taking advantage of others and looking out for 'number one', no matter who is overlooked, trodden on, or hurt in the process, angers the heart of God. We see how the Lord viewed such self-seeking and disregard of other people when He spoke through the prophet Ezekiel:

"Woe to the shepherds of Israel who feed themselves! Should not the shepherds feed the flocks? You eat the fat and clothe yourselves with the wool; you slaughter the fatlings, but you do not feed the flock. The weak you have not strengthened, nor have you healed those who were sick, nor bound up the broken, nor brought back what was driven away, nor sought what was lost; but with force and cruelty you have ruled them. So they were scattered because there was no shepherd; and they became food for all the beasts of the field when they were scattered. My sheep wandered through all the mountains, and on every high hill; yes, My flock was scattered over the whole face of the earth, and no one was seeking or searching for them." Therefore, you shepherds, hear the word of the LORD: "As I live," says the Lord GOD, "surely because My flock became a prey, and My flock became food for every beast of the field, because there was no shepherd, nor did My shepherds search for My flock, but the shepherds fed themselves and did not feed My flock"- therefore, O shepherds, hear the word of the LORD! Thus says the Lord GOD: "Behold, I am against the shepherds, and I will require My flock at their hand; I will cause them to cease feeding the sheep, and the shepherds shall feed themselves no more; for I will deliver My flock from their mouths, that they may no longer be food for them" (Ezekiel 34:2b-10, NKJ).

This attitude of pursuing primarily what is best for ourselves, irrespective of others, has to be crucified and put to death, because it mars the image of Christ in us and will have dire consequences spiritually. At its worst it thinks

163

nothing of abusing, disregarding and disrespecting those around, and is more interested in how everything affects their personal gain. "What have you done for ME lately?", or "What can I get out of you that will benefit ME" are poisonous, self-seeking attitudes. Although these will probably never be expressed openly, they hide, lurking, unspoken beneath the surface in the heart of self-seeking people. They give birth to all manner of relationship-destroying behaviours and are contrary to the principle of love we are commanded to live by.

When people give, in whatever way, from selfish motives, they expect a return for their 'investment.' When a genuine, Spirit-filled Christian gives, they do so, not for what they can get, but for the joy of knowing they are enriching the person they have given to. They understand that the vain pursuit of pleasure is built on self-seeking, but true joy is based on self-sacrifice. The more we pursue our own gratification, the emptier we feel. Someone once said, "If a pint of pleasure gives momentary happiness today, a gallon of excitement and thrills is necessary for the same effect tomorrow." A life of lasting and overflowing joy however, is based on the sacrificial giving of ourselves, which is why the Bible says, "...*it is more blessed to give than to receive*" (Acts 20:35b).

When talking about love, Paul plainly states in 1 Corinthians 13:5, "... *it is not self-seeking*" (NIV). We will know we have died to this problem when our lives reflect the characteristics of love that the apostle outlines in verse 4-7 of this chapter. Here he speaks of having attitudes that express patience and kindness; not being envious, or boastful. Paul talks of relating to others with a manner that isn't proud, rude, easily angered, or keeps a record of wrongs. He goes on to say, love does not delight in evil but rejoices in the truth. Then he concludes by saying, our love for another should always be protective, trusting, hopeful and persevering. This means we are never to take advantage of others. In fact, Christ teaches us to love our neighbour as we would ourselves. Love therefore serves with no false intent, and doesn't worry about who gets the credit.

In John 13:1-15 we see a powerful demonstration of what it means to die to self-seeking as Christ the Lord, stoops down and washes His disciples' feet. He was completely aware of His sovereign authority, His origin, and coming destiny; yet He voluntarily took the place of a slave and served His disciples in this extraordinary way. This act of humble self-effacing modesty was followed by Jesus teaching that, with humility, we are to serve one another:

"If I then, your Lord and Teacher, have washed your feet, you also ought to wash one another's feet. For I have given you an example, that you also should do as I have done to you" (verses 14-15).

We learn how to die to self-seeking by asking God to change our attitudes towards those around us. This becomes possible as we first repent of all selfish motives and thoughts for our own advancement, and instead we seek the best for others. The Bible shows us plenty of ways we can do this, for example: *"... outdo one another in showing honour"* (Romans 12:10). *"Be kind to one another, ..forgiving one another..."* (Ephesians 4:32). *"Be subject to one another"* (Ephesians 5:21). *"Encourage one another, and build one another up"* (1 Thessalonians 5:11). *"Do not grumble against one another..."* (James 5:9). *"Confess your sins to one another, and pray for one another"* (James 5:16), *"Practice hospitality ungrudgingly to one another"* (1 Peter 4:9), and *"... love one another"* (1 John 3:11).

Dying to all we are in ourselves and putting others first, may mean the risk of being taken advantage of. Undoubtedly there are those in life today that would jump at the chance to make prey of people that go out of their way, seeking to benefit their fellow man. Even though we may be anxious about being 'used', we are called to sacrifice our time, energy and resources for the good of others.

We must be prepared to go the 'second mile', to 'turn the other cheek', and like Christ, even be willing to suffer at the hands of unjust men. If we do get taken advantage of and are mistreated, by dying to self we are able rest in God. We can remain at peace, rather than becoming resentful and being wearied by the need to 'stand up and fight for our 'rights'.

As we die to self, then God, who sees the whole picture, will give us all the grace we need to rise in the dynamic power of resurrection life.

(e) Self-Promotion

One other major area, closely related to self-seeking, which we need to die daily to, is the tendency we have of promoting ourselves. Until we've crucified the flesh in this matter, we will continually be trying to find recognition from others for our lives to feel of any importance. The apostle Paul refused to have anything to do with promoting himself or his own ministry. He took an uncompromising stand on this issue and said,

"For what we preach is not ourselves, but Jesus Christ as Lord, with ourselves as your servants for Jesus' sake" (2 Corinthians 4:5).

Unless we die to the temptation of self-promotion, we will be striving to gain the approval of those around us and struggling to maintain an appearance of success, even at the cost of our integrity. It has to be said, that there is within most people, an inclination to embellish the truth in order to promote themselves and impress their peers. This is part of the culture, or 'spirit of the age' in which we live, where image and acceptance are so important to a person's existence.

In our efforts to stay ahead, or at least keep pace with others, we often feel the need to build ourselves up in their eyes. In doing so we are inclined to exaggerate almost everything, except our own mistakes. This is amusingly illustrated by something I read recently about two intrepid travellers trying to out-do one another as they boasted of their great exploits: "It was so cold where we were," said one Arctic explorer, "that the candle froze and we couldn't blow it out!" "That's nothing," said his rival. "Where we were, the words came out of our mouths in pieces of ice and we had to fry them to hear what we were talking about!!"

Obviously this is a caricature of the absurdness of self-promotion, nevertheless within it there is an unfortunate element of truth. Whether talking about our academic qualifications; responsibilities at work; various aspects of ministry; the size of our church; some past achievement; a future project, or the position we hold in our social circle etc., exaggeration comes naturally to most people. We must avoid thinking about ourselves in a way which expresses an attitude that everything is about us. The Bible addresses the issue when it says, *"... Do not think of yourself more highly than you ought"* (Romans 12:3).

Christ's disciples needed to be taught this as they argued over who was the greatest and who would have the highest position in Heaven (Mark 9:33-35). Two of them, James and John, the sons of Zebedee, in their ambition to promote themselves, allowed their mother to get involved! She intervened for them, asking for seats on the right and left hand of Jesus in His Kingdom, (Matthew 20:20-21).

In a contrast to the way the world seeks promotion through pushing ahead, stepping on people and grabbing the limelight, Jesus taught that the path to true greatness is found via the road of humility, servitude, and sacrifice. This is the peculiar paradox of God's Kingdom; more often than not its principles are completely the reverse of human logic. Self-promotion is totally alien to Kingdom living. Jesus illustrated this by saying, *"The last will be first, and the first last"* (Matthew 20:16). Furthermore, to the disciples who were getting agitated by James and John's shameless act of self-promotion, Jesus said in verses 26-27,

> *"... whoever would be great among you must be your servant, and whoever would be first among you must be your slave."*

John the Baptist had a totally different attitude and understanding as he expressed one of the most significant keys in dying to self-promotion. Speaking of his own importance, in relation to Christ, he said, *"He must increase, but I must decrease"* (John 3:30). This law of dying to self that Christ might be magnified is the secret of maintaining spiritual freshness, because it brings our lives into harmony with the principle that, *"... He alone in everything and in every respect might occupy the chief place..."* (Colossians 1:18b, Amp). Conversely, when Christ is small and self is large, we feel restless and unfulfilled because we are never satisfied. Many things can begin to annoy us and we can grow impatient about whatever may disrupt our comfort. We resent whatever would hinder or stand in our way.

It is a delusion to ever think that self-promotion is the answer to our success, recognition and ultimate happiness. When we look at the example of Jesus, He did not grasp at His rightful role to be equal with God, rather the Bible says He made Himself of no reputation. Because He was willing to humble Himself, become a servant, live and die for the benefit of others, God highly exalted Him! This teaches us the wonderful reality that promotion comes from the Lord! He is the one who exalts, promotes and causes us to find favour, all that we must take care to maintain is a humble attitude: *"Humble yourselves, therefore, under God's mighty hand, that he may lift you up in due time"* (1 Peter 5:6, NIV).

Of course, ambition and motivation are important in developing our potential, and achieving the very best we can be for God; we have no need though to push ourselves forward or catch the eye of anyone but Him. It is His favour upon our lives that causes us to prosper, and we can find reassurance in the fact that, *"... man looks on the outward appearance, but the Lord looks on the heart"* (1 Samuel 16:7b). Rather than wearing ourselves out trying to 'be somebody' the wisest of all men, King Solomon, states a simple truth we can rest in, and that is, *"A man's gift makes room for him and brings him before great men"* (Proverbs 18:16).

The Pathway To Death And New Life

Dying to self must always come out of intimacy with Christ, and our desire to please Him. No amount of religious fervour, on its own, will mean anything to God. When this isn't the case a person will be driven by legalistic striving, producing either delusion, or a sense of failure, condemnation, and even mental exhaustion. The latter was so with Martin Luther, who, due to his unenlightened religious zeal, practiced self-flagellation and harshly punished his body, in his quest to conquer sin. His misguided concept of self-denial brought him much torment as relentlessly he battled with his guilt, until eventually coming into a 'personal relationship' with Jesus as Lord.

To avoid such vain strivings, the pathway to death and new life involves at least three things, each of which starts with a living faith in the finished work of Christ: **Supplication**, **Sanctification** and **Subjugation**. A deeper study and understanding of these areas, which unfortunately we have no time for in this book, is something every Christian would do well to pursue. The benefit of them to the vibrancy of our relationship with God is incalculable as we will see briefly now:

(a) Supplication

In whatever form the self-life raises its ugly head, it is cut down and put to death when we come in sincere, humble supplication to God. The Bible identifies supplication as a specific way of seeking the Lord, particularly in times of need. This is found as a distinct and special form of prayer in the scriptures, which is why it is usually referred to separately. For example, in Ephesians 6:18a (NKJ), Paul speaks of, *"Praying always with all prayer and supplication in the Spirit..."*

Thanksgiving, praise and worship must always characterise our approach to God. Supplication however, is an earnest attitude and passionate state of heart that accompanies our prayers, as we bring our petition to the only one who is able to help. Such fervent praying is spoken of when the writer to the Hebrew believers refers to the manner in which Jesus prayed to His Father:

"In the days of his flesh, Jesus offered up prayers and supplications, with loud cries and tears, to him who was able to save him from death..." (Hebrews 5: 7).

We cannot force this attitude, or produce the emotion at whim; it is a divine work of grace that comes through self-effacing surrender. In supplication we humble ourselves to seek God and die to our own vain sufficiency and resources. We submit our will, laying our own agenda and our entire lives before Him, to be used in whatever He wants. In doing so we are yielding the self-life and saying to God, as Jesus did, *"... not My will, be but Yours, be done"* (Luke 22:42, NKJ).

The apostle Paul was often driven to his knees, particularly by the pressure of persecution. He understood that without God there was no hope; adversity only made his supplications more heartfelt. Problems have the effect of sharpening our focus upon the Lord and, as a consequence, even in the most stressful situations, we remain untroubled. When we have died to ourselves and have learned to wholly trust in God, it will be evident in our approach to Him in prayer. The benefit of this is what Paul wanted the Church at Philippi to discover when he wrote,

"Have no anxiety about anything, but in everything by prayer and supplication with thanksgiving let your requests be made known to God" (Philippians 4:6).

It was American President Abraham Lincoln who once remarked, "I have been driven many times to my knees by the overwhelming conviction that I had nowhere else to go. My own wisdom, and that of all about me, seemed insufficient for the day." In supplication we express that we are dying to our understanding; we have no answer in our own wisdom, nor power in our own might, but are affirming our absolute dependence upon God. Therefore, as we pray, we are actually accepting that without His help and intervention we are hopeless. This acknowledgement is expressed not merely at a time of crisis, but every occasion we come to make our requests known to God.

Furthermore, as far as any breakthrough is concerned, a lifestyle of self-denial, humble reliance and desperation in prayer is one of the major keys to experiencing change. The Lord is willing to pour out His Holy Spirit and bring transformation to the barren situations that surround us, but surrender and sacrifice on our part, is an inseparable element to this.

The Azusa Street revival meetings that began in 1906, led by William Seymour, were born out of humble, earnest supplication and were characterised by powerful, supernatural manifestations of the Holy Spirit. Much of the time, as these things were taking place, Seymour, an African American preacher sat with his head inside an old shoe box praying and seeking God to move in even greater ways. Such a hunger for God was in his heart that initially he prayed for five hours a day, for two and half years. When he got to Los Angeles the hunger was not less, but more. He asked God what to do and the Holy Spirit directed him to pray more. He therefore increased his time in prayer to seven hours and prayed like this for a further one and half years!

Unconditional availability and abandonment to God in prayer is a rare thing these days and yet it is the basis on which great things are accomplished. The apostle's plea to the Roman Christians was, *"I appeal to you therefore, brethren, by the mercies of God, to present your bodies as a living sacrifice, holy and acceptable to God..."* (Romans 12:1). This offering of our lives is expressed as we take time to come aside from all distractions, focus on Him and devote ourselves to wholehearted supplication.

Through spirit-led supplication we steer clear of vain struggling and self interest. It helps us avoid the tendency to pray too often for ourselves and not much for others. Our intent to die to self must have, at its heart, not simply the needs we have, but also our burden for others. The 17th Century British preacher and writer John Bunyan said, "You have not lived today until you have done something for someone who can never repay you." The very least we can do for others is prayerfully bring them before the Lord. This directs and strengthens our desire to practically apply what it means to be a *'living sacrifice,'* serving God and our fellow man. To the Church at Ephesus Paul wrote, "... *keep alert with all perseverance, making supplication for all the saints"* (Ephesians 6:18b).

The Psalmist David said, "... *I will not offer to the Lord my God that which costs me nothing"* (2 Samuel 24:24b). Prayer should always involve a personal cost to us. The sacrifice of our time, comfort, and convenience, we ought to gladly lay on the altar as we come to God. Pride, however, draws us away from Him and we become confident in ourselves, complacent in our worship and careless in offering to the Lord. There is nothing like the discipline and sacrifice of prayer to keep us reliant upon God on a daily basis. We read in the scriptures of Jesus,

"And in the morning, a great while before day, he rose and went out to a lonely place, and there he prayed" (Mark 1:35).

Paul taught that we should, *"Pray without ceasing"* (1 Thessalonians 5:17, NKJ). It is this selfless dependence on God which enables us to stay spiritually fresh even in the most challenging circumstances. The old adage, **'Seven Days Without Prayer Makes One Weak'** is not only a catchy phrase to remember, it is basic to our spiritual strength. If we are to re-direct our lives away from ourselves and on to God then there is no short cut – we cannot build a bypass around the importance of prayerful supplication and expect to thrive as a Christian!

(b) Sanctification

Although sanctification is often perceived as a religious notion too complex to comprehend, and appears less than enthralling, it is a major key to staying spiritually vibrant. This is because, what we are talking about, is not merely a doctrine, but a dynamic power! It is a liberating truth, teaching us, yet again, that with God, new life comes out of death!

Initially, sanctification is a sovereign act of God's grace, but it is one that leads to personal holiness. Paul, referring to this, wrote,

> "May God himself, the God of peace, sanctify you through and through. May your whole spirit, soul and body be kept blameless at the coming of our Lord Jesus Christ" (1 Thessalonians 5:23, NIV).

It is presented in the Bible as both an **event** and also a **process**. The event occurred instantly we put our trust in the death and resurrection of Jesus Christ. At that moment we were sanctified by God; cleansed, forgiven, set free from the power of evil and saved from a lost eternity. It was entirely His doing! The writer to the Hebrew Christians speaks of this when he says, *"For by one offering He has perfected forever those who are being sanctified"* (Hebrews 10:14, NKJ).

The process however is progressive, and one that every believer must apply themselves to each day of their lives. The word sanctify originates from the Greek word *hagiazo*, which means to be 'separate' or 'set apart for a sacred purpose.' Therefore it does not stop with the moment of salvation, but rather it continues in a Christian's life as they take responsibility to walk in a way pleasing to Him: *"For God called us not for uncleanness, but in sanctification"* (1 Thessalonians 4:7, ASV).

This is why Jesus said to his disciples, *"If any man would come after me, let him deny himself and take up his cross daily, and follow me"* (Luke 9:23). We do this by daily choosing to reject all there is in our self-life that conflicts with God's Word, and is contrary to His Holy Spirit. We take up our cross, willingly identifying ourselves with Christ's suffering - even to the commitment of death. This is then accompanied by a choice to reverently walk in the fear of the Lord, having a teachable spirit and following His example closely.

This is not the work of a moment, an hour, or a day - but of a lifetime. Nor is it dependent on feelings, but is the result of constantly deciding to die to sin that we might consistently live for Christ. Progressive sanctification is the process in our daily lives by which we are being conformed to the image of Christ. It is the principle referred to in Ephesians 4:22-24, which involves putting off of the old sinful habits and putting on the Christ-like qualities that express holiness. The believer's ongoing sanctification is therefore a matter of choosing not to yield to temptation:

"If a man therefore purge himself from these, he shall be a vessel unto honour, sanctified, and meet for the master's use, and prepared unto every good work" (2 Timothy 2:21, AV).

Progressive sanctification is accomplished as we are filled by the Holy Spirit and are submitted to the Word of God. We see this in Paul's teaching when he says, *"Walk by the Spirit, and you shall not fulfil the lust of the flesh"* (Galatians 5:16, NKJ). Also, when Jesus prayed for His disciples He said, *"Sanctify them by Your truth. Your word is truth"* (John 17:17, NKJ). Furthermore, Paul, when he wrote to the Church at Ephesus referred to the cleansing power of God's Word:

"… Christ loved the church, and gave himself up for her, that he might sanctify her, having cleansed her by the washing of water with the word" (Ephesians 5:25-26).

The clearest example of the meaning of sanctification, and the most critical to our understanding, is found in Romans 6 when Paul teaches about water baptism. Here he illustrates that through this act of obedience to be baptized, the believer is symbolically identifying himself with Christ's death, burial and resurrection. In baptism they are declaring to God, the devil, and to their fellow man that they are dead to sin; no longer responding to its attraction, and are now living in the power of resurrection life:

"How can we who have died to sin still live in it?... We were buried therefore with him by baptism into death, so that as Christ was raised from the dead by

the glory of the Father, we too might walk in newness of life." (verses 2 and 4).

In baptism a person goes under the water, and figuratively they are buried with Christ. Then rising out of that watery grave, symbolically, the believer is showing they are resurrected to live in the power of a new life! Many that assume the name of Christ, but who are not living a holy life, may have been baptized, but if they are not then daily dying to self, they will never know the victory of walking in a new life of resurrection power!

In verse 11, Paul's instructions are, *"So you also must consider yourselves dead to sin and alive to God in Christ Jesus."* Furthermore, in Colossians 3:3 we read, *"You have died, and your life is hid with Christ in God."* The appeal of sin should therefore strike us as it would a corpse! Dead people do not sin, nor take offence or seek to retaliate and justify themselves, nor should we!

Practically then, dying to self is something we need to choose the moment we wake up in the morning, as we first open our eyes to a new day. Before we do anything we take a moment and thank God for the day and make the conscious choice to completely yield our lives to Him. This is a personal act of commitment on our part; a willingness to die to ourselves, that we might live fully for the glory of God.

(c) Subjugation

If we are to maintain our spiritual freshness, and practice dying daily, we must bring our flesh under subjection. This means we are to make our carnal desires a slave to the goal of finishing triumphantly the course God has set for our lives. One of the metaphors the scriptures use to speak of the Christian life is that of a long-distance race, and the disciple of Christ as an athlete, running with endurance (Hebrews 12:1).

When we look at anyone committed to being their best in the area of sports, we see how important the principle of discipline and personal subjugation is. Likewise, we ought to live our lives with all the earnestness and determination of a world-class athlete. To grow in spiritual stamina and enjoy the vitality and fitness of an athlete it is necessary to be serious, single-minded, self-controlled, and prepared to make personal sacrifices. Paul had this in mind when he wrote to the Christians at Corinth saying,

> *"Every athlete exercises self-control in all things. They do it to receive a perishable wreath, but we an imperishable"* (1 Corinthians 9:25).

Consider the example of the Olympic Games; in thinking of a major event like this, tremendous feats of athleticism are witnessed; wonderful victories are accomplished and amazing records are broken. Some finish as victors, receiving awards of gold, silver and bronze medals. Every individual returns home, to applause, with the pride of knowing they have given their all, and done their best. Long before the actual event ever takes place, each athlete involved has trained at least four years for the one opportunity to fulfil their dream, see their potential realised, and honour their country.

Throughout those four years, and in some cases, even longer, Olympic competitors have personally and practically died to themselves on a daily basis. By subjugating their bodies they have died to that extra hour in bed, the temptation of unhealthy foods, and the attraction of partying and late nights. The softer option and easier alternative has been rejected and they have chosen a strict, harsh and unrelenting regime; their own comfort and desires have been brought into subjection in pursuit of their goal to be a winner!

On an individual basis, every athlete has to personally make a decision and commitment to discipline themselves; their trainer cannot do this for them. Their relatives and fans are not able to share this responsibility either. Even on the actual day of their 'big event' it is a battle of personal discipline that they must win. No amount of encouragement from the stadium, filled with admiring supporters, will make any difference, if they have not been diligent, and disciplined in preparation.

The principle of personal subjugation is that the competitor must die to themselves and choose a narrow path of determination, hard work and sacrifice. Their attitude must be positive and their objective clear and focused. Paul understood the importance of this responsibility, and the consequences of failing to do so, when writing to the Corinthian Church, bringing correction to them. Knowing that he was addressing people who were carnal and spiritually lax, he spoke of his own spiritual need to be disciplined. He said,

"I disciple my body and bring it into subjection, lest, when I have preached to others, I myself should become disqualified" (1 Corinthians 9:27).

Paul's admonishment to others was reinforced by explaining that even he, as an apostle, could end up a loser in the Christian life, if he didn't take personal discipline seriously. Let us never assume we are eternally safe if we are living careless, undisciplined lives; this is a very dangerous position to be in. We have to value our salvation so much that we are always mindful that without personal restraint being exercised, we can, and will, drift away from God. This is what the writer to the Hebrew Christians was explaining when he said, *"We must pay the most earnest attention to what we have heard, lest we drift away from it"* (Hebrews 2:1). Moreover, in verse 3 the writer poses the challenging question,*"How shall we escape if we neglect such a great salvation?"*

Bringing our emotions and thoughts into subjection is particularly necessary when we don't feel like being disciplined or the circumstances around make it hard. In my younger days, as a competitive boxing champion, there were many times I would rather not have done the circuit training in the gym. Frequently on wet, cold days, it would have been easier to have given the outdoor running a miss. However, ignoring the temptation to duck out on these disciplines was not an option if I was going to triumph in the tough world of boxing. This is made much more important for all of us when we understand that our destiny hangs on our decisions.

The self-discipline we see in an athlete, who wants to compete at a level of excellence, is not only about strenuous training and a life of arduous denial. It also involves common sense, and a right balance of thinking; taking care that the body receives what it needs to function at maximum capacity. If we are to stay spiritually fresh, be alert and give our best, then bringing our lives under subjection is necessary to make sure we don't burn out and become obsessive. Whoever we are, in whatever walk of life we come from, self-control is needed. We must learn to exercise regularly, have sufficient sleep, be disciplined about a balanced diet, and also learn how to relax, laugh and enjoy life!

The Greeks had a race in their Olympic games that was unique. The winner was not the runner who finished first. It was the one who finished with his torch still lit. Let us all have that same determination as we learn how to die daily. In doing so we will run all the way, and finish the race, with the flame of our torch still lit for the LORD! Moreover, we will be able to confidently say, like Paul, who nearing the end of his days could declare,

"I have fought the good fight, I have finished the race, I have kept the faith. Henceforth there is laid up for me the crown of righteousness, which the Lord, the righteous judge, will award to me on that Day, and not only to me, but also to all who have loved his appearing" (2 Timothy 4:7-8).

Chapter 7

Develop A Consistent Attitude Of Praise And Thankfulness

American Zig Ziglar was the tenth child of twelve, born into a poor family in Alabama. His father died when he was five, then two days after the funeral his 14-month-old baby sister also died. In spite of many other tough and painful experiences in his life, he learnt the importance of gratitude and committed his life to Christ on July 4th 1972. Although he came from humble beginnings, he went on to become a very successful motivational speaker and best selling author of over twenty five books, including **'God's Way Is Still The Best Way'**. There is no other assertion than this, that could better introduce the chapter we are about to consider, nor indeed the whole of the book before us.

In a day and age where so many ways to success are offered, and enthusiastically tried, the Bible states, *"There is a way which seems right to a man, but its end is the way of death"* (Proverbs 16:25). Zig Ziglar believed in only one, true, and meaningful way worth living, and that was a general lifestyle of gratitude that had its foundation first and foremost in thanksgiving to Jesus as Lord. He once wisely said, "Of all

183

the attitudes we can acquire, surely the attitude of gratitude is the most important and by far the most life-changing." This is not only true in terms of changing the direction and potential of our lives, but certainly is also the case if we are to stay spiritually fresh.

Without doubt there is nothing quite like grumbling, complaining and fault finding to quench the Holy Spirit, darken someone's perspective on life and bring barrenness into an individual's soul. These are not only signs of unhappiness, but also symptoms of poor spiritual health. Whether it is a disposition of constant dissatisfaction where nothing is ever good enough, or less frequent murmurings, expressing discontent; the resulting weariness will always be the same. It is vital for our wellbeing that we maintain a joyful state of heart because the Bible says, *"A cheerful heart is good medicine..."* (Proverbs 17:22).

Sad though it is to say, my own parents, particularly my dear mother, unfortunately never had a good word to speak about anyone or anything – least of all God. Nothing was ever praise-worthy; in fact there is not a day I can remember, when they both didn't find something or someone to complain about. This resulted in them having no friends and never getting on with any of the neighbours either side of the family home, who, over the years, moved in, and then eventually moved on. As a consequence their lives became extremely insular, and at the end of their time here on earth, regrettably, no more than two acquaintances attended each of their funerals.

If we are not careful it is so easy to slip into a grumbling mode and find ourselves complaining. In our own eyes things can either be too slow, too fast, too big or too small. We may consider something doesn't taste, smell, or feel right. We can be uncomfortable that certain things have changed, and irritated because we're not accustomed to doing things in a different way. The weather can be too hot or too cold, too dry or too wet. Maybe fuel prices have just increased again, or, in our opinion, we consider an item we've seen is too expensive, or the quality too poor. Perhaps the hotel we're staying at is not quite what we expected or the holiday disappointing etc – the list can be endless!

The amusing story is told of a little old lady who walked into a department store and, just as she crossed the threshold, an enthusiastic employee handed her £200 and congratulated her on being the millionth customer! "By the way", he asked, "what brought you to our store today?" She answered very sheepishly, "I came to make a complaint." - How embarrassing! No one is exempt from this, there are times we can embarrass ourselves, others and the calling we have to be witnesses for Christ, by not being careful about what we express. Solomon wrote, "... *there is a time to keep silence, and a time to speak*" (Ecclesiastes 3:7). This isn't to say when something is wrong; if there has been an injustice, or we have cause to raise a matter of concern, that we shouldn't speak out about the issue, where appropriate. In expressing our dissatisfaction though, we must always guard against doing so in an ungracious way and avoid an attitude of ingratitude.

For good spiritual health one of the defining principles for us all to develop is taught by Paul when he said, "... *I have learned, in whatever state I am, to be content*" (Philippians 4:11). This of course doesn't come automatically, but is a process of learning, and the bottom line is that we seek consistently to have a thankful heart. Whether at work struggling with difficult people and circumstances; in church frustrated by its shortcomings; or at home in a situation where we feel taken for granted and unappreciated, the Bible says we are to, *"Do all things without grumbling or questioning ..."* (Philippians 2:14).

Developing a consistent attitude of praise and thanksgiving is the very foundation of a spiritually vibrant life, because by doing so, we are learning to avoid the pitfall of ingratitude that makes both ourselves and others miserable. We should always aim to honour God with our words and let them express the faith we profess to have. Psalm 19:14 says, *"Let the words of my mouth and the meditation of my heart be acceptable in your sight..."* This is especially important when acknowledging God's faithfulness; we must endeavour to maintain a thankful heart for His goodness and grace in our lives. We soon forget the wonder of what the Lord has already done for us in the past, and the way in which His grace is sustaining us in the present. The exhortation that the Psalmist gives therefore is one that applies to us all, *"Let everything that has breath praise the Lord"* (Psalm 150:6, NKJ).

Lack of thankfulness to God for His miraculous deliverance out of Egypt led the children of Israel on a downward spiral of unrighteousness. Their ingratitude in spite of all He had done for them was evident in the way they soon turned to idolatry and sexual immorality. Amongst all their sins in the wilderness, Paul warns of this very serious and underestimated character flaw in 1 Corinthians 10:10. The negative attitude he speaks of is judged with great severity and can be found at the heart of all moral and spiritual failure. The apostle says we are not to, *"...grumble, as some of them did and were destroyed by the Destroyer."* 14,700 died as a result of grumbling in this one incident!

Failing to appreciate God's grace brings dire consequences and is the start of a slippery slope into all manner of depravity. Paul goes on to tell us these things are written for our admonition. We are therefore plainly cautioned to beware of losing sight of our debt of gratitude and not to be a complainer!

The Malady Of Ingratitude

It was a presidential election year and the Republicans at their national convention in Chicago had just nominated Abraham Lincoln as their candidate for the presidency. That same year, on September 8th 1860 in Chicago, some partygoers chartered a luxury boat and went out for a cruise on Lake Michigan. As they were heading back in the dark, a schooner, fully loaded with logs from the North, was running without lights and smashed into the luxury steamboat, cutting it in half. The steamboat began to sink quickly with its 393 passengers and crew on board. Of that number, 279 drowned. It wasn't far off shore and soon a crowd formed, watching the people trying to get to land on pieces of wreckage left over from the boat. Looking on that night was a student from nearby Northwestern University, Edward Spencer. Without hesitation he threw off his jacket, jumped into the cold water and began to swim out to the struggling people.

He brought one back, and then went out again. He brought back another, and another, and the people on the shore were actually telling him "Don't go back anymore and risk your life!" Edward made 16 trips into the freezing water that night, saving 17 people. However, his bravery cost him dearly, as being in that cold water for so long took its toll. He collapsed with exhaustion and was left with severe and permanent nerve damage to his legs. For the rest of his life he was restricted to a wheelchair as an invalid. Many years later when he was 80 years old, somebody asked him "What is the most vivid memory you have of that fateful night." His response was simple, yet poignant: "No one ever came back to thank me for saving them... not one."

The attitude of ingratitude towards one another is hard to understand and yet it goes on everyday. Slowly and subtly it creeps in between husbands and wives, as characteristics they once treasured in each other, gradually are taken for granted. Unique differences initially appreciated, and which at one time sparked and kept burning the excitement of their love, begins to dwindle. Over the years this deteriorates further with their spontaneous gratitude becoming exchanged by fault-finding and irritation.

Absence of appreciation is also commonly seen between children and parents as growing independence in the teenage years silences the simple 'Thank you,' leaving mum and dad feeling hurt, used and abused. Frequently, the same happens between church members amongst themselves, and from them towards their leaders. Discontent and complaining replaces the harmony and thankfulness that once marked their unity and appreciation, even though the Bible commands,

> *"Do not grumble, brethren, against one another, that you may not be judged; behold, the Judge is standing at the doors"* (James 5:9).

However harmful the malady of ingratitude is in relationships, ingratitude towards God is more shocking. Not until we see it as a serious spiritual disease, eating away at the potential of our lives, will we appreciate its danger. It was something that saddened the heart of Jesus when He healed ten lepers in Luke 17:11-19 and only one said 'thank you.' You would have thought no person had more reason to thank God than those lepers who stood afar off crying out for help.

Afflicted with a degrading and tormenting disease, they were hopelessly incurable. They were cut off from their family and friends; made to leave their own homes, and banned from entering the houses of men, or the churches of God. They were forbidden, for fear of spreading infection, to go near any human being; keeping no company but that of helpless lepers like themselves and forced to struggle for a living by begging.

In this lonely, wretched state, certain only of living and dying miserably, they met the Lord and He healed them as they called out for mercy. These lepers were re-established within their families and homes; their ability to work was regained, and their rights as citizens reinstated. All that had been stolen from them by their terrible affliction was restored. In spite of the amazing miracle they had experienced, we read that only one of the lepers, the Samaritan, returned to express his gratitude. He threw himself down at Jesus' feet, praising Him with a loud voice! At this, the response of Jesus was,

> *"Were all ten cleansed? Where are the other nine? Was no-one found to return and give praise to God except this foreigner?"* (Luke 17:17-18, NIV).

Developing an attitude of gratitude expressed in praise and thankfulness to God is deeply meaningful to the Lord, but also essential for us, because, *"... the joy of the Lord is our strength"* (Nehemiah 8:10b). The responsibility to maintain this must be seen as entirely our own and independent of other people or our circumstances. We see David's grasp of this principle when he said in Psalm 34:1, *"I will bless the Lord at all times; his praise shall continually be in my mouth."* Here we see that developing thankfulness and praise is both a choice of our will and also a commitment of our heart: the choice is, *"I **will** bless the*

Lord," and the commitment is, *"I will bless the Lord **at all times**; his praise shall **continually** be in my mouth."*

The Bible teaches us that we are to thank God from the moment we wake up in the morning, until we lay our head down to rest at night: David says, *"From the rising of the sun to its setting the name of the Lord is to be praised!"* (Psalm 113:3). Our thanksgiving is to be continuous, not broken up by the 'ups and downs' of everyday difficulties. David's commitment to this as a lifestyle is seen when he declares,

"I will sing to the Lord as long as I live; I will sing praise to my God while I have being" (Psalm 104:33).

An old poem that I came across, from an unknown author, helps remind us to live in a constant state of gratitude rather than whining about the things we feel disadvantaged by:

"Today upon a bus, I saw a lovely maid with golden hair.
I envied her – she seemed so bright –
And wished I were as fair.
When suddenly she arose to leave,
I saw the cruel braces as she hobbled down the aisle;
A victim of polio was she,
But as she passed – a smile!
Oh, God, forgive me when I whine.
I have two straight feet.
The world is mine!

And then I stopped to buy some sweets.
The lad who sold them had such charm.

I talked with him. He said to me,
"It's nice to talk with folks like you.
You see," he said, "I'm blind."
Oh, God, forgive me when I whine.
I have two eyes.
The world is mine!

Then walking down the street, I saw
A child with eyes of blue.
He stood and watched the others play.
It seemed he knew not what to do.
I stopped a moment, and then I said,
"Why don't you join the others, dear?"
He looked ahead without a word
And then I knew...he could not hear.
Oh, God, forgive me when I whine.
I have two ears.
The world is mine!

With feet to take me where I'd go,
with eyes to see the sunset's glow;
With ears to hear what I would know –
Oh, God, forgive me when I whine.
I'm blessed indeed.
The world is mine!"

There are many situations when it comes to knowing God's will, that we can find ourselves being uncertain. Developing a consistent attitude of praise and thankfulness though, is one area the Bible leaves everyone in no doubt about; it is always His intention for us! There is no room for confusion that this is what our way of life should be. Paul says,

"Rejoice always, pray constantly, give thanks in all circumstances; for this is the will of God in Christ Jesus for you" (1 Thessalonians 5:16-18).

The Habit Of Thankfulness

If you want to establish the habit of doing something worthwhile, you must be determined to do so at every opportunity, and avoid whatever is inconsistent with this goal. The only possible way to keep out bad habits is to form and maintain good habits. To develop the habit of thankfulness we simply begin by being thankful! The discipline is established by doing it – not next week, not tomorrow, but right now! It does not have to necessarily be for some great event or experience, but for where we are at the moment; for what we have; for whom God is; for what He has done and all He has promised to do. Just press on with a resolve, continuing to be thankful, hour-by-hour, and day-by-day.

The importance of habit is well illustrated by the celebrated Norwegian violinist and composer Ole Bornemann Bull who lived in the 19th Century. He was, according to Robert Schumann's estimation, among "the greatest of all" and on a level with Niccolò Paganini for the speed and clarity of his playing. Bull once said, "When I stop practicing just one day, I see the difference; when I stop two days, my friends see the difference; when I stop a week, everybody sees the difference!" In the same way, even by just going for one day without practising the discipline of giving thanks, it ought to be evident to ourselves.

Let us therefore consider some of the steps that are necessary to help us develop a thankful heart so that it becomes a godly habit we form in our lives:

1. Repent Of Complaining

Complaining is like bad breath, you notice it when it comes out of somebody else's mouth, but seldom your own. We must recognize that all of us, from time-to-time, suffer from this problem, and it is an even more offensive odour in the nostrils of God than to those around us. This is the case whether it is grumbling and complaining about other people; personal circumstances; discontent in terms of our lives as Christians, or our outlook in general.

Having a joyful and thankful disposition is refreshing to everyone, especially the Lord who inhabits the praises of His people. Therefore, where Psalm 149:6 tells us, the *"high praises of God"* should be in our mouths, but instead there is grumbling and complaining, we must seek to remedy the matter. When words of praise aren't expressed, the obnoxious breath of ingratitude is usually evidence of unbelief towards God. This is something He detests, and only genuine repentance will bring change, giving us spiritually good 'oral hygiene!'

Murmuring and complaining, rather than thanksgiving and praise, were serious enough matters to incur the wrath of God upon His covenant people Israel in the Old Testament, and still are today. Moreover, Hebrews 3:19 tells us that it was also sufficient cause to prevent a whole generation from entering the Promised Land. Likewise, unless we repent of this problem it will always keep us out of the fullness of God's provision, which we need to stay spiritually fresh.

The issue in relation to God though is not straightforward, because there are examples in the Bible of faithful men who did complain and call out to the Lord, questioning Him. In their distress and with their troubled thoughts, they found it hard to always be full of praise and thanksgiving. They were not struck down by God though, nor rebuked for their wavering. This is because their ultimate intention was to hold fast in faith, until they came through their time of bewilderment; they did not become bitter, or abandon their love for the Lord.

There may be times in our own lives when, for example, as Proverbs 12:13 says, *"Hope deferred makes the heart sick..."* Perhaps difficult circumstances remain unchanged, even though much prayer has been made to see a breakthrough. As a result of grief, injustice, bafflement etc, we may find ourselves weakened, especially when we've trusted the Lord for something and have felt let down. Whatever the situation, God understands our feelings of being overwhelmed, and also knows if we are sincerely relying on Him.

We cannot shock God by crying out in complaint, when we have an honest longing for assurance, and a desire to grasp why events have unfolded in the way they have. It is the stubborn expression of continued ingratitude which is so offensive to Him. Our heart attitude is what determines the difference, and sometimes there is simply the need for patience in the situation, and a willingness to wait for God to reveal His purpose and perfect timing. In our waiting all we can do is hold on to His promises, trust His character and always remember that with the Lord, IT IS NEVER OVER, UNTIL IT'S OVER!

The prophet Habakkuk wrestled with three big questions about God's silence and apparent lack of action. He came through his journey from scepticism to faith, from confusion to confidence, and from despair to joyful praise, because his search for an answer was with honesty and in reverence. The three things he struggled with in his life are often the same for us. These are: **(a) *Does God care?* (b)**

Is God fair? (c) *Is God there?* (Habakkuk 1:2-4 and chapter 1:13-2:1).

The Psalmist David also, on many occasions, did not shrink back from expressing his troubled thoughts in a similar way: Psalms 10:1, 13:1-4, 44:23-26, 74:1-11, 77:1-9, and 88:1-9. The important factors that make the difference are in what manner and for what reason we are expressing our complaint. Habakkuk and David ultimately came to a place of affirming their faith in God's faithfulness. We must also aim to do the same, even though we may not fully understand, nor yet have all the answers.

2. Count Your Blessings

American, Henry Ward Beecher, a prominent social reformer, clergyman and speaker of the mid to late 19th Century, once said: "The unthankful heart discovers no mercies; but the thankful heart will find, in every hour, some heavenly blessings." Throughout everyday we have so much to be grateful for which is why the apostle Paul says in Colossians 2:7 we are to, *"Abound in thanksgiving,"* and the writer to the Hebrews encourages us to *"...continually offer up a sacrifice of praise to God"* (Hebrews 13:15). Modern-day life however, is lived at such a fast pace that we rarely take the time to appreciate the good, often we only stop and complain about the bad.

We seldom consider what we have, but more easily the things we lack, and it would seem that no matter how much we possess we soon grow dissatisfied and want more. It is helpful for us to be reminded of how substantially better off we are today than those in bygone years, and also than so many in other parts of the world. We need to pause for a moment and take time to count our blessings rather than be despondent about the things we feel deficient in. Today life is so much easier than ever before because of all the modern conveniences available to us. Perhaps an old Kentucky 'process' for washing clothes will help us appreciate the advances we benefit from nowadays:

> "Build a fire in the back yard to heat the rain water and set the tubs so the smoke won't blow in your eyes. Shave a whole cake of soap in boiling water then sort the clothes in three piles – 1 pile of white – 1 pile of colours and 1 pile of rags and work britches. Rub dirty spots hard on a scrub board, spread towels on the grass and hang rags on the fence. Pour rinse water in flower bed and scrub the porch with the soap water. Turn tubs upside down, put on a clean dress, brew some coffee then sit and rock awhile as you count your blessings."

It is a tendency within us all to become preoccupied with our problems, rather than all we have to rejoice about. For example, a tiny splinter in our finger, an ache in one small tooth or a sore toe can consume our thoughts and dominate the whole body. Although the pain may only be in a minor area and not a critical issue, it can make us feel miserable. Consequently we become absorbed in how the ailment is affecting us, so that we forget our blessings.

Rev Johnson Oatman Jr. became one of the most prolific gospel song writers of the late 19th and early 20th Centuries, putting pen to more than 2,000 songs. 'Count Your Blessings' was one of his most well known hymns. In it he wrote: "When upon life's billows you are tempest-tossed, when you are discouraged, thinking all is lost, count your blessings name them one by one and it will surprise you what the Lord has done."

One practical thing we can do is to actually write down and number the benefits we have from God. In doing so we will always find that our blessings far exceed our problems. Making a list of the good things that have happened to us; the prayers we've had answered and all we enjoy as Christians, certainly will surprise us as to what the Lord has done! Also let us never take for granted the simple, everyday things in life such as security, peace, comfort, shelter, warmth, food, health, employment, as well as our families and friends etc.

By adopting this practice we become more grateful for all we have and are persuaded to appreciate every moment of our lives. Counting our blessings helps us keep life's minor irritations in proportion. Problems such as getting stuck in traffic, being kept waiting at the supermarket cash till, not getting the salary increase we wanted, or our car breaking down etc. become smaller matters when we see some of the calamities people face on a daily basis. Setbacks and inconveniences which would normally cause us to complain, then no longer seem that important. From time-to-time we need a 'reality check' to silence our grumbling and fill our hearts with thanksgiving. For instance, it has been so aptly stated:

> "If you woke up this morning with more health than illness...you are more blessed than the six million who will not survive this week. If you have never experienced the danger of battle, the loneliness of imprisonment, the agony of torture, or the pangs of starvation...you are ahead of 500 million people in the world. If you can attend a church meeting without

fear of harassment, arrest, torture or death...you are more blessed than three billion people in the world. If you have food in the refrigerator, clothes on your back, a roof overhead, and a place to sleep you are richer than 75% of this world. If you have money in the bank, cash in your wallet, and spare change in a dish someplace...you are among the top 8% of the worlds wealthy."

3. See Every Problem As An Opportunity For Growth

We must refuse to allow ourselves to be worn down and stressed out by problems because the Bible says, *"A tranquil mind gives life to the flesh..."* (Proverbs 14:30). One of the major keys to staying spiritually fresh is to make a choice to remain in a state of peace rather than being agitated by things that would otherwise disturb us. Choosing to see problems as opportunities for growth develops you instead of draining you. This is something we can only achieve by casting our care upon the Lord and trusting that,

> *"... in everything God works for good with those who love him, who are called according to His purpose"* (Romans 8:28).

Because God is The Sovereign Lord nothing is wasted by Him. Henry Beecher once wisely remarked, "Troubles are often tools by which God fashions us for better things." It takes an act of our will, so that we discipline ourselves to look at life from this spiritual perspective. Our emotions frequently dictate to us, making us feel helpless and rob us of having a heart filled with praise. What we must realise is that we can help how we feel, because how we feel about any situation is simply the result of what we believe about it.

The apostle Paul shows us the difference perspective makes when considering the many trials and adverse circumstances that he was going through. He didn't waste time feeling sorry for himself and getting discouraged. Nor did he allow fear and doubt to rob him of his joy and victory. He could declare that in every negative situation of life he was *"... more than a conqueror..."* (Romans 8:37).

Paul remained strong and spiritually fresh because of the way he viewed his trials. He could say, *"For this slight momentary affliction is preparing for us an eternal weight of glory beyond all comparison"* (2 Corinthians 4:17). The remarkable thing is that Paul's *"slight momentary affliction"* would certainly not be called minor problems by most people; they were in actual fact major, potentially devastating issues. However his perspective caused him to triumph over trouble. The list of afflictions that he gives us is staggering:

"... far greater labours, far more imprisonments, with countless beatings, and often near death. Five times I have received at the hands of the Jews the forty lashes less one. Three times I have been beaten with rods; once I was stoned. Three times I have been shipwrecked; a night and day I have been adrift at sea; on frequent journeys, in danger from rivers, danger from robbers, danger from my own people, danger from Gentiles, danger in the city, danger in the wilderness, danger at sea, danger from false brethren; in toil and hardship, through many a sleepless night, in hunger and thirst, often without food, in cold and exposure" (2 Cor.11:24-27).

Evangelical Christian pastor and author Chuck Swindoll says, "Every problem is an opportunity to prove God's power. Each day we encounter countless golden opportunities, brilliantly disguised as insurmountable problems." The key therefore to dealing with our problems is perspective. When the Israelite soldiers saw Goliath, they thought, he was so big they could never kill him. When David, armed with a sling and a few pebbles saw Goliath, he thought, he was so big he couldn't miss him!

Journalist, satirist and author Malcolm Muggeridge, who died in November 1990 once said, "Contrary to what might be expected, I look back on experiences that at the time seemed especially desolating and painful, with particular satisfaction. Indeed, I can say with complete truthfulness that everything I have learned in my 75 years in this world; everything that has truly enhanced and enlightened my experience has been through affliction and not through happiness."

We must remember that times of trial and suffering have a purpose; they will be used for our ultimate benefit, and the good of others, as we keep a right perspective towards them. It is in acknowledging that God is the only one who can bring good out of evil; even turning around what Satan intends for our harm so that it used for good, that we can rejoice and maintain thankfulness. Growth out of difficulties is one of the major principles taught in the scriptures. Problems are not meant to take the strength *out* of us but put strength *into* us. James tells us,

"Count it all joy, my brethren, when you meet various trials, for you know that the testing of your faith produces steadfastness. And let steadfastness have it's full effect, that you may be perfect and complete, lacking in nothing" (James 1:2-4).

The sharp contention between Barnabas and his best friend and ministry partner Paul, in Acts 15:36-41, is a good example of growth coming out of a problem. These two godly men could not reach an agreement about whether Mark should be allowed to join them on a mission trip, because of how he had previously deserted them in Pamphylia, and not continued with them in the work. The difference of opinion was so strong that it caused a split between Paul and Barnabas and they went their separate ways.

As far as we know these two remarkable men never saw one another again, however, it resulted in the ministry being doubled in its manpower and effectiveness. Instead of one missionary party consisting of two; now there would be two missionary parties consisting of four (Paul with Silas, and Barnabas with Mark). Therefore more work could be done and new churches planted in a wider area. At the time, I'm sure neither of them could have seen the problem as a positive incident, yet growth was the result as they continued to spread the gospel throughout the known world. Paul's original proposal to Barnabas was merely to revisit the churches they had already started. However, God had other plans and wanted the work to expand into Macedonia and Greece.

We also see growth coming out of problems with the persecution that came upon the New Testament Church. Their devotion was not diluted nor were their numbers diminished, quite the opposite; it became the means of their expansion and effectiveness. We read of how trouble resulted in the spreading of the gospel when Luke writes,

> *"Now those who were scattered because of the persecution that arose over Stephen travelled as far as Phoenicia and Cyprus and Antioch, speaking the word..."* (Acts 11:19).

201

The same growth is true today right across the world wherever the Christian Church is under attack; it always increases and will never be defeated! One such example is the phenomenal growth of the Church in China, which, in spite of severe persecution, is estimated to be over 100 million strong. Current growth is said to be at the rate of 35,000 people a day or over 12 million a year!

4. Confess Faith In Negative Circumstances

In difficult circumstances, one of the most destructive things we can do to ourselves, and others, is be negative; this always brings spiritual dryness, if left unchecked. We undermine our own faith by coming into agreement with the devil rather than God's Word, and we damage the faith of those around us. The Bible tells us that *"Death and life are in the power of the tongue..."* (Proverbs 18:21). We therefore need to be careful about the words we speak, so that there is no contradiction between what we claim to believe, and what is spoken out of our mouths. Everyday, especially when times are challenging, we must practise speaking faith-filled, Holy Spirit anointed words. By doing this it will help keep us consistent in our attitude of praise and thankfulness.

While away on holiday recently, and having lots of spare time available, I was able to discover more about the amazing life of George Muller, through reading his fascinating autobiography. This remarkable man never stopped affirming his faith in God to provide financially, or in kind, for every aspect of the great work God had called him to. For most Christians the area of financial need quickly robs them of joy, and is one that brings stress and weariness into their lives. George Muller is an example to us all of someone who kept a positive confession of faith, even under immense financial pressure. As a result he was able to maintain an attitude of praise and thankfulness as he prayed and trusted God.

He accomplished many things for God as a pastor and evangelist, but is best known for his tireless work in establishing Christian orphanages in Bristol, for several years, from 1836. He also founded the 'Scriptural Knowledge Institution for Home and Abroad', with the goal of aiding Christian schools and missionaries; distributing the Bible and Christian tracts; and providing Day-Schools, Sunday-Schools and Adult-Schools, all based on a Scriptural foundation. Without any government support and refusing to tell anyone of his needs, in his lifetime he received from God, and spent wisely, the equivalent of over £200 million in today's terms.

He believed for the rent, food, clothes, medicine, staff and daily running costs of four orphanages housing 130 children, in Wilson Street, Bristol, over a period of 13 years. He then went on, in stages, to build 5 homes in 7 acres of land on Ashley Downs, outside the city and by May 1870, a total of 1,722 children were being housed there. Throughout his life he cared for over 10,000 orphans and trusted God on a daily basis for every penny to come in that the children might be fed, clothed and educated in the Christian faith.

With relentless regularity there were times he and his staff were faced with ruin and the possible closure of their work because no money was left. He never went into debt though and God always met their need. Frequently they were down to their last loaf of bread to eat, or final lump of coal on the fire to keep the children warm. On one occasion he and all the children sat down for a meal at an empty table with not a scrap of food in the Home. He continued to speak out in faith though, declaring that the Lord would supply, and simply prayed for God's provision. This confession of faith resulted in much praise and thankfulness when a knock on the door was heard and the local baker, who had been 'sent by God' appeared with sufficient fresh bread to feed them all!

If we want to develop a consistent attitude of praise and thankfulness we need to believe we have the same God as George Muller, and confess our conviction accordingly. We need to be speaking out our faith in prayer to God; speaking faith within to ourselves, speaking faith around us to others and speaking words of faith to the 'mountain' of any problem that confronts us. Paul said,

> *"Since we have the same spirit of faith as he had who wrote, 'I believed, and so I spoke,' we too believe, and so we speak..."* (2 Corinthians 4:13).

We must, at all times, confess with our lips The Word of God and rely on His faithfulness, especially in times of deep darkness, injustice, and despair. In doing so we will be speaking faith into situations that our feelings, intellect, sight, ears, and circumstances would otherwise bring fear and doubt into. This confession of faith supernaturally fills our lives with praise and thanksgiving, even when there appears to be nothing whatsoever to be thankful for.

In her book, *The Hiding Place*, Corrie ten Boom tells about an incident that taught her the principle of speaking faith into negative circumstances and giving thanks in all things. It was during World War II that Corrie and her sister, Betsy, were found to be harbouring Jewish people in their home, so they were arrested and imprisoned in Germany, at Ravensbruck Camp. The barracks were extremely crowded and infested with fleas.

One morning they read in their tattered Bible from 1 Thessalonians 5:16 the reminder to *"Rejoice always."* Betsy said, "Corrie, we've got to give thanks for these barracks and even for these fleas." Corrie replied, "No way am I going to thank God for fleas." But Betsy was persuasive, and they did thank God even for the fleas. During the months that followed, they found that their barracks were left relatively free, and they could do Bible study, talk openly, and even pray in the barracks. It was their only place of refuge. Several months later they learned that the reason the guards never entered their barracks was because of the infestation of those fleas!

5. Be Separate From The Company Of Grumblers

Not only must we live free from all grumbling and complaining ourselves, we need to separate ourselves from the company of people who have this attitude. Considerable stress is experienced, which wears us down, because of extended interactions with unhappy people who grumble. These individuals have the ability to make you tired, angry and frustrated if you have to spend any length of time with them. It is for this reason the Bible says, *"Do not be deceived, bad company ruins good morals"* (1 Corinthians 15:33).

Praise and thanksgiving elevates us into God's presence whereas listening to grumbling only drags us down and drains our lives of all enthusiasm. Our thankfulness should never be determined by negative people or adverse circumstances, but by the presence of the Holy Spirit in our lives. There is a mutual benefit that comes from being with people that are sensitive to the Holy Spirit, and who practise 'building one another up.' This is why the Bible teaches us to,

"Speak to one another in psalms, hymns and spiritual songs. Sing and make music in your heart to the

Lord, always giving thanks to God the Father for everything, in the name of our Lord Jesus Christ" (Ephesians 5:19-20, NIV).

Praise and thanksgiving must be spoken verbally if it is to benefit ourselves and others, and one thing the grumbler finds hard to cope with is the expression of a grateful heart. A lifestyle of affirmation and praise, rather than listening to grumbling, is refreshing and powerful! Avoiding those that grumble though, is not always as easy to achieve as it might seem. Human nature is such that you'll find them everywhere, as this amusing tale illustrates:

> A monk joined a monastery and took a vow of silence. After the first 10 years the Abbot called him in and asked, "Do you have anything to say?" The monk replied, "Food bad." After another 10 years the monk again had opportunity to voice his thoughts. He said, "Bed hard." Another 10 years went by and again he was called in before his superior. When asked if he had anything to say, he responded, "I quit." To this the Abbot replied, "It doesn't surprise me a bit. You've done nothing but complain ever since you got here!"

Even if we were to shut ourselves away in the most secluded place we could think of we might well find ourselves in the company of the grumbler! As far as it is possible it is important for our spiritual well-being that we do not to keep company with these people, unless of course we believe God has called us to speak into their lives and bring change. If it is impractical and unavoidable for us not to have contact with them, then to speak out graciously and make our faith clear, as quickly as possible is essential.

Failing to do this will only result in being drawn in ourselves, dragged down and drained by those of a thankless heart.

If we can't avoid the grumbler then we need to adopt an attitude of faith towards such people, not simply in church but also in the workplace, at school or college and amongst our neighbours, friends and family etc. In this context we must pray for wisdom to speak something positive into their lives, sowing good seed into their hearts and having a godly influence. By doing so, if people are grumbling and complaining about something, our aim should be to lift the conversation and turn it around. We can help preserve the purity of their time with us and even bring words of healing to the one that is grumbling. The Bible says,

"Let your speech always be gracious, seasoned with salt, so that you may know how you ought to answer every one" (Colossians 4:6).

Salt water helps to heal mouth sores when we gargle with it. This is exactly what happens when our words are seasoned with salt; our words help bring comfort and healing to those who have the sores of grumbling and complaining. To speak with grace is to speak words that are wholesome, fitting, sensitive and purposeful. The Bible says,

"Do not let any unwholesome talk come out of your mouths, but only what is helpful for building others up according to their needs, that it may benefit those who listen" (Ephesians 4:29, NIV).

To influence people in a positive way, we must always seek to find the good in others rather than being quick to see their failings. With the analogy of salt in mind we need to be asking ourselves, 'does my speech flavour the conversation and bring out the best in people, or is my talk merely *'idle chatter?'* 'Do I contribute something from God's Word when someone opens their heart to me, or do I sit there and join them in their pity party?' Our words need to preserve the atmosphere of holiness at all times.

Best selling author Dr. Robert Bramson, a psychologist and management consultant, had a client list that included major corporations such as IBM, Hewlett-Packard, and the Bank of America. He put years of observation and research into understanding behaviour and formulating the most practical solutions to day-to-day problems we all encounter. One of the books he wrote is entitled, 'Coping With Difficult People' and in it he writes,

> "Grumblers think that *their* job is to *find* the problems of the world, while *your* job is to *fix* the problems. Most Grumblers feel helpless and never take responsibility for their own problems. The trick with Grumblers is to get them to think as problem-solvers, and not to waste your time with pointless complaints. Grumblers tend to focus on what is wrong with their lives, but they rarely do anything but grumble. If you try to solve a Grumbler's problems, you will probably get treated to more grumbling. So, you must ask them to solve their own dilemmas."

He suggests some of the ways to handle grumblers:

• Don't try to solve their problems! They will only respond with all the reasons why your solutions won't work.

• Never verbally agree with a Grumbler. Even if you do agree with them, avoid admitting your agreement. Grumblers usually take your verbal agreement as an open invitation for more grumbling.

• Whenever they grumble, ask them open-ended questions to make them problem-solve. Questions like, "So what would you like to do about it?" or "What do you think caused the problem?" or "Why haven't you spoken to the person responsible?"

• Reply to every statement, complaint and grumble that they make with a question. Put the responsibility for changing things squarely in their laps.

6. Find At Least One Positive Thing You Can Focus On

In order to not merely survive, but to thrive, we must make an effort to guard our spiritual life – to nurture and strengthen it. No matter what circumstances we are in, and regardless of our problems, there will always be at least one thing we can focus on that is positive and for which we can give thanks. As someone once said, "Some people are always complaining because roses have thorns; I am thankful that thorns have roses!"

When thinking about focussing on that which is positive so that we walk in victory and maintain our commitment, Jesus is our perfect example. He could easily have become absorbed with the rejection, humiliation and torment that confronted His life, and yet He chose to dwell upon that which would strengthen His faith. The Bible encourages us to do the same:

"Let us fix our eyes on Jesus, the author and perfecter of our faith, who for the joy set before

> *him endured the cross, scorning its shame, and*
> *sat down at the right hand of the throne of God"*
> (Hebrews 12:2, NIV).

When we look at the example of King Jehoshaphat in the book of Chronicles we see the answer to overcoming and even rejoicing when facing major problems. Three great nations that formed the eastern border of Judah had all joined forces to fight Jehoshaphat; the armies of the Moabites, Ammonites and some of the Meunites. The situation seemed impossible and there didn't appear much hope for God's people. We read though that Jehoshaphat set his face to seek the Lord; amidst impending gloom and certain defeat he focused on God's strength, and he prayed, *"...We do not know what to do, but our eyes are upon you"* (2 Chronicles 20:12, NIV). This great principle of dwelling on the positive resulted in great joy and victory for Jehoshaphat, as God brought a remarkable defeat to his enemies.

Sometimes we can find ourselves in impossible situations where there seems no possibility of a way out. At such times, even when we feel trapped and imprisoned by hopelessness, there will always be something of worth we can focus on, not least God's faithfulness. Acknowledging that in and of ourselves we don't know what to do, but our eyes are upon the Lord, is the beginning of any breakthrough. We must choose not to be overwhelmed by the negative circumstances surrounding us. Instead, concentrating on the light we have in our darkness, will always transform our outlook on life, bringing liberty into the despair of our prison.

General Robbie Risner illustrates this so well. He was a fighter pilot in the Vietnam War and a double recipient of the Air Force Cross, the second highest military decoration for valour in United States Air Force. This was awarded to him for extraordinary heroism and willpower, in the face of the enemy. He described the seven years he spent as a prisoner of war of the North Vietnamese as 'the essence of despair'. He said, 'If you could have squeezed the feeling out of the word despair, it would have come out lead-coloured, dingy and dirty.'

What's amazing is how he survived. He prised the cover off a floor drain in his cell and lowered his head into the opening. There he noticed a solitary blade of grass, the only smidgeon of colour in his colourless world. Calling it a blood transfusion for the soul, Risner began each day in prayer, lying on the floor of his cell with his head down the vent, focused on that single blade of grass and giving thanks to God.

For ourselves, if there is nothing else we feel we have to be thankful about, we can always be glad and rejoice that the situation is not more serious than it is. The old Negro's philosophy was wise and good: *"Bless de Lord, 'taint no wuss."* Having an attitude that even though things might seem grim at times, they could always be more serious, helps us to be grateful in every circumstance. This is well illustrated by Englishman Matthew Henry, a Presbyterian minister and commentator on the Bible. One day after having his house burgled, he wrote in his diary, "Let me be thankful **(a)** He never stole from me before **(b)** he did not take my life **(c)** it was he that did the robbing and not I.

7. Regularly Use The Gift Of Tongues

As we have previously said, we need to discipline ourselves to give thanks at all times. With the various pressures that go on in our daily lives though, and particularly with everything that races round in our minds, this is not always as easy as it might seem. God however has given to us one of the greatest gifts of all to help us stay spiritually fresh – the supernatural 'gift of tongues.' This gift is an expression of the Holy Spirit within us. It is independent of our mind, though of course, the person speaking in tongues does not lose control of his mind, or himself. It is a powerful means of maintaining joy and spiritual strength, particularly in situations of difficulty and busyness. The Bible teaches us,

> *"But you, beloved, build yourselves up on your most holy faith; pray in the Holy Spirit..."* (Jude 20).

Even if we're at the sink washing dishes; on the floor changing the baby's nappy; confronted by stressful circumstances at work; or in the frustrating situation of motorway queues in our car, nothing need prevent us expressing thankfulness and praise. Paul wrote to the church at Corinth explaining the personal benefit of this gift, saying, *"He who speaks in a strange tongue edifies and improves himself..."* (1 Corinthians 14:4, Amp). The Greek word translated "edifies" is "oikodomeo," which means to construct, build up or to restore. The one who speaks in a supernatural tongue builds himself up like an edifice; he is restored and strengthened.

Through the gift of tongues we become revitalised and our lives are charged up like a battery! We strengthen our 'inner man'; the spiritual part of our being is built up because we are not trying to make sense of problems with our own human logic, rather we are worshipping God. When faced with challenges and problems are weighing heavily on our minds, praying or singing in the spirit enables us to be lifted up; we become connected to a supernatural dimension of power. Our spirit-man is automatically fixed on God as Paul explains,

"For one who speaks in a tongue speaks not to men but to God; for no one understands him, but he utters mysteries in the Spirit" (1 Corinthians 14:2).

It is clear the part of our being that is praying as we are using this gift, is our spirit, when we read, *"For if I pray in a tongue, my spirit prays, but my mind is unfruitful"* (1 Corinthians 14:14). There are times when we can be overwhelmed by situations and simply don't know how to pray about them. This anxiety very often is the cause of making people feel weary, and bringing them to the point of despair. As we pray in tongues though, God's Holy Spirit enables us to express that which is inexpressible with our mind. His Spirit prays in us and through us, bringing us closer to God and releases our frustration:

"In the same way, the Spirit helps us in our weakness. We do not know what we ought to pray for, but the Spirit himself intercedes for us..." (Romans 8:26, NIV).

We see this gift was something Paul longed for all Christians to experience when he says, *"Now I want you all to speak in tongues..."* (1 Corinthians 14:5). Also, it is evident, this was a gift that Paul valued greatly in his own life for he states in verse 18, *"I thank God that I speak in tongues more than you all."* Regardless of whatever may be going on around us, as we pray and sing in tongues, we bring into our lives the necessary sustaining strength, to rise above every situation trying to weaken us.

Jesus taught His disciples, *"These signs will accompany those who believe... they will speak in new tongues"* (Mark 16:17). This is a vital gift for all believers, but it has to be said that although every Christian can speak in tongues, not everyone does. The normal Spirit-filled Christian life is for every child of God to experience such an invaluable gift. For this to happen though, they must accept:

- **(a)** it is clearly based in scripture
- **(b)** it is enabled by the Holy Spirit, through faith
- **(c)** it involves the exercise of their will and therefore needs their co-operation
- **(d)** they must not allow themselves to be restricted by human reason, ruled by fear, or robbed by doubt.

8. Refuse To Let Adversity Silence Your Praise

Even in times of dire circumstances we can maintain an attitude of praise and thanksgiving. The clearest example of this is seen in the life of Job. He had lost everything that was dear to him in terms of his health, wealth, reputation, and children. Also in the eyes of his so called friends he'd lost his integrity, and even as far as his wife was concerned, he'd lost her support. However, he still continued to praise and worship God. Immediately after hearing of the death of his ten children, on top of all the other bad news he'd received, we read that Job,

> *"... fell upon the ground, and worshipped. And he said, 'Naked I came from my mother's womb, and naked shall I return; the Lord gave, and the Lord*

has taken away; blessed be the name of the Lord"'
(Job 1:20-21).

A positive praise-filled environment robs Satan of his ultimate victory over the believer; it stops him dead in his tracks because he knows God is enthroned on the praises of His people! This atmosphere of thanksgiving and praise not only brings God's presence, but keeps our focus upon the one who is the source of our spiritual freshness. In every circumstance of life we have a choice in how we respond. We can refuse to let our praise be silenced, or we can withdraw into self-pity, doubt and bitterness - that choice will either develop us or destroy us! The Psalmist said,

"... that my heart may sing to you and not be silent.
O Lord my God, I will give you thanks forever"
(Psalm 30:12, NIV).

Joni Eareckson Tada is an outstanding modern-day example of maintaining an attitude of thankfulness and praise. After a diving accident in 1967, she was left a quadriplegic in a wheelchair at the age of 17. In spite of her heartbreaking circumstances she went on to become an international speaker, artist, musician and author. More recently, in June 2010, she was diagnosed with malignant breast cancer, and still Joni says she is determined not to waste her experience of cancer, but use it for the benefit of others. From a deep understanding of personal tragedy she wrote, "Most of the verses written about praise in God's Word, were voiced by people faced with crushing heartaches, injustice, treachery, slander and scores of other difficult situations."

British Prime Minister and novelist Benjamin Disraeli said, "There is no education like adversity." One of the greatest things it teaches us is a resolve to depend on God. Paul spoke about not letting adversity silence our praise when he said, *"Rejoice in the Lord always. Again I will say, rejoice!"* (Philippians 4:4, NKJ). Not only did he teach this, he demonstrated it time and time again in his own afflictions of imprisonment, beatings, false accusations and consistent persecutions. In fact his words to the Christians at Philippi were made more powerful because they were written, not from the comfort of a palace, but the cruel atmosphere of a prison cell!

Without question, life can seem unfair at times and deal us some very cruel blows; however the song of God's praises will always strengthen us to rise above adversity. Johann Sebastian Bach is proof of this. By the age of ten, both his parents had died. He was raised reluctantly by an older brother who resented another mouth to feed. His wife died after 13 years of marriage. 10 of his 20 children, from two marriages, passed away while they were still infants. One died in his 20's, and one was mentally deranged. Eventually, this outstanding musician went blind, and was paralyzed with a stroke. However, he never lost his faith and continued to maintain an attitude of thankfulness and praise to God, becoming one of the greatest ever composers of religious music.

There are occasions when we have to take responsibility ourselves, to create an atmosphere that will refresh us, rather than oppress us. For example when coming home tired and perhaps discouraged at the end of the day, maybe all we feel like doing is sitting down in the comfort of our armchair, to watch television. There is nothing wrong with that in itself, but if we feel somewhat downcast when we come home, the last thing we should do is switch on something that is negative, dark and oppressive. The alternative of slipping on a CD of worship, and simply taking time to be spiritually refreshed will be of far greater benefit.

The importance of seeing our responsibility is best understood in the initiative that God expects us to take, if we are to experience His presence and refreshing in our lives. James 4:8 says, *"You draw near to God, and He will draw near to you."* The way we draw near to God is the very essence of worship, as the Psalmist David explains:

> *"Enter his gates with thanksgiving, and his courts with praise! Give thanks to him, bless his name! For the Lord is good; his steadfast love endures for ever, and his faithfulness to all generations"* (Psalm 100:4-5).

Chapter 8

Understanding Unanswered Prayer

Another of the major causes of becoming weary and spiritually dry for many people is the puzzle of unanswered prayer. Of all the things that weigh us down, perhaps no burden is greater for the Christian than the apparent silence of God. The disappointment, frustration, heartbreak and doubts that can arise out of this can be considerable in people's lives. It is therefore very important, if we are to stay spiritually fresh, that we look at this issue and endeavour to come to a better understanding of what many believers struggle with today.

The difficulty is made much harder because of some misguided Christians who bring false prophecy to people, making promises, allegedly from God, that never come to pass. Another influence that only compounds the problem is some of the extreme 'Faith Teaching' that approaches such a complex issue, with a blanket presumption of a 'Name it and Claim it' philosophy. Very often such a simplistic view only leaves people feeling guilty they didn't have enough faith, or that there must be sin in their life, which resulted in them not receiving what they believed God for.

219

Good people can pray sincere prayers that sometimes appear to remain unanswered by God. I know of Christian friends, who, because of infertility, received prayer and expectantly trusted God over several years to conceive. Their faith and practical action however, remained unanswered. I've come across others who have suffered the agony of watching a loved one die of cancer, even though, they, their family and their church prayed, fasted and believed for healing. Conversely, I've had the privilege of personally praying for several couples who were childless and God miraculously answered prayer; where it was impossible for them to conceive, they have had the joy of giving birth! Also, over the years we've seen hundreds of sick people, including those with cancer, healed through our ministry.

In spite of every negative set-back it is essential that we have faith in our approach to God and we never stop believing in His miraculous power to make a way where there seems to be no way. We must always trust His infallible promises and expect His Word to be fulfilled in our lives. In doing this though, we need to come to a balanced position on what for many is a very painful and perplexing part of their relationship with God.

The dilemma is made more difficult, because God emphatically promises us in His Word, that He will answer our prayer when we seek Him. He clearly says, *"Call to me and I will answer you and will tell you great and hidden things which you have not known"* (Jeremiah 33:3). There is no doubt God is prepared to demonstrate His power in Miracles, Signs and Wonders. He delights to bring breakthroughs and daily help in the needs we have for ourselves and others.

This same willingness is stated categorically five times by Jesus in three chapters of John's gospel when He says, *"Whatever you ask in my name, I will do it, that the Father may be glorified in the Son"* (John 14:13). *"If you abide in me, and my words abide in you, ask whatever you will, and it shall be done for you"* (John 15:7). *"...whatever you ask the Father in my name, he will give it to you"* (John 15:16b). *"... Truly, truly, I say to you, if you ask anything of the Father, he will give it to you in my name"* (John 16:23), and also verse 24, *"... ask, and you will receive, that your joy may be full."*

With such clear promises in mind, why is it, therefore, that despite the Lord's evident assurance and unmistakable willingness to answer prayer, it is undeniable that we do not always receive what we pray for. Moreover, when we've prayed in faith, sometimes things may even get worse!

Although the Holocaust in Germany during World War II is an extreme example, nevertheless the glaring and unavoidable question is, 'Why were so many legitimate prayers unanswered?' The same puzzle is experienced in numerous other areas we can all identify with: our prayers for loved ones being saved; sickness being healed; guidance being found; financial provision being released; bondages being broken; relationships being restored and revival being experienced etc. Unless an answer to the mystery of this conundrum is at least attempted, we can find ourselves feeling confused, discouraged and worn down.

As we address this subject we must firstly be aware that many of the promises of God are conditional. The blessings of God don't just fall on us like ripe fruit off a tree. We have our part to play; our responsibility is to maintain a right relationship with the Lord and *"... hold fast the confession of our hope without wavering, for he who promised is faithful"* (Hebrews 10:23). Let us first start then by considering some of the major blockages to answered prayer. In doing so we probably will be surprised as to how many there are. If these can be identified and removed this will go a long way to helping us come to a clearer and stronger position on the matter:

1. Unforgiveness

Prayer will not work without forgiveness. Whether it is hate, resentment, or holding on to a grudge, these attitudes will be a hindrance to our prayers. The apostle Paul tells us in Galatians 5:6, *"... faith works through love."* If we have wrong attitudes to anyone, and harbour unforgiveness in our hearts, then this will quench the Holy Spirit and stop our faith from being activated. Unforgiveness will not prevent us from praying, but it will stop our prayers from being answered. Mark 11:25 says, *"Whenever you stand praying, forgive, if you have anything against anyone..."* Also in Matthew 5:23-24 we read,

> *"So if you are offering your gift at the altar, and there remember that your brother has something against you, leave your gift there before the altar and go; first be reconciled to your brother, and then come and offer your gift."*

Forgiveness, as taught by Jesus in 'The Lord's Prayer', emphasises the need to extend to others what we expect from God: *"... if you do not forgive men their sins, your Father will not forgive your sins"* (Matthew 6:15, NIV). When we choose to be in a position of withholding forgiveness from anyone, for any reason, we will be in an unforgiven state ourselves and therefore be living in sin! Unforgiveness is always self-defeating. It was the 18th Century English poet and artist William Blake who so rightly said, "The glory of Christianity is to conquer by forgiveness."

After the Civil War, Robert E. Lee, General-in-Chief of the Confederate army, visited a Kentucky lady who took him to the remains of what at one time was a majestic old tree in front of her house. There she bitterly cried that its limbs and trunk had been destroyed by Federal artillery fire. She looked to Lee for a word condemning the North or at least sympathizing with her loss. After a brief silence, Lee said, "Cut it down, my dear Madam, and forget it." This is how we must deal with all matters of what we consider to be injustice against us. We must deal with the issue through forgiveness and move on. To do otherwise will only give rise to bitterness taking root, poisoning our lives and blocking answers to our prayers.

2. Neglecting God's Word

The story is told about a new minister of a church who was asked to teach a boys' class in the absence of the regular teacher. He decided to see what they knew, so he asked "Who knocked down the walls of Jericho?" All the boys strongly denied having done it, and the preacher was appalled by their ignorance. At the next deacons' meeting he told them about the experience. "Not one of them knows who knocked down the walls of Jericho," he lamented. The group was silent until finally one seasoned veteran of disputes spoke up. "Preacher, this appears to be bothering you a lot. But I've known all those boys since they were born and they're good boys. If they said they didn't know, I believe them. Let's just take some money out of the repair and maintenance fund, fix the walls, and let it go at that!"

While this does sound amusing there is, without doubt, an amazing lack of knowledge concerning God's Word in the lives of some Christians and churches today, simply because of neglect. When this is the case, it is like a room that once was filled with light slowly giving way to darkness. We are in danger then of simply stumbling into situations, guided by mere logic and rational thinking. God's will is revealed in His Word, and when we are unaware of what the Bible has to say, then we can easily be led into deception, even on basic matters. Ignorance of God's Word, through neglect, is the reason for many Christians and churches getting themselves into all manner of confusion and error, and why prayers remain unanswered.

Jesus makes clear in John 15:7, *"If you abide in me, and my words abide in you, ask whatever you will, and it shall be done for you."* As we've previously seen, twice in John 15, the Lord gives assurance of God answering our prayers. Inseparably linked to this though is the instruction to keep the commandments of God and abide in His Word. We must therefore be careful of being so busy that we don't spend time meditating on His Word and becoming complacent about its vital importance to our daily living. Doing so will inevitably lead to the deception of finding ourselves living contrary to it and missing the joy of answered prayer.

It is essential that we not only have an abiding intimacy with Christ, but our love for His Word is continually growing and abiding in our lives. One way of developing this is by memorising scripture. This strengthens our faith, helps keep us from error, and makes meditation possible when we can't actually be reading the Bible. It shapes the way we view the world and circumstances around us by bringing our thoughts and perception into line with God's. For His Word to abide in us though, is far more than simply memorising scripture. His Word must take root and bear fruit through our obedience and daily hunger for it.

3. Lack Of Compassion

King Solomon writes in Proverbs 21:13, *"He who closes his ear to the cry of the poor will himself cry out and not be heard."* Looking beyond ourselves and seeking to meet the needs of others is part of the responsibility of every Christian. John Wesley, the great revivalist of the 18th Century was not only a powerful preacher but also a man that understood the need for compassion. He said, "Do all the good you can. By all the means you can. In all the ways you can. In all the places you can. At all the times you can. To all the people you can. As long as ever you can."

Lack of compassion is something few would admit to, yet this is blatantly evident in terms of reaching out to the unsaved; a responsibility which should be of utmost importance to all. For many churches a local evangelistic strategy falls well down the order of their priorities and thinking. The problem of being too parochial also becomes obvious in the silence heard when it comes to any global missionary emphasis, or prayer for the persecuted Church. This lack of compassion becomes more obscene when viewed against the background of disunity and petty internal disputes amongst believers. While Christians are busy fighting one another their focus is obscured. As a consequence, those in their community remain bound by the devil, oppressed by despair and left going to hell, never having heard the gospel!

In James 4:17 we read, *"Whoever knows what is right to do and fails to do it, for him it is sin."* How can anyone expect God to answer their prayers if they have little or no regard for the needs of those suffering? Our receiving from God is determined by our willingness to give to others, as is seen in the principle of Luke 6:38, where Jesus taught, *"...*

For the measure you give will be the measure you get back." This not only includes the giving of our money, but also of our time, help, interest and compassion for the disadvantaged, poor, lonely and lost.

Greatness in the kingdom of heaven is measured by small acts of kindness. Even a cup of cold water given in Jesus name produces high commendation from the Lord. Jesus declared in Matthew 25:40, *"... as you did it to one of the least of these my brethren, you did it to me."* If we responded to the needs around us as if we were ministering to Christ Himself, then no doubt our concern, conduct and care would be very different, and our prayer life far more productive. There is an inseparable link between the compassion we show to others and the compassion we receive from God. This is made clear in the teaching of Jesus when He says, *"Blessed are the merciful, for they shall obtain mercy"* (Matthew 5:7).

4. Unconfessed Sin

The Psalmist wrote, *"If I had cherished sin in my heart, the Lord would not have listened"* (Psalm 66:18, NIV). Here is a problem that must be taken into account when people are trying to understand unanswered prayer. It is something that can't be ignored and swept under the carpet, because sin separates us from God's blessing. This verse doesn't, of course, mean we must be perfect to pray, but it does teach us that, as best as we know how to, we must seek to have a pure heart before God. If sin is not confessed, it is like a dark cloud that comes across our relationship with the Lord, and will always be a hindrance, which is why Solomon said, *"He who conceals his sins does not prosper..."* (Proverbs 28:13, NIV).

There may be times when wilfully we have sinned and have not confessed that wrong, just like King David who thought he could get away with his lust and act of adultery. On other occasions, through denial or self-deception, we can have 'blind spots' in our lives; things that we are completely unaware of, but nevertheless are still just as offensive to the Lord. All sin distances us from God. Therefore, while we must avoid the danger and indulgence of being too introspective, we do need to learn to cry out as David ultimately did and say,

> "Search me, O God, and know my heart! Try me and know my thoughts! And see if there be any wicked way in me" (Psalm 139:23-24).

Peter teaches that when we desire to live righteous lives, we will have God's full attention and know His willingness to respond to our needs: "For the eyes of the Lord are on the righteous and his ears are attentive to their prayer..." (1 Peter 3:12, NIV). There is absolutely nothing hidden from God, and therefore, knowing this fact should cause us to take swift action regarding our sin. A crucial key to seeing answers to prayer is living assured of God's favour. Such confidence that God is both aware and actively responding to the righteous is reflected in the words,

> "For the eyes of the LORD run to and fro throughout the whole earth, to show Himself strong on behalf of those whose heart is loyal to Him" (2 Chronicles 16:9, NKJ).

In view of the fact that God is aware of every aspect of our lives, it is a wise thing to walk in the positive fear of the Lord at all times, and in all we do. When we become complacent about dealing with our personal sin we dishonour and grieve the Holy Spirit. Only when our conscience is not accusing us, can we have any assurance of God answering our prayers. The apostle John makes this point when he writes,

> *"Beloved, if our hearts do not condemn us, we have confidence before God; and we receive from him whatever we ask ..."* (1 John 3:21).

5. Wrong Motives

There are occasions when our prayers are not answered because of the self-interest behind our asking. God does not hear when we ask to satisfy our own selfish pleasure, or prosper our personal short term agenda. He has a plan and purpose for our lives that is greater than us, and He sees the bigger picture. Asking with the wrong motive is praying in conflict with the Holy Spirit; it is asking beyond our need and God only promises to supply our needs, whether great or small. James states,

> *"When you ask, you do not receive, because you ask with wrong motives, that you may spend what you get on your pleasures"* (James 4:3, NIV).

Also God simply cannot answer every prayer with a 'Yes' because at the same time there may well be two people asking and believing for opposite things. For instance, a farmer could be earnestly praying for rain upon his dry ground while another person is asking for sunshine to enjoy their family picnic or wedding! There is nothing wrong, in itself, in asking God to bring pleasant weather for such causes; it is perfectly reasonable and good to commit daily concerns to Him. Our understanding and acceptance though, of how God answers prayer, needs to have a wider perspective than merely our own personal desires.

The basis on which we pray must be first and foremost for whatever advances Christ's Kingdom, and not simply our comfort and convenience. When this becomes a foundational principle in our daily living, then as Jesus taught in Matthew 6:33 everything that we need in our lives will be given to us by our heavenly Father.

As our lives are freed from selfish motives we will experience God's remarkable and powerful answers to our prayers. This is well illustrated by the Captain of a ship which was taking George Muller to Quebec for a preaching engagement. He tells of an incident, when faced with thick fog. His life was challenged and changed as he witnessed the power of prayer offered to the Lord from a life consecrated in service for Christ. He recounts:

"George Muller came to me, and said, "Captain I have come to tell you that I must be in Quebec by Saturday afternoon." "It is impossible," I said. "Very well" he replied, "if your ship cannot take me, God will find some other way. I have never broken an engagement for fifty-seven years. Let us go down into the chart-room and pray." I looked at that man of God and thought to myself, what lunatic asylum can he have come from? I never heard of such a thing as this. "Mr Muller," I said, "do you know how dense this fog is?" "No," he replied, "My eye is not on the density of the fog, but on the living God, who controls every circumstance of my life."

He knelt down and prayed one of the simplest prayers, and when he had finished I was going to pray, but he put his hand on my shoulder and told me not to. "First, you do not believe God will answer; and second I believe He has, and there is no need whatever for you to pray about it." I looked at him, and he said, "Captain, I have known my Lord for fifty-seven years, and there has never been a single day that I have failed to get an audience with the King. Get up Captain and open the door, and you will find the fog gone." I got up, and the fog was indeed gone and on Saturday afternoon, George Muller was in Quebec for his engagement!"

6. Pride

All forms of pride create a blockage to our prayers being answered because it provokes divine resistance that is impossible to overcome: *"God resists the proud, but gives grace to the humble"* (1 Peter 5:5b). If the Lord Himself is opposing our prayers there is absolutely no chance of them ever coming to pass! The attitude of pride comes in many forms but more commonly it is putting confidence in our own ability and resourcefulness, rather than having a complete reliance on God. It is offensive to the Lord because in effect we are saying (although as Christians we would never articulate it) either, God is in need of our help to bring about His will, or we can manage perfectly well by ourselves.

The proud often only turn to God as a last resort, in a time of crisis, and give little thought or effort to cultivating a deep relationship with Him. They are always too busy with their own personal development, comfort and pursuits, to see God as the most important priority in their lives. The principle Jesus taught is totally contrary to this. He said,

"Truly, Truly, I say to you, unless a grain of wheat falls into the earth and dies, it remains alone; but if it dies, it bears much fruit" (John 12:24).

Occasionally pride comes in the form of wanting to preserve our image before other people; to make ourselves seem better than them or at least appear to keep up with them. It is an unhealthy preoccupation with our own self-importance to impress, and not to be thought of as having less or being less than others. The advertising world certainly takes advantage of this egotism in our character. An example of feeding such vanity is the clever salesman who successfully manipulated hundreds of sales with this line: "Let me show you something several of your neighbours said you couldn't afford."

Sometimes pride might come to the surface through an innocent mistake which exposes an anxious concern we have not to lose face in a situation. This was the case for Ronald Reagan on an occasion after making a speech as governor of California, in Mexico City. He recalls: "After I had finished speaking, I sat down to rather unenthusiastic applause, and I was a little embarrassed. The speaker who followed me spoke in Spanish – which I didn't understand – and he was being applauded about every paragraph. To hide my embarrassment, I started clapping before everyone else and longer than anyone else until the ambassador leaned over and said, "I wouldn't do that if I were you. He's interpreting your speech!"

God is willing to answer prayer; there is no reluctance in His heart to do so, but the condition He makes for the Church today is the same as it was for His people in the Old Testament in 2 Chronicles 7:14 (NKJ). Here the Lord is speaking to Solomon, calling Israel to prayer, and the prerequisite to blessing remains unchanged. We can read about national revival, long for revival and even pray for revival, but the first thing God requires is, *"If My people ...will humble themselves..."* When pride is renounced it clears the way to dealing with all other issues that prevent us receiving what God promises, and ultimately results in our petitions being answered.

7. Wavering Faith

Single-minded certainty is the very essence of faith, without which we cannot please God. There are occasions for us all when we ask and believe for something, having no doubts whatsoever, then the passage of time takes its toll and discouragement weakens our confidence. This is particularly so if we've been stirred by an inspirational sermon to have faith; encouraged in a meeting by anointed worship to expect a response from God; or uplifted by the counsel and prayers of others to trust in the Lord. It may be a promise we've received and held onto from scripture, where we've had a clear sense of God speaking to us. At the time we were fully assured, but the delay eventually gave way to doubt.

Delay in our prayer being answered introduces confusion, uncertainty and fear which Satan quickly seizes upon, whispering questions and sowing all manner of lies. When our faith begins to waver, it weakens, bringing us into a position of being unable to receive from God. This is a problem that James warns us about when referring to our prayers. He states,

"But let him ask in faith, with no doubting, for he who doubts is like a wave of the sea that is driven and tossed by the wind. For that person must not suppose that a double-minded man, unstable in all his ways, will receive anything from the Lord" (James 1:6-8).

Notice here that having two minds about what we are asking for, creates an inner conflict that not only makes us unstable, but stops God's provision being received. Wavering occurs sometimes because our faith is based on feelings or circumstances, which will always be unreliable because they frequently change. This is also the case when we bring our thoughts down to the level of human logic and rational reasoning and why Proverbs 3:5 says, *"Trust in the Lord with all your heart and do not rely on your own insight..."*

Another cause for wavering, is simply because we can't see as clearly as we feel we need to, for us to boldly trust God. If that's the case for you, be encouraged by this illustration:

One night a house caught fire and a young boy was forced to flee to the roof. The father stood on the ground below with outstretched arms, calling to his son, "Jump! I'll catch you!" He knew the boy had to jump to save his life. All the boy could see, however, was flames, smoke, and blackness. As you can imagine, he was terrified to leave the roof. His father kept yelling: "Jump! I will catch you!" But the boy protested, "Daddy, I can't see you!" The father replied, "But I can see you, and that's all that matters!"

We need to remind ourselves that there will be times when we may not be able to see clearly, and as a consequence feel confused and anxious. However, God sees us, and wants us to abandon ourselves to His care. We must ask God's forgiveness for our doubts, and be reassured by His mercy and understanding of our frailty. Just like the father in Mark 9:24 (NKJ), we need to come to Jesus saying, *"... Lord, I believe, help my unbelief!"* The man recorded in this account of scripture believed, yet doubted, but the Lord granted his request because of his confession and honesty.

8. A Wrong Perception Of God's Character

Being fully persuaded that the Lord hears, and is willing to respond to our prayers, is an essential part of the assurance needed to receive from Him. When we don't have this, it can be a significant blockage to experiencing answered prayer. As we more accurately understand the loving character of God, our confidence grows and our prayer life becomes more fruitful. The writer to the Hebrew Christians, taught them this important aspect of His willingness to respond when he wrote,

> *"But without faith it is impossible to please Him. For he who comes to God must believe that He is, and that He is a rewarder of those who diligently seek Him"* (Hebrews 11:6, NKJ).

Sometimes our prayers remain unanswered because we just cannot relate to God as a rewarder of those who come to Him. Unless we see Him as our 'Heavenly Father', we will be unable to appreciate that He delights to answer our prayers, and be involved in every aspect of our lives. The perception we have of God, may well be distorted by the poor parenting we've received as a child by our natural father. Painful memories of neglect, harshness, abuse, lack of encouragement or negative words spoken over us, can be extremely damaging. Having a father that was too busy to be involved, too emotionally distant to care or frequently absent etc. all has a major effect on how we view God as our Father.

As the child of our heavenly Father we have special favour and access to Him at all times; no-one can prevent that access. When we believe this we can boldly approach Him knowing, because of our relationship, our petition will be heard, even when we come on behalf of others in need. We don't have to beg and plead or feel uncertain, because we are confident His nature is to gladly give to His children. Jesus said,

> *"Ask, and it will be given you;... If you then, who are evil, know how to give good gifts to your children,*

*how much more will your Father who is in heaven
give good things to those who ask him!"* (Matthew
7:7 and verse 11).

The confidence a child can have about their father's
response, is well illustrated in an incident that occurred during
the US Civil War. Abraham Lincoln had issued an order, that
for a certain time no man was to go home on furlough. During
the period this order was in force a solider made his way to
Washington to see the President, but he was refused access,
even though he said his wife was dying and he needed to go
home and see her. He turned from the White House with his
head bowed and walked away discouraged.

As he made his way down the grounds President Lincoln's
small son, Tad, came up to him and taking his hand, asked,
"What is the matter?" He turned to the boy and said, "My
wife is dying and I wanted permission to go home, but they
won't allow me to see the President." "Very well," said the
little fellow, "you take my hand, I am President Lincoln's boy,
and I will take you in."

He led him up the steps to the President's room, but the
guard would not allow him to open the door. He said, "The
President is busy." But the boy was not to be put off, and still
held on to the man's hand. Just then the door to the Oval
office opened and Tad cried out, "Father, tell this man to let
me come in." Abraham Lincoln dropped his pen and said to
the officer, "Let him in." The boy entered with his new found
friend, and the soldier told his story. Abraham Lincoln dipped
his pen in the ink, signed the order of furlough and sent the
man home.

Believing in our sonship with the Father gives us greater
confidence of full access, a listening ear and a willing response
from the one who has ultimate power and authority!

9. A Lack Of Perseverance And Determination

One very common reason why prayer goes unanswered is simply because our determination weakens, and we give up far too quickly. This is particularly so nowadays in the 'Instant Age' in which we live, where people have grown accustomed to expect everything in moments, without any delay. We are used to instant foods; immediate communication through e-mails, web cams, and text messages; split-second information - courtesy of the 'World Wide Web' - fast online purchases, and internet banking transactions all at the click of a button. Wonderful though these things are, we've become impatient and reluctant to wait very long for anything.

It was Albert Einstein who somewhat modestly stated, "It's not that I'm so smart, it's just that I stay with problems longer." If only we had that attitude of perseverance as Christians, we might well discover answered prayer more likely. The truth is that few have this mindset to persevere. Therefore, as a consequence, if our prayers aren't answered as swiftly as we think they should be, we begin to lose heart and feel the answer is never coming. As long as we have the promise of God's Word we need to be patient and determined; we must keep believing, and never give up, no matter how long it takes!

Jesus used a parable in Luke 18:1-5, to teach His disciples they *"...ought always to pray and not lose heart."* The illustration was about a persistent woman, who continually came before a judge to be vindicated against her adversary. In this story He explained that the judge granted her request, because of her perseverance and determination. God has a *"due season"* (Galatians 6:9); if we don't give up, then what we have believed for, shall come to pass. In Romans 12:12 (NKJ), Paul says we are to be, *"Rejoicing in hope, patient in tribulation, continuing steadfastly in prayer."* Moreover, in Ephesians 6:18 (AV), the apostle tells us to, *"pray with all perseverance."*

Another example of determined perseverance in prayer is found in Daniel 10:10-13. Here Daniel prayed and fasted for three full weeks before he got the answer to his prayers. The reason for this was because a demonic power was hindering the angel of God from getting through to him. We just do not know what resistance there is in the demonic realm hindering our prayers coming to pass. In view of this we must always remain vigilant, and with fortitude not cease to persevere in prayer. Hebrews 6:12 teaches us to imitate, *"... those who through faith and patience inherit the promises"* (NKJ). Faith lays hold of the promise, and patience holds on until it comes to pass!

While continuing to pray we must learn to be patient in seeking God, because the answer might be closer than we think. The breakthrough we have been waiting to see might suddenly happen with just one more season in prayer. For example, you can watch a stone cutter hammering away at a rock a hundred times without so much as a crack showing in it, yet at the 101st blow it splits in two! The principle of perseverance is clear here. We need to remind ourselves that when it comes to seeing a breakthrough in our prayers, often it isn't just the one blow that accomplished the desired result, but includes the culmination of all that has gone before.

10. A Lukewarm Relationship With God

We are instructed in Jude 21, *"... keep yourselves in the love of God."* Every Christian needs to take this personal responsibility seriously. We must be alert, watching out for the danger of growing half-hearted or apathetic in our relationship with the Lord, because that is an abomination to Him. God feels so strongly about such spiritual indifference that He says to the Christians at Laodicea,

> *"Because you are lukewarm, and neither cold nor hot,*
> *I will spew you out of my mouth"* (Revelation 3:16).

In the light of this, it would seem obvious to mention that one reason our prayers are not answered, is because our love has grown cool towards God. The obvious however, does have to be stated, because we can neglect our relationship without realising the consequences. Over the course of time and due to a gradual process, we can find ourselves unaware of the critical nature of our position, until a crisis occurs to awaken us out of our spiritual slumber.

It's easy to drift; it takes no effort at all. If you have ever laid down on an air mattress in a pool or a calm sea and then closed your eyes for a short while, you'll understand how simple this is. When you open your eyes again, you often discover that you're far from where you first started. You have drifted away. Drifting is dangerous because it doesn't happen all at once. It occurs very slowly, and because of that, it often goes unnoticed until it is too late.

In the same manner, we can find ourselves drifting away from our initial commitment to God; trying to keep up a traditional religious facade which is meaningless. Insincerely bowing the knee out of formality, and going through an empty ritual of devotion in a careless or half-hearted way, is rather to mock God than to worship Him. Dull and heartless praying at meal times, nightly repetitive prayers, or superficial Bible reading can become just a religious habit; a formal duty rather than a fulfilling heartfelt joy.

It is for this reason the Bible warns that, *"... we must pay the closer attention to what we have heard, lest we drift away from it"* (Hebrews 2:1). Our love for the Lord is evident in how we respond in glad obedience, to do the things that please Him. We can say, sing and pray, professing our love for God. The reality of our relationship though, is seen in that we give earnest attention to what we hear, and then enthusiastically apply it to our daily lives. This reality check is taught by Jesus when He says to His disciples, *"If you love me, you will keep my commandments"* (John 14:15).

If our children or loved ones only made contact when they wanted something, and for the rest of the time they ignored us, we would be hurt and offended. How much more our Creator and Saviour? The promises of God to answer our prayers are based on having a deep, intimate relationship with Him, which is why David says in Psalm 37:4, *"Take delight in the LORD, and he will give you the desires of your heart."* When this love is absent, or has grown lukewarm, then God our heavenly Father is grieved, and a blockage in our relationship results.

11. Not Asking According To God's Will

God does not answer prayers which are contrary to His plan for our lives, or might in any way be harmful to us. Several such instances of this can be found in the scriptures: Elijah, out of weariness and fear, prayed that he might die (1 Kings 19:4). Moses, due to discouragement and rejection, prayed not only for the burden of leading Israel to be removed from him, but that God would take away his life as well (Numbers 11:15). Jonah and Job also expressed similar prayers, when they were experiencing various stresses.

Being unsure, misguided, or presumptuous about what we think God's will is, results in a person praying for the wrong things, and therefore the prayer remains unanswered. We can't rely on our feelings or what might appear to be a good idea; there needs to be full assurance of faith in our prayers. This can only be experienced when we have the firm basis of God's Word guiding our request, the witness of the Holy Spirit in our hearts, and a clear focus to our living. Whimsical desires, vain imaginings or mere opinions are dangerous, and lead to a very shaky foundation as well as 'flaky' praying and disappointment.

Before a person makes any request to God, or bold statements to man regarding His will, they need to have taken the time to seek the Lord first, for clarity and confirmation on the matter. To do otherwise can lead to situations that reveal short-sighted foolishness. This was so for a Bishop, over a century ago, who pronounced from his pulpit and in the periodical he edited, that heavier-than-air flight was both impossible and contrary to the will of God. The irony was that Bishop Wright had two sons, Orville and Wilbur Wright who went on to prove him wrong! They changed the course of the 20th Century and beyond, by inventing the first powered air machine to achieve controlled sustained flight with a pilot aboard.

Not knowing God's will when we pray is a significant reason for failing to receive an answer to our request. The clearer we are about God's mind in any situation, the greater our assurance will be to see fruitfulness in our praying. Paul's letter to the Colossian Church, expresses his burden for them, that they might not only know God's will, but be *"... filled with the knowledge of his will in all spiritual wisdom and understanding"* (Colossians 1:9). Also the apostle John tells us,

> *"This is the confidence which we have in him, that if we ask anything according to his will he hears us. And if we know that he hears us in whatever we ask, we know that we have obtained the requests made of him"* (1 John 5:14-15).

12. Conditional Commitment

This is certainly a contradiction in terms, and yet a problem that is not uncommon in the lives of some Christians today. The truth is, we cannot simply live for God as and when it is convenient for us, and then expect that He will answer our prayers. Surprisingly though some people do. Their attitude is, so long as God responds favourably to them, in the way they want Him to, then gladness characterises their lives. While life runs smoothly and there's no need to make any great sacrifices, they are satisfied. However, when this isn't the case they become less enthusiastic about God.

The mind-set of comfortable, part-time Christianity on a 'My Terms' basis prevails in many churches: 'Don't expect me to be involved in outreach, take on practical commitments or be regular at the prayer meeting if it impinges on my social life – I'm content to be a Christian as long as it doesn't cost too much and no inconvenience is caused me.' Spiritual 'Couch Potatoes' are happy while little is asked of them. However, the moment any responsibility, pressure or conflict arises, their praise is silenced; their attendance spasmodic, and eventually they slip out of sight. This is not true Christianity, and those who live in such a way should not be surprised that their prayers remain unanswered.

Unconditional commitment is the basis for normal Christian living. David Livingstone, the pioneer, medical-missionary and explorer understood this well. A missionary society once wrote to him when he was working in Africa, and asked, "Have you found a good road to where you are? If so, let us know so we can send other men to join you in the ministry." Livingstone characteristically wrote back, "If you have those who will come only when they know there is a good road, I don't want them. Send me men who will come if there is no road at all!"

Having a lifestyle of unconditional commitment is one of the ultimate ways of showing a living faith, genuine love, and deep appreciation to God for all He has done for us. Such devotion, where we are not counting the cost, but are seeking to live righteously before God at all times, will be assured of His response. He is always ready to answer those who don't look for the soft option in life, but are completely yielded to Him. The Psalmist makes this point when he writes,

"The eyes of the Lord are towards the un-compromisingly righteous and His ears are open to their cry" (Psalm 34:15, Amp).

Job is an example of someone who experienced horrendous problems of personal loss, injustice and betrayal, by those who once supported him. His unconditional commitment though was remarkable. Amidst the torment of all his adversity, his reaction was to declare, *"Though He slay me, yet will I trust Him"* (Job 13:15, NKJ). Although it seemed to take a long while for God to respond to the heart cry of his prayers, ultimately he was vindicated. His unconditional commitment was rewarded when the Lord restored back to Job twice as much as the devil had taken from him (Job 42:10).

This attitude is more clearly seen in the commitment of Shadrach, Meshach and Abednego. When faced with the choice of betraying their love for God or being thrown into a fiery furnace, there was no hesitation in their response to King Nebuchadnezzar's threat. They didn't doubt God could answer their prayers and deliver them. However, regardless of whether or not the Lord intervened on their behalf, their commitment was unconditional. They boldly said,

"If we are thrown into the blazing furnace, the God we serve is able to save us from it, and he will rescue us from your hand, O king. But even if he does not, we want you to know, O king, that we will not serve your gods or worship the image of gold you have set up" (Daniel 3:17-18, NIV).

This same loyalty is what Christ looks for today from those who claim to be followers of Him. An attitude of consistent dedication, love and worship so we remain faithful, irrespective of whether our lives are easy or difficult, attracts the favour of God. Even though He may not respond as quickly as we want Him to, or in the way we think He should, still our commitment remains unchanged. It is on this basis we will experience His promise which says, *"...those who honour Me I will honour..."* (1 Samuel 2:30, NKJ).

13. Disharmony Within Marriage

An area that is rarely considered in terms of things hindering our prayers is conflict in the home, specifically within marriage. In today's society, disrespect of women is common and this attitude is also the case sometimes within the Church. Irrespective of a man's achievements and reputation amongst his peers; his status at work or the seemingly powerful ministry he has before crowds, if at home his relationship with his wife is not right, then it grieves the Holy Spirit. The Bible makes very clear that neglect in this area brings a blockage to prayer:

"Husbands, live considerately with your wives, bestowing honour on the woman as the weaker sex,..in order that your prayers may not be hindered" (1 Peter 3:7).

If we want our prayers to be helped and not hindered, we have the responsibility to live harmoniously with our wife, in a way consistent with God's Word. No husband can expect an effective prayer life unless he does so. Scripture puts the onus on the man to set the standard of respect, reconcile conflict and be the peacemaker. This may seem to some men as an unbalanced and unreasonable task, bringing unfair pressure upon them, but it is all part of their priestly role and leadership in the home. An important part of the man's role is to study their wives; to get to know their needs thoroughly; living together with them with understanding, and taking the initiative to honour and cherish them at all times.

The standard God has for a man is extremely high, and it is that they show great respect and value for their wives. Paul's teaching makes it very clear: *"Husbands, love your wives, as Christ loved the church and gave himself up for her"* (Ephesians 5:25). This is certainly a high calling. It is an instruction to love our spouse sacrificially, unconditionally and unilaterally. Many wives who may well be taken care of by their husbands in material goods, are desperately lonely in other ways: wanting their partner's attention; needing to be appreciated; waiting to be remembered, and simply longing for their husbands to give them time and communicate with them.

Writing just over 300 years ago, Bible commentator Matthew Henry, made some interesting comments on the care of a husband for his wife. He said the husband's duty to his wife consisted in "Giving due respect to her, and maintaining her authority, protecting her person, supporting her credit, delighting in her conversation, affording her a handsome maintenance, and placing a due trust and confidence in her."

Even in today's age of 'Modern Marriages' such love is not outdated. Whenever this consideration and honour is neglected because of familiarity, overlooked due to busyness, dismissed because of selfishness, or ignored as a result of indifference, then prayer to God is significantly hindered.

Having looked at all these negative blockages to answered prayer, we must search our hearts, being careful at the same time not to be condemned. If there are any areas we need to put right, repentance is essential, as this could be the reason our prayers have remained unanswered. In addition to these things there are other more positive aspects we must take into account. These are: **Timing, Trust** and **Taking Action.**

Timing In The Delay

God's delays are not necessarily His denials. There is a perfect timing in all that He does, and it could well be just a case of learning to wait for the appointed moment of His season for our lives. Psalm 30:5 is such an encouragement in this respect, *"... Weeping may tarry for the night, but joy comes with the morning."* The time of breakthrough will arrive, but we must accept He has a much broader and clearer picture of our true situation. Paul refers to how limited our understanding is when he says in 1 Corinthians 13:12, *"For now we see through a glass, darkly;... now I know in part; but then shall I know, even as also I am known"* (AV). The reality is, we can just barely see out of the tunnel, He can see the whole matter. He knows how it all fits together and really does know better than we do.

One helpful example when our prayers seem to take so long to be answered is found in the book of Exodus. Israel had been praying for God to deliver them from the suffering of their oppression, as slaves in Egypt. The people were left for several hundred years wondering why God had not intervened. This ordeal must have seemed agonizingly endless, but God was fully aware of their need. The Bible says,

"And God heard their groaning, and God remembered his covenant with Abraham, with Isaac, and with Jacob. And God saw the people of Israel, and God knew their condition" (Exodus 2:24-25).

What we learn from their experience of waiting can help us the next time we are struggling with delays in our own prayers.

Firstly, it is important to remember that God already has His answer in place even before we are sufficiently aware to know our need, or articulate the words of our prayers. We discover this is true concerning our own salvation because the Bible refers to Jesus, in Revelation 13:8b, as *"... the Lamb slain from the foundation of the world"* (NKJ). Before we were ever born our redemption was already secured and in place. In like manner the Lord's deliverance for Israel was also in God's mind, long before His people ever prayed for help. God had already begun the process of providing a deliverer. The fact is though, the answer often does not come when we expect it, nor in the way we think it will happen. A baby at the beginning of Exodus chapter two, is the unknown answer to Israel's prayer at the end of the chapter.

God is the Sovereign Lord and knows the beginning, middle, and end of every situation. Nothing will ever take Him by surprise, and He is mindful of our circumstances. This is something that Jesus reminds us of in Matthew 6:7, *"...your Father knows what you need before you ask him."* Also in Isaiah 65:24 we read, *"Before they call I will answer..."*

Secondly, no adverse circumstances can stand in the way of the timing God has set. Even when Moses goes from being a Prince in Egypt to a fugitive in Midian, there is an indication that God had a special purpose for his life. In Exodus 2:16-17 while in Midian, Moses did not become preoccupied with his own troubles, but drives away the oppressors who were harassing the seven daughters of Jethro, and he waters their sheep. In the same way, and in due time, Moses was to rise up as God's deliverer for Israel; he was going to confront Pharaoh, the oppressor and tormentor of the Israelites. He would then spend 40 years of his life taking care of God's people who would be wandering like sheep in the wilderness.

There are also occasions we have to accept God saying 'No' to our prayers when we are trusting His timing. It is often only in retrospect, that we discover His decision was the best thing that could have happened for us. Looking back, if we had pressed on impatiently, according to our timescale and grasped what we wanted, we would almost certainly have missed God's best. Billy Graham's wife, Ruth, recounts the story of how she prayed for the man she thought she wanted to marry. She speaks of how today she is so grateful that God did not answer her prayer. At that time she had not yet met Billy and now realises what a disaster the other marriage might have been.

Trusting In The Darkness

Having tried to understand with our finite minds the infinite, Almighty God, it has to be said that sometimes there is just no adequate answer, as to why we've not received what we prayed and believed for. After all, He is not a divine vending machine that we walk up to with our spiritual coin; put it in and out pops the answer! We can only therefore continue to trust, while in the darkness of the unknown, and refuse to allow what we don't understand to affect our faith.

One thing we can be absolutely sure of though, is that by trusting God in the darkness of uncertainty, we will never lose out. David says, *"Look to him, and be radiant; so your faces shall never be ashamed"* (Psalm 34:5). Faith has its own rewards far beyond what we can fully appreciate; these are not only spiritual but also physical. By trusting in the Lord with all your heart the Bible says, *"... Your body will glow with health, your very bones will vibrate with life!"* (Proverbs 3:8 TM) – How's that for staying Spiritually Fresh!

One marvellous example of trust that I came across recently was while ministering in Lincolnshire. A 92 year old lady came forward for prayer, asking for her daughter to be healed of advanced cancer. She had previously lost two other daughters to this dreadful disease. Also a son who had been killed in a car crash when he was 18, and she'd buried two husbands - yet her faith was unwavering! I asked her in the light of her past experiences of such devastating disappointments with unanswered prayer, how she still remained confident in asking God for this need. Her reply was that, although she didn't understand why God had not responded to her faith before, she did not doubt His faithfulness, and was still going to trust His promises!

Continuing to believe when we don't understand the silence of God to our pain, is expressed so well by a minister by the name of A.M. Overton. He was a pastor of a church in Mississippi with a wife and three small children, two girls and a boy. His wife was pregnant with their fourth child, but when it came time for delivery, there were complications and both she and the baby died. While sitting in the pew at her funeral service in 1932, he wrote a remarkable poem. Born out of great personal sorrow, it has spread around the world, and speaks so eloquently of trusting God in times of deep darkness:

"My Father's way may twist and turn, my heart may throb and ache,
But in my soul I'm glad I know, He maketh no mistake.
My cherished plans may go astray, my hopes may fade away,
But still I'll trust my Lord to lead, for He doth know the way.
Tho' night be dark and it may seem that day will never break;
I'll pin my faith, my all in Him, He maketh no mistake.
There's so much now I cannot see, my eyesight's far too dim;
but come what may, I'll simply trust and leave it all to Him.
For by and by the mist will lift and plain it all He'll make.
Through all the way, tho' dark to me, He made not one mistake."

God indeed makes no mistakes. He does hear every prayer, even the ones He chooses not to answer. This is something we must hold on to, particularly when going through trials and difficulties. As hard as it is at the time to believe, when our trust is in God, pain can prosper the soul! Suffering is a great mystery but it uncovers hidden depths in ourselves, and also enables us to discover hidden depths in God. Unanswered prayer in our adversity does therefore have a significant purpose. There are experiences we have to go through that God will not intervene in, because He knows a greater benefit for our lives will be the ultimate outcome. These manifold blessings are:

(1) To deepen our experience in helping others (2 Corinthians 1:3-4).

(2) To make us rely more fully on God (2 Corinthians 1:8-9).

(3) To keep us protected from pride (2 Corinthians 12:7).

(4) To develop our character (James 1:2-4).

(5) To purify our faith (1 Peter 1:6-7).

Taking Action In Our Dilemmas

One final area that must be clarified in our understanding is the importance of taking personal action to express our faith. We cannot simply be waiting on God in prayer, and do nothing practical ourselves. There is no doubt of our need for prolonged periods of prayer, to enable us to listen for His direction; giving time to seek His guidance must always be our first priority. Occasionally though, unanswered prayer can be the result of misguided passivity on our part.

Prayer also requires personal action at times, and without this it is powerless! We cannot just shut ourselves away, worship, meditate and wait - then expect God to do everything for us. While relying on Him we must be proactive too, so we are doing something to see our requests come to pass. Bible faith is always active and James is very clear on this point when he plainly says, *"So faith, if it has no works, is dead"* (James 2:17). There is a correlation between praying for the potential of our lives to move forward, and the need not to overlook our practical and obvious responsibility. The reality of the matter is, how can you steer a ship until it lifts anchor and leaves harbour?

Some Christians, though sincere and outwardly very spiritual, can be easily deceived about the way in which God directs their lives. To get them to leave the comfort and security of their 'harbour' can be extremely difficult. This is particularly so if they've received false teaching, or even read inspirational biographies, about how God answered the prayers of great men and women of faith in the past. Encouraging though these accounts are, the way He led others is not necessarily how He will lead us. Also, some may have hidden fears which hold them back from doing anything but pray, and wait for God. Another problem can be if they are simply spiritually lazy, and reluctant to take personal responsibility for decision making.

Corresponding action on our part needs to be seen in the faith we claim to be expressing, as we pray. To live any other way results in dithering and delusion, leaving our lives barren, while thinking we are walking closely with God. When Jesus spoke about prayer, He instructed His disciples that they were not only to *'ask'*, but also they were to *'seek'* and *'knock.'* The imagery here is that we should be doing something active and physical, in a progressive way, to receive the answer we are looking for. Rather than just mystically expressing our need in words or silent thought, we must also be taking steps of faith; keenly searching and knocking on doors of possibilities to discover God's will.

American Michael Jordan, who was considered to be the greatest basketball player of all time, once said, "Some people want it to happen; some people wish it could happen, others make it happen!" Being proactive or passive are characteristics within our nature. They are also learned behaviour patterns that we develop from the mistakes and successes we've made in our past, and also what we've picked up from others. Having the courage to take risks, to create desired results, and to move ourselves forward, rather than just waiting for things to happen, is extremely important. It was Hudson Taylor, founder of the China Inland Missionary Society who once said, *"Unless there is an element of risk in our exploits for God, there is no need for faith."*

When we look at the example of Abraham, he didn't merely pray about God's direction for his life, the Bible tells us, *"... he went out, not knowing where he was to go"* (Hebrews 11:8b). With Gideon, in Judges 6:36-40, practical action was expressed as part of his prayers for God's guidance. He laid out a fleece twice for the Lord to confirm the direction he was to take. The Apostles in Acts 1:26 determined who would replace Judas, not only by praying, but by casting lots. In Acts 16:6-10 the apostle Paul was continually moving in one direction or another on his missionary trips. He actively kept trying various 'doors', searching to see where God was at work. In doing so, the Holy Spirit answered his prayer about the right decision to make, by either keeping those doors closed or allowing them to be opened.

As well as seeking God in prayer, and listening to the Holy Spirit, one practical step when a course of action needs to be decided upon, could be to write a 'balance sheet.' Draw a line across a piece of paper and note down all the reasons for doing a particular thing on one side, and all the reasons against it on the other. Then, having done that, continue to commit the matter to prayer. Another practical step of action, is to seek the wisdom and council of other trusted and more mature Christians. The Bible says, *"... in an abundance of counsellors there is safety"* (Proverbs 11:14b). The very act of seeking out confirmation and advice from others brings clarity. It gets us out of our indecisiveness and confusion, because at least we are doing something to counteract the apparent silence of God to our petitions.

In all that we have attempted to consider concerning unanswered prayer, we need to examine our heart and put right anything that could be a hindrance. Having done this we must come to God in faith, with absolute confidence in the infallible truth of His Word. Let there be no uncertainty; we can be fully assured He does love us and is intimately aware of our need. He cares about our struggles and delights to answer prayer – in His time and in His way. If we must doubt anything, let us doubt our doubts, but let us never doubt the unchanging nature of His Character and His unfailing, steadfast loving commitment towards us.

Chapter 9

Eliminate Chaos From Your Life

It is extraordinary the number of Christians who live in a constant state of chaos, and wonder why they feel stressed out and worn down. One of the major things preventing people from staying spiritually fresh is chaotic and disorganised living. This is so whether it's internal, scattered thoughts buzzing around their heads, or the external muddled chaos they allow to accumulate around them. Clutter distracts, weighs a person down, drains energy from their lives and generally invites more chaos. We have been created after the image and likeness of God, and will never function at our best, nor to our full potential, in an environment of turmoil; it is alien to our divine DNA and therefore causes inner tension and weariness.

The Bible states *"God is not the author of confusion but of peace"* (1 Corinthians 14:33, NKJ). The devil, however delights to bring disorder and chaos, spoiling God's created harmony, and he has been doing so since the Garden of Eden. Having said this though, we cannot blame everything on our adversary. Often we are our own worst enemy, and must take responsibility to live in a well-organised and

255

disciplined way; bringing our daily lives into line with God's will, by choosing to follow His instructions.

Ordered systems or structures do not simply happen by chance; they are the outcome of deliberate choice. We never observe orderliness occurring spontaneously, without an intelligent cause to direct it. No amount of power or energy in itself is sufficient to bring order out of chaos. The specifications and symmetry of a building, for example, is the end result of the detailed and clear thinking of an architect. It is his blueprint that aims to make possible a construction which is functional and aesthetically pleasing to the eye. The same is true of a wrist watch; the only order found in its intricate workings, is that which the maker originally and intelligently put there. Likewise with God, He is the ultimate architect; maker of heaven and earth – the hallmark of His creative hand is all around us and should be reflected in our lives.

There are many intriguing facets which make up God's character; one of which is His attention to precise and remarkably thorough detail. This is evident in the divine order which can be found studying the magnificence of the universe; observing the beauty, diversity and balance of nature; examining the fascinating complexity within the human body, and not least, in seeing the amazing new creation a person becomes, once they are converted and fully yielded to Jesus Christ as Lord.

God doesn't just want to 'save us', His purpose is to reorganise our lives; restoring back to Himself what the devil has stolen and spoilt. The most remarkable act of divine order coming into chaos is evident in the miracle of being 'born again.' Paul, whose own life had been dramatically transformed by Jesus, writes, *"If any one is in Christ he is a new creation, the old has passed away, behold, the new has come"* (2 Corinthians 5:17). Speaking of this change, theologian, author and teacher, R. C. Sproul says, "He is intangible and invisible, but His work is more powerful than the most ferocious wind. The Spirit brings order out of chaos and beauty out of ugliness. He can transform a sin-blistered man into a paragon of virtue. The Spirit changes people. The Author of life is also the transformer of life."

God's meticulous attention to both precise and orderly detail can be found on numerous occasions throughout the Bible. Examples of this are seen in the building of Noah's Ark and the gathering of the animals to enter it (Genesis 6:14 to 7:4); The Tabernacle and its furniture (Exodus 25:9 to 27:1-21); also, Solomon's Temple (1 Chronicles 28:11-19 and 2 Chronicles 3:1 to 4:22). Furthermore, with Bible Prophesy, not one incident occurs randomly, particularly the exact timing of events surrounding the birth, death, resurrection, and return of Jesus Christ.

There is nothing haphazard about God's thinking and actions, nor should there be about our own. He brings order out of chaos just as He did at the start of creation when the world was a desolate and an empty waste. In Genesis 1:1 we read, *"In the beginning God created the heavens and the earth."* This very first chapter of the Bible tells us that God created, not merely the world, but the universe, by organizing it and bringing a structured order that wasn't previously there; separating things from each other: darkness from light, earth from sky, water from dry land, etc. At each stage of God's creative work He reflected on what had been done then pronounced, *"It is good."* – And all that in just six days!

The Dash Between Arrival and Departure

With God, a great deal can be accomplished in a very short space of time. This is important to remember because a short period of time is all that any of us have got, and then it is over all too quickly. The pace of life today is extremely fast, so much faster than we actually realise. Did you know, every day you and I are rushing along at an incredible 66,660 mph, as we speed around the sun! In the past 7 minutes we've travelled almost 8,000 miles through space – talk about life in the fast lane! If only we could see how fast we were moving, we wouldn't be in such a hurry to get everywhere!! The most significant 'dash' that we need reminding of though, is that little hyphen we see between the record of a person's birth and their death.

Everyone can easily state the day, month and year of when they were born and delivered into this world, the date though of departure is something completely unknown; it remains a mystery to us all. The 'dash' in-between these two momentous events represent our span of life; all our achievements as well as our disappointments. With that dash being so short we cannot afford for it to be one of muddle, confusion and chaos. As someone once said:

> "There'll be two dates on your tombstone and all your friends will see 'em, but all that's gonna matter is that little dash between 'em."

By being preoccupied, rushing everywhere, our lives get cluttered with shallow, trivial and unhelpful things, distracting us from our primary purpose of living for God's glory. The prayer of the Psalmist is therefore extremely noteworthy: *"Teach us to number our days that we may get a heart of wisdom."* (Psalm 90:12). God's Word shows us here two crucial things, **(a)** we must have a teachable spirit to make the most of our lives, and **(b)** we need wisdom from God to use our time in the best possible way. It is true to say there are some things that we have no control over at all, but we do have control over how we use our time.

All too often it is the frenetic pace of 21st Century living which creates pressure, hindering people from reflecting God's nature of order, harmony, excellence and attention to detail. The very brevity of life though, should motivate every Christian to eliminate whatever chaos is obstructing their destiny and draining their energy. James says, *"What is your life? For you are a mist that appears for a little time and then vanishes"* (James 4:14). As our time on earth is relatively brief we must make the most of the fleeting span allotted to us; this is impossible unless the problem of being disorganised is addressed.

The benefits of adopting a more disciplined lifestyle are considerable: it will reduce the stress that chaos creates and we will feel more energised, relaxed and spiritually fresh. Time will be saved and frustration avoided in not having to continually search for lost items, which in itself causes considerable weariness. We will be able to arrive for appointments on time; prepared and in a state of peace rather than shambles. Also, it will save us money in not being penalised for late bill payments or bank letters informing us we're overdrawn. Moreover, our productivity will increase because we become more efficient in what we are doing, and this will result in a greater sense of achievement, fulfilment and self-esteem.

Paul when speaking to the Christians at Ephesus urged them to be, *"... making the most of the time, because the days are evil"* (Ephesians 5:16). To do this we must start becoming proactive as we deal with the clutter from our lives in three main areas: **(a)** our mind, **(b)** our emotions **(c)** the environment around, that we live and work in.

Firstly, DE-CLUTTER YOUR MIND

American Robyn Coffman, a committed Christian and life coach has said, "Clutter isn't only what you can see; it's also what you can't see. It perpetuates your overload schedule with endless commitments and overwhelming fears. A cluttered mind means over-thinking, over-reacting, over-analysing, over-worrying and over-committing." It should not be a surprise therefore that when our thoughts are not sanctified, single-minded and set on God we can become extremely weary in our Christian walk.

'Memory Almost Full' is Paul McCartney's 14th studio album, selling well over 2 million copies worldwide. The former Beatle explained the inspiration for the title came from a sentence that appeared on his mobile phone, and he thought the phrase summed up the state of modern life. In a recent interview from Paris, the 69-year-old musician said, "It seemed symbolic of our lives today. Your messages are always full and your mind is constantly crowded. It doesn't matter if you're my age, or 20, I think that we all need to delete stuff every so often."

There certainly is a good measure of truth in that statement; something we would all benefit from doing. Let us therefore look at some of the ways we can de-clutter our minds:

1. Decide To Be A Better Steward Of Time

We all have twenty-four hours in a day, but not everybody gets the same return on them. While in one sense time cannot be controlled because it marches on no matter what we do, we can be better stewards of our time. People talk about trying to 'find time', but they need to stop looking; twenty four hours is the most any of us are going to get. We must stop making excuses, saying, "I've not got enough time!" We have exactly the same number of hours in a day that were given to physicist and mathematician Isaac Newton; composer George Handel; painter, sculptor, architect, poet, and engineer Michelangelo; novelist Charlotte Bronte etc. What we do with that time makes the difference between mediocrity and greatness, frustration and achievement.

There are many different things that waste our time, some of which we could reason are legitimate forms of relaxation. The television, internet, video games, newspapers, and magazines etc can be helpful and good. However, they've created minds that have short attention spans which are unable to focus on tasks requiring discipline for longer periods. Time seems to evaporate as we get absorbed with shallow interests that produce little substance. This prevents necessary jobs being accomplished and meaningful responsibilities being finished, which only increases the chaos.

You would think today's technology offers many time-savers, letting us do things we've never been able to do before. Nonetheless, they can become addictive; we can be tied to them in ways that are exhausting! In the modern age in which we live the benefits of things like mobile phones, laptops, hand-held PCs, electronic organisers, instant messaging, 'twittering' and global social networking are wonderful, but they can also become slave drivers. They are able to slowly dominate our lives, and eat away at our time. One of the consequences of this is that we make it extremely hard for God to get our attention.

It's easy to contact anyone, anywhere and at anytime. Also with information always available on-line, we can keep 'surfing' endlessly and fall into the trap of passive browsing. It is wise therefore to restrict web activity, e-mails, and instant messages. Dipping in and out of the internet when engaged in other tasks is classic self-interruption and time-wasting. Things like 'Facebook' and chat rooms quietly but quickly steal away time. After a short while texting, 'twittering' or on the internet we need to ask ourselves, 'Should I be doing this now?' Lack of discipline in these areas will inevitably lead to time vanishing and having nothing very productive to show for it.

2. Prioritise What Needs To Be Done

Focus on what is important. Think on paper and plan each day by simply spending ten minutes making a list before you go to bed, or just prior to the start of a working day. For some, the morning will be a better option, to avoid thoughts racing at night and causing sleeplessness. You'll then be more focussed and ready to begin the day with clear objectives. An organised plan is always better than trying to carry things around in your head. Itemise the most important jobs you have to do for the day. Number them in order of their priority. When starting the day begin at number one and stick to it until it is completed, then begin the second, and so on. Setting a schedule and not deviating from it will be a positive step forward.

By writing things down we bring a clearer perspective to our workload, so it doesn't get blown out of proportion in our thinking. At times we can be stressed out because our mind tells us we have so much that needs to be done. Actually though, when we write down those jobs we discover there aren't so many as we imagined. Making a list of the objectives and goals we're seeking to fulfil, keeps our thoughts on a track going in a purposeful direction. Be very clear about your goals and your strategy, both short term and long term. There is no question that people who set goals accomplish much more than those who don't.

In considering what needs to be done, take care to always seek God first. While Jesus didn't walk around with a list of things He needed to accomplish, He did prioritise His life, starting with seeking God's will first. He said *"I can do nothing on my own authority;... I seek not my own will but the will of him who sent me"* (John 5:30). One of the major keys here is that Jesus was not driven by the needs that confronted Him, nor was He pressurised into meeting every demand that arose; He was directed by what God wanted Him to do. The guiding principle we must adopt is expressed well by King Solomon, who stated,

> *"Many are the plans in the mind of a man, but it is the purpose of the Lord that will be established"* (Proverbs 19:21).

One idea is to start with a dream or vision you may have, and work backwards to see how you believe God wants it fulfilled. Writing down personal goals gives them a sense of permanency, plus it energises you, giving you something of substance to pray into. As part of your planning, it will be necessary to eliminate activities from your schedule that do not contribute to your life priorities, and that have no significant importance. Wisdom and discipline here will always pay off, which is why the Bible says,

> *"The plans of the diligent lead surely to abundance..."* (Proverbs 21:5).

3. Make A List Of What Not-To-Do

A 'Not-to-do' list is just as important as a 'To-do' list because it keeps us alert to things that will hinder our desire in getting the most out of our lives. It helps us deal with our own bad habits and weaknesses, as well as the distractions that consistently encroach upon our lives every day. These are things that either hide in the background of our minds, or interruptions that suddenly jump out at us during the course of the day. Being clear and able to identify these, will help protect us from intrusions that otherwise would hijack our attention and wear us down. Furthermore, they will serve as a reminder to trigger our thoughts and actions back to our priorities.

The list will, of course, vary from person to person but it could include things like: Not to feel over-responsible for everyone else's wellbeing; Not to answer the phone after a certain time each night; Not to mull over your own or other people's mistakes; Not to engage in negative self-talk; Not to worry about things you cannot change; Not to compare yourself with others; Not to e-mail first thing in the morning or last thing at night – the former scatters your priorities and plans for the day; the latter can give you insomnia!

Unimportant things become a distraction, taking up our time and our energy. The good has always been the enemy of the best. Our adversary will be perfectly happy if he can fill our lives up with doing good things, to cause us to be diverted away from God's best. The way we spend our time, energy and resources may not necessarily be sinful in themselves. However, if the enemy can distract us from walking in God's will, he can accomplish the aim of restricting our potential and robbing us of our destiny.

We therefore need to take an honest look at each area of our lives, and consider all of the things that occupy our time. This can be quite an eye-opening experience. By evaluating our commitments we are then able to make adjustments. The aim is to reduce anything creating pressure and causing chaos, by eliminating habits we've developed which are unhelpful to our overall objective of having an organised life.

4. Avoid 'Butterfly Thinking'

Take care not to get distracted by trivial things, or diverted away from priority matters that are important to focus upon. This means being alert to the problem of 'butterfly thinking', because of how it greatly hinders our ability to be organised and minimises productivity. With some people, all the different stimulation and distractions about them, cause random thoughts, concerns, and ideas to race about in their mind. They find it difficult to slow down in their thinking, enough to focus. As a result of scattered, wandering and undirected thoughts, disorder is something they become prone to.

Refuse to allow your mind to be cluttered by trying to do several things at once. There is no doubt that multitasking is something that certain people, particularly women, can do very well. Nevertheless, it can lead to distraction; interrupting our priorities, causing important tasks to be delayed or remain unfinished, as thoughts flit haphazardly from one thing to the next. As a result, disorganisation occurs, and often people find themselves doing a lot of work, but actually achieving relatively little of significant value. Those who struggle with this problem always talk about how busy their day has been, but when you ask them exactly what has been achieved, their response is vague and uncertain.

People who have a tendency toward 'butterfly thinking' do not have to accept that this is just how they are; if someone wants to change, by God's grace they can. It is not a case merely of personality, but of the power of God enabling them to have the mind of Christ. There must be willingness to co-operate with the divine order that He wants to bring into their lives. The instruction of Philippians 2:5 is, *"Let this mind be in you which was also in Christ Jesus"* (NKJ). God's Word even tells us how to do this when it says, *"... take every thought captive to obey Christ"* (2 Corinthians 10:5), and *"Be transformed, (changed) by the [entire] renewal of your mind, [by its new ideals and its new attitude]..."* (Romans 12:2, Amp).

5. Be Prepared To Say 'No' Occasionally

Here is a matter that I readily admit is a weakness in my life, but fully acknowledge its importance, and am beginning to make greater progress. Getting our lives organised and de-cluttering our minds, requires that we are wise and firm in not being so quick to respond to every need. The danger of 'overload' is only too common, for those who are overly compliant to every request. We must therefore learn to say 'no' sometimes to the pressures of other people's expectations and the demands that they put upon us. This undoubtedly is hard, because we don't want to offend and we should desire to help others.

The more we are prepared to do, the more people will want us to do. Because of this, helpful strategies need to be thought through, to strengthen our resolve in saying 'No' when necessary. This is a matter that applies in every sphere of life, whether it's within the network of our loved ones, friends, neighbours, work-place or church.

Responding to a request honestly is important, and so we could say with a sympathetic yet firm tone, "I'd love to, but it is just not possible because of other commitments." Alternatively, we could make it clear that we'd like to help, but now is not the best time, though we will get back to them when we can. This is a positive response and one that releases us from being under pressure. Also to say, "Let me pray about it," is a simple, immediate and reasonable reply that causes the person to back off at the mention of a 'higher authority' being consulted! Furthermore, it gives us the time to review our schedule, as well as our feelings about saying 'Yes' to yet another commitment.

If Jesus had tried to heal every sickness, He would have burnt Himself out. If He had attempted to drive out every demon and meet every need He never would have survived. As we previously mentioned, He only did what His Father was showing Him to do. In fact, on one occasion, in Luke 5:16, Jesus was surrounded by multitudes who had gathered to hear Him and to be healed, yet we read, *"...but he withdrew to the wilderness and prayed."* We too must take time out, to be still before God, that we might renew our strength and complete the purpose He has for our lives. Central to this goal is the acceptance that we cannot fix every problem.

6. Don't Allow Yourself To Procrastinate

Procrastination is one of the biggest contributors to disorganisation, and is characterised by indecisiveness and inactivity. It is a mind-set that is in conflict with an orderly life and the tension, therefore, of these two positions create frustration, confusion and weariness. A common trait will be choosing to avoid high-priority tasks, by being occupied with those of lesser significance, resulting in leaving important jobs to a later time. In daily life it can be seen in not paying bills on time; completing income tax returns late; leaving shopping for special events till the last minute; putting off decorating the house etc.

Someone once said, "Procrastination is the bad habit of putting off until the day after tomorrow, what should have been done the day before yesterday." If you constantly put things off for a later date, you set yourself up for chaos and stress, because jobs will pile up and eventually become overwhelming. Dealing with important matters as they arise, or at least sorting them in order of their urgency is essential, otherwise we just allow tasks to accumulate and drain our lives. We cannot avoid the responsibility to get organised, it is for that reason we must address this issue and build it into our schedule.

It was Leonardo da Vinci who said, "Iron rusts from disuse and water loses its purity from stagnation, even so does inaction sap the vigour of the mind." Sometimes we can be worn out more by doing nothing, or by having unfulfilled goals and objectives, than anything else. Eric Hoffer, an American social writer and philosopher remarked that "The greatest weariness comes from work not done."

Procrastination has serious and lasting effects. These go beyond creating chaos and a disorganised life and often include: eroding our self-esteem; lowering our expectation; lost opportunities; unfulfilled dreams; diminished self-respect; restricted career and life opportunities; stress-induced damage to health; invention of barriers that prevent our destiny being achieved, and most significantly, spiritual inertia.

Allowing ourselves to procrastinate will result in struggling on with the malaise of apathy which saps our spiritual strength and motivation. Something dies within us, and spiritual barrenness spreads, whenever we are not actively seeking to fulfil our full potential. Decisive development in our calling and making clear, consistent decisions in life is not only necessary, but fundamental to staying spiritually fresh.

7. Establish A Deadline

One of the ways in which we can help with the previous point of procrastination, and eliminate some of the disorder in our lives, is to set a deadline for important tasks. Without a definite beginning and end to the things that need to be done, we will have no sense of time-scale, and therefore find ourselves drifting aimlessly along. It's easy to put things off for another day, but we will be saved so much frustration and disappointment in the long-run, if we have a deadline to work towards.

Setting a definite time to complete tasks propels you to action. This creates a sense of urgency because it is written in black and white in your diary, or on a 'to do' list, rather than just being a notion in your head. A deadline in your mind is just a whim, putting it onto paper gives it power! Most people are reasonably good and are motivated when someone else imposes a timeframe they have to work towards, but find it difficult to instigate one personally. Often they have trouble achieving what they want simply because of not planning ahead sufficiently.

The discipline of writing a book for example is a long haul and a lot of hard work. This would be so much more difficult, if a structured approach was not adopted, and specific deadlines set. We may well miss a few of our desired timescales, but that should never discourage us. Most people tend to underestimate the time it will take to accomplish things; unplanned obstacles may occur and slow them down. However, without at least aiming to complete what needs to be done, tasks will certainly take much longer, and in some cases probably never get finished.

Secondly, DE-CLUTTER YOUR EMOTIONS

We are emotional beings with a very complex human psyche. The mind and emotions are inseparably linked, and some of the points previously made relating to the mind will inevitably cross over to the emotions. However, there is a distinction between what we think in terms of rational, mental judgments, and what we feel. Very often negative issues deeply rooted in our emotions, which we may have only a little understanding about, as far as logical thought is concerned, have a significant impact upon our daily living, creating chaos.

We have the capacity to reason, plan, arrive at conclusions, and to make decisions. God intends our spiritual, sanctified and sound minds to direct our actions. However, unless we do something about the things which create conflict and stress in our emotions, we will find ourselves considerably worn down by them. Out of control emotions can interfere with, and even prevent rational thought. It is for this reason we can find ourselves reacting without thinking in terms of anger, resentment, fear, lust, greed, jealousy, disgust and feelings of rejection etc. Therefore, some of the necessary steps we need to take are:

1. Sort Through Emotional Baggage From The Past

Present day problems caused by past events are all too common in the lives of people, resulting in spiritual and physical fatigue. If we ignore this, the emotional baggage we carry around will inevitably be a hindrance, slowing us down and holding us back from fulfilling God's plan for our lives.

We cannot delete the painful events that have happened to us of abandonment, betrayal, abuse, neglect, humiliation, rejection etc, but we can be healed and delivered from their negative influence upon our present. Simply suppressing the issues and living in denial will only result in carrying the consequences of them around with us, now and into our future.

It is necessary to prayerfully devote time to seeking God, and establish why we react to situations and certain people in the way we do. We must ask the Lord to reveal the 'trigger' to our hurt, anger, fears, sense of inadequacy etc. There may well also be anger or disappointment we have towards God, resulting from unanswered prayer or an incident that has happened to us, which we find hard to understand. As the Holy Spirit reveals theses painful issues, it is important to forgive people who we've been hurt by. Also, we must forgive ourselves of any blame we feel, and repent of any negative attitude we may have towards God.

2. Let Go Feelings Of Guilt And Condemnation

The emotion of guilt and condemnation when we have failed at anything, or know we've not done what we should have, can certainly be draining. There are many reasons we carry guilt, one common cause results from the failure of not having spent more time with our family, particularly when they were young. Lost years can never be recovered and will only leave us with regret.

Having a full diary of church engagements, attractive ministry invitations and social events may feel good. Spending time 'net-working' to climb the ladder of success and developing our career might seem important. Taking on another job and working extra hours perhaps appears necessary, but it will all amount to nothing, if we are continually denying the people most important to us, their need of our time.

In our quest to eliminate chaos from our lives and with our determination to make the most of the potential we have, we must watch out for the danger of neglecting those closest to us. It is possible to become so single-minded, disciplined and obsessed, with maximising our time, in terms of pursuing our ambitions, career, education etc, that we forget about those who need our time the most. Whether this is our elderly parents, marriage partner or our children, we must have a right balance to give time to those whom God has given us responsibility for. To do otherwise will ultimately bring an underlying feeling of guilt and failure, creating the turmoil of emotional chaos.

Such a situation is well illustrated by the personal life of American singer Harry Chapin. In 1974 a folk rock song, sung by him called, "Cats in the Cradle" became a number one hit in the charts. It was about a father who was too busy to spend time with his son. As the son grows he asks his father to spend time with him, but he always postpones the son's request to the future. The son idolises him and wants to become like his dad. At the end of the song, the father realises his son has become just like him. Here are a few verses:

My child arrived just the other day.
He came to the world in the usual way.
But there were planes to catch and bills to pay.
He learned to walk while I was away.
He was talking before I knew it, and as he grew
He said, "I'm going to be like you, Dad.
You know I'm going to be like you."

My Son turned ten just the other day.
He said, "Thanks for the ball, now come on lets play.
Can you teach me to throw?" I said, "Not today,
I've got a lot to do." He said, "That's OK."
And he walked away and he smiled and he said
"You know I'm going to be like you, Dad,
You know I'm going to be like you."

The final verse says:

I've long since retired and my son's moved away.
I called him up just the other day.
I said, "I'd like to see you, if you don't mind."
He said, "I'd love to, Dad, if I could find the time.
You see, my new job's a hassle and the kids have the
flu,
But it's sure nice talking to you, Dad.
It's been real nice talking to you."
And as I hung up the phone it occurred to me,
He'd grown up just like me.
My boy was just like me.

Harry Chapin's wife, Sandy, actually wrote the words to the song. Her thoughts were inspired by watching her ex-husband try to reconnect with his absent father. Chapin wasn't that much interested in the words until after their son Josh was born, but it became a self-fulfilling prophesy.

When their son was seven, Harry was performing 200 concerts a year and Sandy asked him when he was going to take some time to be with their son. Harry promised to make some time at the end of the summer. He never made it. That summer, when Harry was on his way to a business meeting, a truck drove into his Volkswagen, it burst into flames, and he was killed.

3. Refuse To Be Worn Down By Fear

Fear, in all its complex forms, is an incredibly powerful emotion, that begins with unease, grows into worry and then can explode into panic. Even just low-level anxiety can wear us down over a long period, and produce physical ill-health and spiritual fatigue. Underlying fears make us dwell with apprehension on decisions we've made, or are about to make; on things that have already happened and even on things that may never happen. Any perceived threat to our well-being, irrespective of the rationale behind it, takes up valuable energy as well as wasting our time.

Fear is a major culprit for creating inner emotional clutter, and hinders people in achieving their goals and dreams. It holds people back from taking steps of faith, by keeping them confined to the safety of the 'known', rather than launching out into unchartered waters, and allowing themselves to be stretched. The self-doubt we permit to shape our expectations will always produce negative emotions, because of the frustration that accompanies them.

Jesus met many who were repressed, oppressed or distressed by events in life, and one of the most common phrases He used when ministering to them was, *"Fear not,"* or *"Do not be afraid."* When Christ said this, it wasn't merely with a *passion* to persuade people about their freedom from fear, it was with a *power* to make possible that liberty. He imparted to all who would believe, the ability not to be afraid. To His own disciples Jesus said, *"Let not your hearts be troubled"* (John 14:1).

In considering this simple instruction from Jesus, the Prince of Peace, we are reminded that fear is something we do not have to live with; it doesn't have to be part of our nature. When Jesus said, *"Let not your hearts be trouble"* He was teaching that there is something a person can do about fear – they needn't *'let'* their hearts be troubled or tormented by anything. Paul said something similar when writing to the Colossian Christians. He instructed them, *"Let the peace of Christ rule in your hearts, to which indeed you were called..."* (Colossians 3:15).

We have not been destined to be driven by our emotions, nor doomed to be dominated by our circumstances. The Lord doesn't merely say, *'don't let yourself be troubled,'* He teaches the alternative to being worn down by fear, is to choose to put our trust in Him. Having done this, we then submit to the rule of His government of peace in our lives. It is in seeing this choice from scripture, we begin to understand that our co-operation in applying God's Word, can help or hinder the process of peace.

Stored up in our damaged emotions can be all manner of fears that trouble us: fear of failure; rejection; disapproval; humiliation; the fear of making mistakes etc. It will be useful therefore to identify which specific fears bother us, then face them, and one-by-one renounce the unbelief behind them. By coming to The Cross of Christ with these burdens we are reassured of His unconditional and sacrificial love for us. As we confess our desire to be free from their bondage, and commit ourselves to trusting in the power of His risen life, we can be free!

Our lives are either built on a foundation of love or fear. We must make sure that we have a solid basis of love from which we are seeking to serve God. Without this we always will be prone to self-doubt and insecurity; fears then will cause us to crumble under pressure. There is nothing more powerful to deal with fear than the revelation of God's unchanging love for us. When emotionally we are secure in His steadfast love, we discover an amazing strength against all insecurity that would undermine our confidence. Speaking of this the Bible says, *"... perfect love drives out fear"* (1 John 4:18, NIV).

4. Deal Quickly With Moodiness

Trying to live an ordered life is almost impossible if we haven't learned how to control moodiness. This is because mood-swings will make us their master. They will alienate us from others, making harmony in relationships difficult. Also they will cause us to feel lethargic and de-motivated in our attempt to be more organised.

Understandable mood swings, caused by life-changing events, which involve the loss of something or someone significant to us is fairly common. This might come through bereavement, divorce or loss of employment. Also the temperament change due to hormonal fluctuations in women, during their monthly cycle, or menopausal phase, is a fact of life.

Furthermore, there are mood-swings which have to do with chemical malfunctions in the brain. Those who struggle in this way need Christian care, counselling and prayer, as well as possibly medication, to help them get through the disorder. This is a more complex condition and not just the general moodiness that we are looking at here. More common is the tendency to be moody, which is extremely self-indulgent; its root is selfishness, and it must be seen as a spiritual problem as well as an emotional one. Whatever the circumstances are, even when people seem to have little control over their emotions, victory by God's grace is possible.

Lack of discipline with the problem of moods, will result in brooding becoming predominant and overwhelming.

Sometimes we'll be happy and excited about life, other times sad, and the world around us will seem empty and dull. If these negative feelings are not dealt with swiftly, we can be dragged down into a dark emotional abyss that is extremely hard to get out of.

When people are moody they become unpredictable, like constantly changing weather conditions. You never know quite when they are going to erupt in anger or react with sullenness, and therefore it can be like walking on eggshells with them. They may use their moods as a way of wielding power and control over another, to gain attention, sympathy or excuse inadequacies and particular patterns of behavior. This emotional blackmail can make others feel somehow responsible for something; though they are not quite sure what.

General moodiness comes unexpectedly, with no obvious reason, but often it is the result of hurt, offence, the feeling of injustice or not being understood by another. The answer is to identify it in us as soon as it comes; recognise that to continue to embrace it is sin; then to break its hold through repentance and surrender to Christ. Swift action, not allowing emotional instability to cause unrighteous behaviour, is very important. This is something we notice with King David, he took responsibility to address his own soul when heaviness tried to overwhelm him. He said, *"Why are you downcast, O my soul? Why so disturbed within me? Put your hope in God..."* (Psalm 43:5, NIV).

On a practical note it will be helpful to remember the following when seeking to overcome moodiness:

(a) Stop dwelling on negative past memories. This is possible by the power of the Holy Spirit, as you focus on living in the present. Remember that being positive is an attitude of choice. You might think what's happened to you is the end of the world, or that your life is totally destroyed, but the reality is, it's not!

(b) Accept that you are probably being oversensitive and that maybe you've misinterpreted someone's words or actions. Seek to be less preoccupied with yourself by thinking of the needs of others, and where you have been self-centered, confess it as sin to God.

(c) Have in mind things that you can consciously do to break the mood, before it becomes overwhelming. Consider things like immediately praying; reading a passage from the Bible; praising God with the gift of tongues; going out for a walk; doing some gardening etc.

5. Watch Out For Perfectionism

Perfectionism, in a person, refers to someone with a set of self-defeating thoughts and behaviours, aimed at reaching excessively high, unrealistic goals. The futility of this can, and often does, prevent them from becoming organised. It is a problem directly connected to self-esteem, and almost always is rooted in past emotional pain and anxiety, of striving to impress those of importance to them. It comes from a desire to gain approval and acceptance through performance, and is usually found where little reassurance and encouragement was given while growing up.

A child learns early on in their development, that other people valued them because of how much they or their siblings accomplished or achieved. The expectations of parents being set very high, and the awareness of what they did, never being quite 'good enough', certainly leaves its mark on the emotions of a growing child looking for acceptance and love. These thought patterns are then carried over into whatever relationships are entered into, and can be extremely draining for all parties involved, not least the individual themselves.

Many good relationships have been destroyed because of perfectionism; this is particularly so in marriage. It can become a killer of love and romance, because the perfectionist is always finding fault; they often expect more from others than they expect from themselves. At the very least they are quick to see faults in another, while minimising their own weaknesses. Such a person must learn to accept the difference in others, and not assume that their way of getting things done is the right way or the only way. Learning to live with change, and to accept uncertainty, is as important as having a predictable routine and well-ordered life.

Not everything can be perfect around us, and therefore in the aim to eliminate chaos, it is necessary also to learn to be both flexible and adaptable. Always struggling to 'stabilise' in a world that is constantly changing, becomes stressful in itself. While wanting to be organised, care needs to be taken not to fall into the trap of trying to make everything happen on our terms. We may have to still learn to live with loose ends, so 'chill out and be relaxed', otherwise striving for perfection will be exhausting and just as draining as living in chaos!

Essentially the fundamental answer is to find security, acceptance and worth in God's love, through faith in His Word. This will enable a person to be themselves, and greatly reduce the anxiety of trying to live up to the standards of other people's expectations, or their own perception of who they think they should be. God has made us all wonderfully different in taste, personality, humour, gifts, ability etc. We are unique individuals. There is therefore no need for anyone to anxiously strive to 'measure up' to their friend, co-worker, or relative. We are all of immense worth to God, and we need to have that same value and view of ourselves and others.

6. Avoid Negative People

If you are serious about de-cluttering your emotions and staying spiritually fresh, then it is important to look at the people you spend time with. Wherever possible, avoid negative, aimless, complaining, draining, unspiritual people. They are like emotional vampires that suck the life out of you. Nothing will make you grow weary faster than being around people who wallow in a sea of negativity. From an emotional standpoint, it simply is not possible for you to associate with such people for any length of time without absorbing some of that negativity into your own life.

These toxic relationships may come from people in the office, church, neighbours, or even family members, and we know that they are unhealthy because they make us feel bad. Invariably, toxic people are opinionated prophets of doom, quick to see the dark side of everything. Their world of gloom is spread by the negativity of judgmental remarks, gossiping, criticism and fault-finding. Through them, our bright outlook on life becomes overcast as they take the joy out of everything. Before you know it, their negativity contaminates you, and you start looking at things with grey-coloured glasses yourself.

In de-cluttering your emotions, you will ultimately have to eliminate those relationships which drain you, and surround yourself with those who love, support, encourage and inspire you! This isn't being selfish, and it doesn't mean ignoring others with needs, but where there is a negative relationship which is having a detrimental effect on us, we need to be wise. The Bible tells us not to be unequally yoked, for light cannot fellowship with darkness. It also says, *"Can two walk together unless they are agreed?* (Amos 3:3, NKJ). The answer of course is 'no'. Therefore, if there is anyone bringing stress to our lives and hindering our walk with God, we need to do something about it.

There will be certain situations, perhaps at work or in the home, where walking away is not practically possible; these are relationships we have little choice about. Even in such circumstances we can still de-clutter our emotions, by making sure we no longer allow the person to drain us in the way they did. The following steps to enable us to achieve this will be helpful:

(a) Set boundaries on the relationship so that the person is clear about your commitment not to engage with them on any area of negativity. They must know that you refuse to listen to them complain. When they try to stretch those boundaries, as they will, be quick to re-state your decision not to criticise, gossip, or be judgemental etc. Be clear that you would rather talk about something more beneficial.

(b) Don't let yourself be manipulated by giving any sign of agreement with their toxic comments. This is particularly so, when they try to draw your response by asking what *you* think or how *you* feel about a matter. They will attempt to make you feel guilty for not giving them the attention they seek, and use your unwillingness to listen as the cause of their hurt. Self-pity is a weapon they can use to manipulate the focus of others back on them. Simply respond with firmness and respect, acknowledging you cannot please everyone, therefore you are not unduly concerned.

(c) In the early stages of any negativity developing, seek to change the tone of the conversation and learn to steer the dialogue in a more optimistic direction. This can be done simply by gentle, loving correction, or just interjecting with a few positive comments. Make it a habit to always look for, and highlight, the best in any situation or person.

(d) Beware of lengthy arguments or in-depth discussions, unless it's about your faith. Some negative people are triggered by certain topics, and are likely to have very fixed views - they are not likely to change these just because of what you say. The positive confidence of your own testimony however, with constructive comments about God's miraculous power to bring change, can counter their negativity.

(e) Maintaining a sense of humour with difficult people helps to lighten the mood of any conversation. If you can slip in a harmless joke before their negative rant escalates, it might just lift them from the downward spiral of their gloomy thoughts; maybe even help them to lighten up themselves. The benefit of laughter to our well-being is stated by Solomon when he says, *"A merry heart does good, like medicine, but a broken spirit dries the bones"* (Proverbs 17:22, NKJ).

Thirdly, DE-CLUTTER YOUR ENVIRONMENT

Addressing the two previous areas of de-cluttering the mind and the emotions, will go a long way to bringing order in the environment of where we live and work. This is because very often the chaos going on *'around'* a person, is simply a reflection of what is going on *'within'* them. It is not necessary, therefore, to spend too much time on this last section, except to say, maintaining this inner order, free from chaos, will require taking some steps to be more organised externally as well. Neglecting this will only allow clutter to agitate us and steal peace from our lives, which in turn will just drain us.

Accumulating 'things' that produce clutter is a problem very common in the materialistic, consumer-driven society we live in. The advertising world consistently bombards us with its message that we just have to have the latest 'gadget', 'convenience' or 'comfort' otherwise our lives will not be complete. The danger of this is, we can become possessed by our possessions and eventually worn down by the clutter they bring into our lives.

Some of the happiest and most fulfilled people I've ever met have been those who lived very sparse and simple lives. This has been so, not only in Africa and India, where they possessed very little indeed, but also during ministry trips to Romania and Bulgaria. There I've had the privilege of preaching to villages of Gypsy Christians, and visiting their modest, ramshackle homes. Even though a family of eight or more would be living in a one-roomed house, there was a remarkable contentment in their uncomplicated lives. Witnessing their cheerfulness and faith, was a good reminder of the truth of Jesus' words when He said, *"... a man's life does not consist in the abundance of his possessions"* (Luke 12:15). Such basic living is a challenge for us to learn to simplify our lives; living quietly and in peace, not getting caught up with the spirit of this age.

The instructions Jesus gave to His followers was, *"Lay up for yourselves treasures in heaven, where neither moth nor rust consumes and where thieves do not break in and steal"* (Matthew 6:20). Also, Paul the apostle taught, *"Set your minds on things that are above, not on things that are on earth"* (Colossians 3:2). One of the great liberating truths of God's Word, which we must never forget is, this world is not our home; eternity is our focus. As pilgrims and strangers in this land, we are just passing through, and therefore need to keep a very loose hold on material things.

Clearing Out The Clutter

Clearing out the clutter has a remarkably detoxifying effect upon us. I experienced this last year when my wife and I moved to our new home in the village of Groby, Leicestershire. Sorting through the old house and clearing out the accumulation of over 25 years, was at first quite an ordeal, as this involved a lot of treasured memories. It was however, also wonderfully liberating, to be free from all the unnecessary clutter that had built up over time, not just in the loft, but the garden shed, and every room of the house.

Making a start is always one of the most difficult parts of any major change. For example, the interesting question could be asked, 'How do you eat an elephant?' The answer of course is 'One bite at a time.' This is also so, when faced with the daunting task of de-cluttering the environment around us, that we live and work in. One bite at a time eventually enables us to get done what initially seems quite overwhelming. The wise words of St Francis of Assisi are a great encouragement in this regard. He said, "Start by doing what's necessary; then do what's possible; and suddenly you will be doing the impossible."

On a practical note, perhaps these simple and achievable steps might help towards that goal of becoming a more organised person, in your own environment:

1. Whether it is your home, the garage, garden shed, office desk, computer or even the car, walk through with Christ, stop, look around, and recognize the clutter that is there. Let Him show you what to hold on to, and the things to let go of. Living in denial is the action of the proverbial ostrich with his head in the sand. As sons and daughters of the living God, we need to prayerfully seek His help to face up to this issue, and to do something about it.

2. Don't put yourself under unreasonable pressure by doing too much too quickly; have realistic goals for each room, and take on a little at a time each day. Just as clutter builds up over years, so it must be tackled over time; it won't be achieved in 24 hours. Beating chaos involves a change of lifestyle, requiring that we form new habits, and apply new organisational skills which may take a while.

3. Systematically go round the house/room, and start with the things that have no sentimental value before taking on the more emotional items. The things which have simply been shelved, dropped, piled-up or left for a later time, will only grow, not disappear. At the bottom of each item of clutter is a decision delayed; the thought, 'I'll deal with that later.' Therefore have a systematic 'deal with it now' approach to things you come across.

4. Identify and rationally rid yourself of what you clearly don't use or need. When you de-clutter it isn't enough to clean and re-organise, the only way to decrease the amount of clutter is to remove it from your home. As far as hoarding is concerned, if you haven't used it for two years, you probably don't need it. Therefore you could put a load in the car for the charity shop, or local dump, perhaps turn it into cash by having a 'Car Boot Sale', or maybe sell it on-line.

5. Designate an 'incoming papers spot' for bills, receipts, post etc. Paperwork of every type, accounts for a large amount of clutter; it builds up very quickly, and much of it is of no use to us. With what is important, few things are more frustrating, time-wasting and draining, than not being able to find things we need, because we've put them in different places. Therefore set up some simple folders, and develop the habit of filing quickly, rather than leaving paperwork lying around.

6. Sort through clothes that you haven't worn for years, and take them out of the wardrobe. Seasonal garments can be stored in a container, and put in the loft, not forgetting to clearly mark what it is. De-clutter shelves, cupboards and under the bed. Old shoes that are just taking up space and never used, can be thrown out. Resist the temptation just to transfer things from one room to another.

7. Take care what you now allow to accumulate around you, by learning to live with what you need, and within your means. Before you buy one more thing, ask yourself whether it will truly enhance your life over the long run, or not. Ask whether it will give you more of an ability to love and serve God, or diminish it. Do you really need it, or just want it, and will you still want it in a year?

As we seek to more clearly reflect God's nature of order and peace in every part of our lives, let us never be daunted or discouraged. This struggle against the forces of disorder in our minds, emotions and environment, is one we all face to some degree, but it is a battle we ultimately will win. Paul taught in Philippians 2:12-13, *"work out your own salvation...,"* but in the same verses he also reminds us that *"God is at work in you, both to will and to work for his good pleasure."* We are not alone; the Almighty God, who brought order out of chaos at the beginning of creation, is the power we co-operate with, depend upon and put our confidence in today.

His will for every Christian is that they live in the full benefit of an abundant life that is not just free from chaos, but is also vibrant, exciting and fulfilling! Such an experience should cause the believer to say with the Psalmist, *"... my cup overflows"* (Psalm 23:5b). This is why over the last nine chapters we've considered, not only the need to stay spiritually fresh, but how to achieve that goal. It is by being honest about where we are at right now, that our hope for the future lies. The necessary steps we've looked at to take each individual believer from dryness, fatigue and barrenness, to fullness of life are:

1. Maintain a close relationship with God
2. Seek out meaningful fellowship
3. Thirst for the fullness of the Holy Spirit
4. Be alert in your thought-life
5. Practice dying daily
6. Develop a consistent attitude of praise and thankfulness
7. Understanding unanswered prayer
8. Eliminate chaos from your life

May God Bless and Encourage You on Your Journey.

Other Publications by Yan Hadley

Available From New Life Ministry Trust
80 Lime Avenue, Groby, Leicester LE6 0EN
Telephone: 0116 235 6992
E-mail yan.hadley@ntlworld.com
Or order online: www.newlifeministrytrust.com

REAPING GOD'S HARVEST
(Equipping the Church For Evangelism)
(£6.99 + p&p)

ANSWERING TODAY'S PROBLEMS
(Helping Ourselves to Help Others)
(£6.99 + p&p)

CONSISTENT CHRISTIAN LIVING
(Four Keys to Remaining in Joy and Victory)
(£3.50 + p&p)

REALISING YOUR FULL POTENTIAL
(Discover God's Purpose for Your Life)
(£6.99 + p&p)

DECISIONS THAT DETERMINE YOUR DESTINY
(Moving From the Ordinary to the Extraordinary)
(£7.99 + p&p)

Teaching DVD's by Yan Hadley
£8.00 + p&p

(10 minute clips can also be seen on YouTube)

FREEDOM FROM UNGODLY ATTITUDES

CONFIDENCE IN TIMES OF DESPAIR

STANDING FIRM AGAINST SATANIC FORCES

THE TRANSFORMING POWER OF FAITH

LIVING BEYOND YOUR LIMITATIONS

DECLARING GOD'S DELIVERANCE

FOUR KEYS THAT UNLOCK GOD'S BLESSING

FREEDOM FROM ANXIETY AND STRESS

STAYING SPIRITUALLY FRESH